The Plantagenets

A volume in the British Monarchy series, which also includes:

Henry Yevele

Gothic England

Dublin

Tudor Architecture

The Gothic World

English Mediaeval Architects

The English Cathedrals

The Cathedrals of Spain

William Worcestre: Itineraries

JOHN HARVEY

The Plantagenets

FONTANA/COLLINS

First published by B. T. Batsford Ltd 1948
First issued in Fontana 1967
Sixteenth Impression July 1979

Revised edition © John Harvey 1959

Made and printed in Great Britain by
William Collins Sons & Co Ltd Glasgow

CONTENTS

ILLUSTRATIONS

NOTE ON THE ILLUSTRATIONS

The pedigree on pp. 18-19 shows the House of Anjou from its foundation to the extinction of the male line in 1499; irrelevant female descents have been omitted. The descent of the Crown from Henry I downwards is shown by a thicker line. The map is diagrammatic, and does not show the state of frontiers at any single date. The boundaries of England are those of 1485. Wales is shown as including the March, excluding the County of Flint administered from Chester. The boundary of the English Pale around Dublin is roughly that of the fifteenth century. In France, the maximum extent of the Angevin Empire in the twelfth century is shown, with the names and extent of the major provinces. The eastern frontier of the kingdom of France is also of the twelfth century.

Fig. 1, the effigy of King John, is generally dated *c.* 1230-40. The tomb on which it rests is much later.

Fig. 2, the bronze effigy of Henry III, was not cast until 1291, but there is reason to think that it was based on the wax effigy made in 1276 by Robert of Beverley, the King's chief mason and surveyor of works.

Fig 3*a* is from a series of English royal portraits executed about the middle of Edward I's reign.

The statue at Lincoln Cathedral traditionally stated to be a portrait of Queen Margaret of France (Fig. 3*b*) has been the subject of controversy, as the head's excellent preservation has been considered as evidence of unauthenticity. It has, however, been conclusively proved by expert examination (see A. Gardner & R. P. Howgrave-Graham in *Antiquaries Journal*, XXIX, 1949, pp. 87-9; A. Gardner: *English Medieval Sculpture*, 1951, pp. 148-9) that the head is an integral part of the figure, and not a replacement like the 19th-century heads of "Edward I" and "Eleanor of Castile" close by; and the degree of weathering of head and face as a whole, compared with that of these new heads, refutes the suggestion of severe recutting (made by Mr. Lawrence Stone in *Sculpture in Britain*, 1955, p. 253). It is clear that this head is one of the most outstanding extant works of portraiture of its period, and that an actual Queen of England is portrayed. While the date of the statue could be as early as *c.* 1280, when this part of the building was completed, the figures are not integral with the fabric, and may well be later additions of somewhere within the next generation. The pair of statues can only represent Edward I and Eleanor, or Edward II and Isabella, and to make sense this queen must represent either Eleanor of Provence, Edward I's mother who died in 1291; or his second wife Margaret (1282-1318); of these the latter is by far the more probable on the score of apparent age, apart from the traditional identification.

The effigies of Richard II and Anne of Bohemia were undertaken by contract of 24 April 1395 (Rymer: *Foedera*, VII, 797) and were to be finished by Michaelmas 1397. The account for payment to the coppersmiths Nicholas Broker and Godfrey Prest (Public Record Office, E.364/35, rot. E) shows that they had been paid the whole of their contract price of £400 by 23 July 1397, while a further £300 was allowed for gilding between 7 December 1398 and 14 April 1399. Linen cloth was among the materials used, perhaps for drawing full-size cartoons. Further details from the records are given in *Archaeologia*, XCVIII, 1961, p. 8, note 6.

ACKNOWLEDGMENT

The author and publishers here express their indebtedness to the following persons and institutions for the illustrations mentioned: the Trustees of the British Museum for Fig. 3a; Mr. W. MacLean Homan for Figs, 4a, 4b; The National Portrait Gallery for Figs. 8b, 9, 10; the late Sydney Pitcher, F.R.P.S., for Figs. 1, 5; The President and Fellows of Queens' College, Cambridge, for Fig. 11b; Messrs. Walter Scott for Fig. 3b (by the late S. Smith); The Society of Antiquaries of London for Figs. 11a, 12; The Warburg Institute for Figs. 2, 6a, 7, 8a (by Dr. Gernsheim); and the late Edward Yates, F.S.A., for Figs. 4c, 4d. Fig. 6b (by Mr. W. Fisk-Moore, F.R.P.S.) is in the publishers' collection. The pedigree and map have been drawn for this book by the author.

PREFACE

Kingship is at a discount. Certainly European kingship, and possibly Asiatic; African kingship has succumbed to the impact of Europe, with the possible exceptions of Ethiopia and the revived monarchy of Morocco. The American continent has had no kings since its ancient states were destroyed by Spain, and the modern empires of Mexico and Brazil did not long survive. In India the most vociferous of political bodies, the Congress Party, has one by one dethroned the independent princes.

It is now little more than a century and a half since the abolition of the French monarchy by the First Revolution, yet to the south of Scandinavia not one of the greater monarchies is now left upon the Continent, and the Asiatic empires of China, Russia, and Turkey are gone as well. Of the significant sovereign states of the whole world only two maintain royal government: Britain and Japan.

Two problems present themselves: why has an institution of immemorial age and sanctity been discarded so suddenly and so unceremoniously; and why should Britain have thus far retained a system which in the seventeenth century she was the first of major European states to abolish? It is too early to answer the first of these questions, for we are living in an age of swift transition towards what may be a new Dark Age, or which, more hopefully, we may diagnose as a new epoch of creative energy, wherein the great advances in knowledge shall be turned to the betterment of humanity instead of its destruction.

To the second question a glance at the atlas will provide a partial answer. The surviving European monarchies of Scandinavia and the Netherlands cluster around the British seas and regard England as the arc of a circle does its centre. It is from these very lands that our Britain derived the most significant sections of its people and its patriarchal kingship. Southern Europe, still Latin in its language and its law, has retained from Rome also a distrust of royalty and a feeling for the republican city-state. The primæval kingdoms were farther off, in the Near East, and from that source cycles of cultural inspiration and successive waves of the ruling caste spread, carrying civilization around the globe. In particular, hereditary kingship was communicated to and became traditional in the peoples of Central Asia and Eastern and Northern Europe, and consequently among their descendants who built the new European polity after the downfall of Rome.

It is no coincidence that it is among the northern peoples of Europe that personal freedom and individuality have been most highly developed. To those to whom all subservience is repugnant, the rule of a single man, to whom appeal can be made, and towards whose person feelings of loyalty are possible, is less objectionable than the domination of an impersonal political group. Besides, the age-old belief in the King's magical possession of *power*, the power to make crops grow, to bring fair weather, to heal disease, necessarily tended to maintain kingship, while the fortunate state of the possessor of such power is reflected in the children's phrase " as happy as a King ".

Natural misfortunes, earthquakes, tempest, plague, and the disasters of Man's own folly, war, misgovernment, bankruptcy, came not unnaturally to be attributed to the shortcomings of the King. Little by little, as accident contributed to the effects of folly, or stupidity to those of crime, royal power has weakened, and still more the popular belief in the reality of that power. To a cycle of scepticism, possibly inevitable, has been added the wilful distortion of history by the political propagandist: all the forces of publicity are now expended in the attempt to make it appear that monarchy, if it be tolerated at all, is but a romantic survival—as if romance, the eternal element of escape, were not in any case one of the direst wants of the twentieth century.

The terms "royalist" (for example, economic royalist) and "reactionary" have become far more effectively abusive than "radical" or "bolshevik" has ever been, and in spite of the fact that royalism is at least a positive creed, and that reaction against crime and folly may be the only form of sanity left to the human race. People should learn to think a little for themselves before rashly accepting these generalizations so assiduously pumped down their throats, and they should be particularly on their guard against the veiled suggestion, coming even from ostensible supporters of kingship, that monarchy is an institution which needs to be rationalized, apologized for, and defended. There is only one worthwhile criterion: actions speak louder than words, and a tree is known by its fruits. The factual records of government, comprising not only what has been written, but the legislative, administrative and, above all, artistic remains of past activity, are what must be examined.

As soon as the facts are sought out, a remarkable thing is noticed. Again and again kings with a truly regal achievement to their credit are found to have been removed from their office, and their memory besmirched by the historians. In England it seems strange that the same Richard II, whose extravagance and misgovernment figure in the books, should have insisted on the right of the bondman to obtain his freedom by education; that the "mad" King Henry VI should have done more than any other for the furtherance of education and scholarship; that it was Charles I who in 1630 sought to bind together his people by bidding the gentry dwell upon their country estates rather than at Court. It was the despot Louis XIV who permitted his meanest subjects to bring their troubles to him at all times; Louis XVI in 1779 abolished the last relics of serfdom from the royal domain, though the clergy and nobles kept their bondmen for another ten years, until the Revolution; the Czar Nicholas II was the chief promoter of the Hague International Court of Arbitration, whose principles have recently been so signally flouted by his murderers and their allies.

These are striking examples, yet examination of the history

of kingship would show that they were not untypical. In the cultural field, monarchy shines forth with equal brilliance, though here its eminence is more obviously the direct outcome of individuality. The party politics of a republican democracy inevitably depend upon methods of attracting votes; upon the spiritual, if not physical, bribery of the electorate. The production of art and literature of a really high quality interests only a minority of the population, and hence never can become a primary interest of so-called democratic government. It is necessity that knows no law; necessity that comes before luxury; but the ultimate reason why art and literature flourish under kingship is that to kings, art and literature are matters of absolute necessity. And it is only where the fostering of the best art is the first object of government that humanity finds its soul.

It is widely recognized that in the modern world, that is within the limits of European culture after the breakdown of the Roman Empire, the most nearly perfect realization of human aims took place during what are loosely termed the "Middle Ages". Stretched to their utmost, these centuries span the millennium from the year A.D. 500 to the year 1500; in England, from the founding of the dynasty of Wessex by Cerdic, a Saxon prince bearing a British name (Caradoc), up to the usurpation by another Briton, Henry Tudor, of the throne of the Plantagenets. But with the earlier and darker of these ten centuries we have no concern; England was unformed, and too much subjected to invasion and civil strife to achieve unity for herself until it was forced upon her by the Norman Conquest. For another century the fate of England as a nation, capable of producing a true culture, hung in the balance; only with the coming of Henry II was the problem resolved. Little more than three of the ten centuries were left, but in those three hundred years the energy of a single family was to give new form, a specific English guise, to the eternal values of Man's knowledge and Man's skill.

This family has no other accepted title than that of Plantagenet, though this was only adopted as a surname towards their end by Richard Duke of York, the father of Edward IV. In origin it was the nickname of Geoffrey of Anjou, Henry II's father, who took for his badge, the *plante genet*, a sprig of flowering broom. Yet there is symbolism in the attachment to the whole family of this floral emblem, torn from the tough brilliance of the wayward shrub with its blazing glory of golden blossom. So the anachronism is welcome, and we come to recognize in the name an epitome of that vital force which typified the whole line from its early dæmonic beginnings through to its extinction on the fields of Bosworth and of Pavia. Changed, developed, and improved as the family was by a chain of fortunate marriages, it retained throughout a certain quality or tone, a note of fierce and flaming intensity giving the key to the character of the house. In it there was little of the calculating craftiness and cold ability to play a waiting game that were at once the secret and the shame of the House of Valois, the makers of France. To the Plantagenets their own qualities: their courage, their foresight, their love of art and indeed their personal genius as artists and provokers of genius in others, their tempestuous anger, their justice; above all, their humanity.

So this book will deal little in affairs of state, and much in smaller but more precious reminiscences of personality and temperament. It is not a work of original research: only an infinitesimal proportion of its contents has been quarried out of original manuscript records, though I have used printed transcripts and calendars of record material in preference to narrative accounts with their bias and their often violent personal animus. There must be a really immense fund of important matter not yet in print, but several lifetimes of solid work will have to be spent before it becomes accessible, so vast are the accumulations of public and private material in which the gems of information lie hidden.

Not counting the child Edward V, there were thirteen Plantagenet Kings of England, just as there were thirteen of the Valois Kings of France. About their public careers has grown up an immense literature: the bulk of solid material is daunting, and in a good deal of it personal matters have been more or less rigidly pushed aside or even excluded altogether. Of all the kings but one there are one or more " careers ", if not " lives " in the strict sense, and it is among these special studies of individual sovereigns that I have found most of my material, apart from the royal wills, letters, and speeches actually in print. The one exception is Henry III, whose paradoxical character should have attracted many students. It is to be hoped that the personal aspects of his life will receive thorough treatment as soon as the publication of the Liberate Rolls, those revelatory journals of his daily doings, has reached the end of the reign.*

The principal sources that I have used will be found in the short bibliography, but it would be churlish not to mention the assistance derived from several books which have most nearly traversed the same ground, and greatly eased my path. First and foremost is the scholarly work *The Kings of England*, 1066-1901, by the Hon. Clive Bigham, later Lord Mersey; this and the slighter, amusing volume *Our Sovereigns*, 871-1937, by Mr. Osbert Lancaster, treat of the Plantagenets as part of a much wider field. Coupled with Edward the Confessor and the Norman Kings, they form the subject of Mr. Philip Lindsay's spirited *Kings of Merry England*, a book which has done a great deal to dispel the mummified atmosphere which is so often allowed to shroud the Middle Ages as a whole.

To the courteous and ever-helpful staffs of the British Museum, the Public Record Office, and the London Library, I tender my grateful thanks. I owe an even deeper debt to the vast and authoritative knowledge of royal genealogy and heredity of my friend George F. Powell, epitomized in his hitherto unpublished work *An Introduction to Cultural Heredity*. Mr. Powell is in no way responsible for the form of this book, nor for its mistakes and imperfections, which are entirely my own.

Other notable help has been received from Mr. George

* This was written before the announcement of Sir Maurice Powicke's great work: *King Henry III and the Lord Edward*.

Smith, who generously gave me a copy of his edition of *The Coronation of Elizabeth Wydeville*, with its valuable biographical notes; Mr. W. MacLean Homan, Mr. R. P. Howgrave-Graham, Sir T. D. Kendrick, the late Professor E. W. Tristram, Mr. Anthony R. Wagner, and Mr. Francis Wormald, all of whom have assisted me in connexion with portraiture.

To my wife I am indebted for numberless ideas and for devoted and patient assistance throughout; without her help the book would not have been written.

Lastly I must express my thanks to the members of the firm of Batsford who contributed so largely to the final result: the late Harry Batsford as presiding genius; the late Charles Fry, who precipitated my cloudy ideas; and Sam Carr, whose abounding energy has overcome so many details and difficulties.

JOHN HARVEY

*Half Moon Cottage
Little Bookham, Surrey,
1st December, 1947*

THE DESCENT OF PLANTAGENE[T]

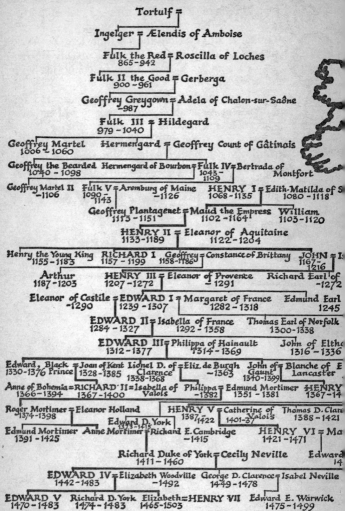

Tortulf =

Ingelger = Ælendis of Amboise

Fulk the Red = Roscilla of Loches
865–942

Fulk II the Good = Gerberga
900–961

Geoffrey Greygown = Adela of Chalon-sur-Saône
–987

Fulk III = Hildegard
979–1040

Geoffrey Martel   Hermengard = Geoffrey Count of Gâtinais
1006–1060

Geoffrey the Bearded Hermengard of Bourbon = Fulk IV = Bertrada of
1040–1098   1043–   Montfort
                                                 1109

Geoffrey Martel II   Fulk V = Aremburg of Maine   HENRY I = Edith-Matilda of S[cotland]
–1106   1090–   1068–1135   1080–1118
                     1143

Geoffrey Plantagenet = Maud the Empress   William
1113–1151   1102–1164   1103–1120

HENRY II = Eleanor of Aquitaine
1133–1189   1122–1204

Henry the Young King RICHARD I Geoffrey = Constance of Brittany   JOHN = Is[abella]
1155–1183   1157–1199 1158–1186   1167–
                                                                   1216

Arthur   HENRY III = Eleanor of Provence   Richard Earl of [Cornwall]
1187–1203   1207–1272   –1291   –1272

Eleanor of Castile = EDWARD I = Margaret of France   Edmund Earl
–1290   1239–1307   1282–1318   1245

EDWARD II = Isabella of France   Thomas Earl of Norfolk
1284–1327   1292–1358   1300–1338

EDWARD III = Philippa of Hainault   John of Eltham
1312–1377   1314–1369   1316–1336

Edward, Black = Joan of Kent Lionel D. of = Eliz. de Burgh John of = Blanche of [E]
1330–1376 Prince 1328–1385   Clarence   –1363   Gaunt   Lancaster
                             1338–1368   1340–1399

Anne of Bohemia = RICHARD II = Isabella of   Philippa = Edmund Mortimer   HENRY [IV]
1366–1394   1367–1400   Valois   –1382   1351–1381   1367–14[13]

Roger Mortimer = Eleanor Holland   HENRY V = Catherine of   Thomas D. Clare[nce]
–1374–1398   1387–1422   Valois   1388–1421
                     Edward D. York   1401–3[7]
                     –1415

Edmund Mortimer Anne Mortimer = Richard E. Cambridge   HENRY VI = Ma[rgaret]
1391–1425   –1415   1421–1471

Richard Duke of York = Cecily Neville   Edward
1411–1460   14[53]

EDWARD IV = Elizabeth Woodville   George D. Clarence = Isabel Neville
1442–1483   –1492   1449–1478

EDWARD V   Richard D. York   Elizabeth = HENRY VII   Edward E. Warwick
1470–1483 1474–1483   1465–1503   1475–1499

100 50 O 100 150 MILES

Edinburgh

Durham

York

Dublin

Chester

WALES

Norwich

Bristol

London

Winchester

Ghent

Calais

Amiens

Rouen

Reims

Caen

NORMANDY

Paris

Chartres

Troyes

BRITTANY

MAINE
Le Mans

Angers

ANJOU

Fontevrault TOURAINE

POITOU

Poitiers

Angou
lême

LIMOUSIN

AUVERGNE

PERIGORD

Bordeaux

GUIENNE

TOULOUSE

BEARN

J.H.H.
1947

NOTE TO THE THIRD IMPRESSION

The text has been revised throughout and a number of corrections made. For criticism and suggestions I am particularly indebted to Dr. K. A. Bisset, Mr. Colin J. Hughes, the late Dr. J. J. Keevil, and Colonel Alfred H. Burne, D.S.O., the last of whom has demolished the legend of the personal responsibility of the Black Prince for a massacre at the sack of Limoges; see his article in *The Fighting Forces*, February 1949, and A. Leroux: *Le Sac de la Cité de Limoges* (Limoges, 1906). The revised text owes much to M. Antoine Gentien who, in producing a French version (Paris, Plon, 1960), drew my attention to a number of obscurities in the original and suggested a few minor omissions which help the narrative.

As stated on p. 15, this is not a work of original research, but in its present form the book to some extent rests upon my own researches in related fields of study. As the technique of reprinting does not allow of extensive changes in the Notes (see pp. 233-239) it may be appropriate here to draw attention to some papers which give the evidence for a different approach to the historical background: for St. Stephen's Chapel and the change to Perpendicular art (p. 135) see "The Origin of the Perpendicular Style" in *Studies in Building History* (edited by E. M. Jope, 1962); for the importance of English painters under Edward III and Richard II (pp. 138, 154), "Some London Painters of the 14th and 15th centuries" in *The Burlington Magazine*, November, 1947; and for the relations between art and personality in the case of Richard II, "The Wilton Diptych —a Re-examination" in *Archaeologia*, XCVIII, 1961, pp. 1-28. On a more general issue of the historical evidence upon which the book is based, see *The Amateur Historian*, IV, no. 7, 1960, p. 281.

16th April, 1963   *J. H. H.*

INTRODUCTION

Within recent years there has been a highly significant trend of thought away from the Darwinian evolutionary conception of biology, and parallel tendencies are affecting the views held by experts in a whole range of linked fields of study. One of the most striking pronouncements is to be found in Lord Raglan's preface to a new edition of *Jocasta's Crime*, published in 1940. He says: "At the time when I wrote this book (seven years ago) I accepted Sir James Frazer's view . . . that magic is a necessary stage on the upward path to religion. . . . I have since come to the conclusion that this view is untenable. It seems to me that magic, as we find it among savages and the superstitious, far from being the stuff out of which religions grow, is really the decayed or fossilized remains of ancient religion. . . . I would ask the reader to think of any given magical practice as being widespread not because it is in any way natural, but because it was once associated with the highest civilization of the day. All magic is, like everything connected with civilization, highly artificial."

In the place of a gradual evolution from lower forms towards higher, a devolution downwards from a higher origin is here postulated, as well as a single higher civilization diffused about the globe. That this *diffusionist* hypothesis of civilization is correct is now almost universally conceded by scientists, following the proofs advanced by Professor W. J. Perry and the late Sir Grafton Elliot Smith. The "Children of the Sun" who carried outwards this single human culture from its point of origin were not necessarily, as Elliot Smith maintained, exclusively Ancient Egyptians. It now seems probable that Sumeria had the elements of civilization earlier than Egypt, and Northern Syria before either. Be this as it may, this one original human culture, which some five or six thousand years ago already comprehended all the essentials of which our own civilization is composed, had as its keystone the institution of Divine Kingship. This extraordinary institution has been traced in all its details by the late A. M. Hocart in his fascinating book *Kingship*. There he shows with the clearest proofs the "identification" of the King with the Sun, as God-Man; his Coronation, a ceremony symbolizing his rebirth as the God; his Marriage, and the Queen's consecration, representing the union of God (Sky) with Earth, of soul with body. Further, he shows that priests have developed out of kings, as their deputies before God; and that the marriage of non-royal persons is a counterpart of the Coronation and Consecration ceremony, designed to have the same beneficial results for mankind as individuals that its prototype secures for the nation or the tribe.

So far, for several thousands of years, notwithstanding the deep cleavage with tradition caused by religious and political upheavals, this theory and the practices deriving from it have persisted in some form or other in every part of the habitable globe, and have contributed most of what is imperishable in mythology, poetry, literature, and art in all forms. Clearly there must be, beneath all this stratified yet integrated tradiion, a sufficient Cause. What it is we do not know, nor is it necessary that we should. The observed facts are in themselves sufficient ground for scrupulous adherence to this Way of Life by every human being who desires the maintenance of higher civilization: the continued existence of those things which differentiate mankind from the rest of the animal creation.

The diffusion of culture was not generally accomplished by mass migrations; folk-wanderings have indeed taken place: the movements of the Germanic and Gothic tribes into the declining Roman Empire, the invasion of Europe by the Huns and later by the Tartars. Such mass invasions were not without effect, but are not typical of the principal means by which higher cultures replace their inferiors. There seems to be an inversion of Gresham's law; while bad money drives out good, it is good blood that replaces bad. Small numbers of men and women endowed with this higher potency transform whole empires, and there is no doubt that this higher blood is that of the Children of the Sun. Further, strong evidence is advanced for what Perry terms " dynastic continuity ", that is to say, the lineal descent of all royal families from the single original stock. It is well known that the royal blood of Egypt was kept free from mixture over long periods by means of sister-marriage, but outside Egypt inbreeding has preserved a distinct royal caste, relatively homogeneous compared with the diversity of the subject peoples.

It is singular, as Perry points out, how seldom usurpations have been lasting: in some way the original ruling family comes back into its own, not necessarily in the male line. Time alone will show how this rule will operate in the case of modern republics, but Julius Caesar claimed descent from the Kings of Rome, and this was probably the main cause of his assassination, which did not, however, prevent the rule of the Empire falling to his line.* Britain's civiliza-tion is due, according to a legend of hoary antiquity and (in outline at least) high probability, to the arrival of a band of exiled Trojans led by Brutus, great-grandson of Aeneas, about the end of the eleventh or beginning of the tenth century B.C. Whether or no we accept the legendary genea-logies, which, like the dynastic lists of Sumeria, India, or the Pacific Islands, bring down the line of Brutus from century to century, we may accept the probability of the dynastic continuity implied. And when, after the interlude of Roman imperial rule, Britain fell a prey to the Saxons, the first Saxon King of Wessex, Cerdic, bore a Celtic name, while his successor Ina, five generations after, seems to have represented the legitimate British Kings as grandson of the sister of the last King Cadwaladr.

* The hitherto unsuspected importance of heredity at a later period of the Roman Empire is shown by Jérome Carcopino: L'Hérédité dynastique chez les Antonins (*Revue des Etudes Anciennes*, t. LI, nos. 3-4, Juillet-Décembre 1949).

Hazy as are the details, these transactions indicate the probable character of dynastic continuity in Britain. From Ina, whose code of laws still survives, the English royal pedigree is a matter of fact. Egbert, sixth in succession from Ina, was the grandfather of Alfred the Great, while Her Majesty Queen Elizabeth II is Alfred's direct descendant in the thirty-sixth generation. Here we are concerned only with ten of these thirty-six generations, the tenth to the nineteenth, counting from Alfred. Those ten generations of the House of Plantagenet gave England its form and character.

Before it is possible to grasp the greatness of the task performed by our Plantagenet Kings, something must be known of the country before the arrival of Henry II. After the invasions of the Saxons and their settlement of England from the fifth to the eighth century A.D., English culture and art, under strong Eastern influences, reached a high level. This flourishing country was completely wrecked by the Danish inroads of the ninth century, so that King Alfred during his lifetime saw both the pre-existent civilization and the chaos left by the war; on the ruins he built up a new culture with a strong literary background. The debt owed by England, and for that matter by the whole of western Christendom, to King Alfred, is among the greatest ever due to a single man. His record is the more impressive in that he was one of the very few soldier kings of history who was never an aggressor. For posterity his greatness lies in his undaunted spirit and grip on essentials, his unswerving and forthright religious sense, his realization of the importance of written history in forming a backbone of tradition, and in his superb grasp of his own language.

In spite of Alfred the decadence of Saxon England had set in, and the continuance of the Danish raids made normal national life an impossibility. The conquest of Canute made England the centre of a wide-flung overseas empire, but Canute the Dane, though he strengthened his dynastic position by a marriage with Emma, widow of Æthelred the Unredy, did not succeed in ensuring the continuity of his line. A truly great King, generous and well served, a lover of poetry and worthy successor to the throne of Alfred, Canute succeeded in repairing the appalling damage wrought by his own ancestors, and made of England a wealthy nation and one of the arbiters of Europe. At his death the country lapsed into chaos, and during the following generation rapidly lost ground: the way lay open for radical change.

It came with William the Conqueror, though the Norman had no wish to effect so violent a change as political circumstances ultimately forced upon him. By the end of his reign, when Domesday Survey was compiled, Saxon landowners were a small minority and their language foreign to the ears of the Court. The Conqueror himself, his boisterous and wayward son Rufus, and his wiser and more diplomatic younger child Henry, maintained a high degree of law and order. At Henry's death, there being no recognized heir, all was confusion, and the legitimist claims of his daughter Maud, widow of the German Emperor Henry V, did not prevent the coronation of Stephen of Blois, grandson of the Conqueror, whose daughter Adela had been his mother.

For almost twenty years English civil life was chaotic; giving rise to the statement that during those years God and His Saints slept. Stephen, a chivalrous gentleman, was quite incapable of dealing with the unscrupulous foes who surrounded him. At one time he was captured by Maud, who was proclaimed lady or queen of England; but her own arrogance alienated her supporters and caused her expulsion from the country and Stephen's restoration. After this, Maud resided in Normandy, which had been overrun by her husband, Geoffrey of Anjou, and left to her eldest son Henry, afterwards Henry II, the prosecution of her hereditary claim to the English throne. From Maud, Henry must have inherited much of his ceaseless energy, and through her some of Henry I's capacity for the arrangement of public affairs, but he escaped the callous and vindictive cruelty of which the Norman kings had been capable. On his father's side he came of different blood: it is time to give consideration to the House of Anjou.

The story of the Angevins has points of resemblance to the Victorian fables of wealth and power attained by diligent self-help. From small beginnings the family increased its heritage by marrying the appropriate heiresses of the neighbouring lands. The tale of increase begins with Ingelger of Anjou, son of the semi-mythical Tortulf the Woodman and contemporary of our Alfred the Great. Ingelger acquired Amboise with his wife Ælendis; their son Fulk the Red added Loches by his union with Roscilla, daughter of Warner lord of Loches, Villentras and Haye, and died in 942. Their son Fulk II, the Good, waged no wars, and seems to have been a Christian Pacifist; his sanctity was proverbial, and a tale was told that, meeting with a poor crippled leper, Fulk carried him to the door of the church, probably St. Martin's at Tours, where Count Fulk was one of the canons. At the church door the leper vanished, but at the midnight service St. Martin appeared in a vision and explained that like St. Christopher, Count Fulk had carried the Lord Christ Himself.

By Fulk's marriage to one Gerberga (his canonry at Tours was honorary) he had a son Geoffrey, known as Greygown, who married twice and died in 987, leaving by his second wife a son and successor, Fulk III the Black or the Palmer, from his crusade to the Holy Land. This Fulk also married twice, first Elizabeth heiress of Vendôme, who in the year 1000 was burnt at the stake in Angers, whereupon the whole city was destroyed by fire by, as was said, supernatural intervention. In spite of this, Fulk was able to find a second wife, Hildegard, by whom he had a son, Geoffrey Martel, and a daughter, Hermengard, who married Geoffrey, Count of the Gâtinais. During his twenty years' reign over Anjou, from 1040 to 1060, Geoffrey Martel acquired Saintonge, Touraine, Vendôme, and Maine. All of these were lost again, except the vitally important Touraine. Geoffrey left no son, and was succeeded by his sister's elder son, Geoffrey the Bearded, soon ousted by his younger brother Fulk IV Rechin, the Quarreller, four times married, who abdicated in 1103 and died in 1109. His son by Hermengard of

Bourbon, whom he abandoned in 1075, was Geoffrey Martel II, but he died before his father in 1106; Geoffrey was succeeded by his half-brother Fulk V, son of Bertrada of Montfort, who had in 1093 served her husband as he had served Hermengard, and eloped with King Philip of France.

Fulk V, by his marriage with Aremburg of Maine reunited Maine with Anjou, but thereby came into collision with the interests of Henry I of England and Normandy. Peace was in the end made in 1119, Henry's son William being married to Fulk's daughter Matilda, only to perish in the White Ship soon afterwards. After further tension between Anjou and England, Fulk's son Geoffrey married the widowed Maud, Henry's only surviving child, and heiress to both Saxon and Norman claims to the English throne. Fulk resigned Anjou to Geoffrey and left for Palestine, where he married Melisende, daughter and heiress of Baldwin II, King of Jerusalem; on Baldwin's death in 1131, Fulk became King of Jerusalem. This abandonment of Anjou for Palestine by the head of the Angevin House played a considerable part in giving to Richard Cœur-de-Lion, Fulk's great-grandson, a prominent place in the Crusade of 1190-3.

In this brief sketch of the pedigree of Anjou we have caught no glimpse of the demon ancestress for whom the family was famous. The story was accepted by the time of Henry II and Richard, for Gerald the Welshman records their joking remarks on the subject, but similar legends are found of other families, and it is by no means clear which count of Anjou could possibly have been the victim of the beautiful but soulless vampire. Not that her behaviour seems so bad, for all that we are told is that she was wont to avoid the mysteries of the Mass by leaving chapel immediately after the Gospel, and when restrained by force, vanished and was no more seen of men. Such tales were very generally believed in the Middle Ages, and an even more famous one accounted for the notorious fact that Englishmen were equipped with small tails. St. Augustine and his missionaries arrived at Cerne in Dorset, where the inhabitants (proud of their heathen sanctuary, whose tutelary figure on the neighbouring chalk down may still be seen) fastened cows' tails to their garments. For this they found their fitting punishment: they and their descendants should have tails for evermore.

Demon ancestress or no, we may agree with Miss Norgate that the whole Angevin line was a very remarkable race: "there is a strong family likeness . . . the first thing that strikes one about them is their thoroughness; whatsoever their hands found to do, whether it were good or evil, they did it with all their might. Nearly all of them were men of great and varied natural powers." Immense physical energy was a distinguishing character of Geoffrey, the first Plantagenet and father of our Henry II. Born on 24 August 1113, he married the widowed empress Maud, who was eleven years his senior, on 2 June 1129, when he was not yet sixteen years of age. Within the year he had succeeded his father as Count of Anjou and immediately made preparations for expansion. As soon as his father-in-law, Henry I, was dead he attacked Normandy, and in less than ten years had made himself its master; on 19 January 1144 he received the ducal crown in Rouen Cathedral. Five years afterwards he handed over the duchy to his son Henry, who thus gained actual experience of government during the impressionable years between sixteen and twenty-one, when he attained the English crown.

It was fortunate that Henry took after his father, not so much in looks (for Geoffrey was known as " the Handsome ") but in temperament. Maud the empress, at any rate in her younger days (she lived on to sixty-two, surviving her husband by thirteen, and her son's accession by ten years), exemplified the less pleasant traits of her Norman forebears. Energetic but tactless and arrogant, she herself lost her power over England to Stephen, weakest and most easily outwitted of opponents. What is to her credit is that in later life she gained the common sense to step back out of her son's path; she was capable of attempting to keep him in tutelage while she established herself as a queen regnant in England, but fortunately for Henry and for England she decided to shun the public stage and to devote herself to works of charity and religion. Thus it was that, endowed with energy and ambition by both his parents, Henry came completely unencumbered to the English throne.

Before we can turn to the life of Henry II we must know something of his country, Anjou, and of his birthplace, Le Mans. Le Mans, ancient capital of Maine, had only been Angevin for a little over twenty years at Henry's birth. It lies on the forty-eighth parallel of latitude about 250 miles to the south of London, and almost on the Greenwich meridian. Angers, the ancient capital of Henry's ancestors, lay fifty miles to the south-west. Anjou was and is a wine-producing country, far enough to the south to enjoy real heat in summer and to endue its grapes with solar geniality. In the twelfth century it lay far enough from the narrow orbit of the King of France round Paris to be able to form a genuine centre for a different circle of power; though not metropolitan, it was hardly provincial, for Anjou lay on the march of Brittany, a buffer state between Celt and Gaul. In this capacity it secured its own practical independence. Yet Anjou, though from England it seems a warm southern land, belongs to Northern Europe. South of the Angevin dominions lies Poitou, and on the southern frontier of Poitou lies the real South, the limits of the Langue d'Oïl or Northern French, and of the lands ruled by custom in the old northern manner. The true, deep South was ruled by written Roman law and preserved the Langue d'Oc, the Provençal tongue of the troubadours.

Henry's own marriage to the heiress of Aquitaine brought him into the closest contact with this southern sphere of Provençal, troubadour culture. He and his son Richard were to wield power over a heterogeneous empire of North and South, stretching from the Cheviots to the Pyrenees, constantly shaken by the jealousies of its own rulers and the steadfast policy of the Kings of France. This enormous realm was united by only two things: the personal force of character of its rulers and the fact that it was knit together by the Atlantic Ocean at its back. Through it ran a great cultural artery, linking the Mediterranean coast through Carcassonne to Toulouse on the Garonne, and thus to Bordeaux, the lands reached by way of the western sea and the rest of the Angevin dominions. By this route came to the West strange knowledge from the East, Byzantine architecture and Byzantine enamelling, and a brilliant tradition of lyric poetry and music.

Henry himself was not brought up within this sphere, but upon its outer edge, the divide between the valleys flowing into the Bay of Biscay and those that run into the English Channel. So Henry partook of two climates, two outlooks, two ways of thought; the background of two races, the Nordic Franks and Normans, the Mediterranean Latin people of the South. Starting from that wonderful focal point, the valley of the Loire and its tributaries, he had a world within his grasp. It would have been too great an anticipation of history for such an empire to endure; though the temperament of Henry's son Richard led southward, his career was not such as to consolidate this extended territory; Richard's younger brother John, too indolent to exert himself against the steady encroachment of Philip Augustus of France, retired to his northern island kingdom. His successors were driven back into that island more and more; in spite of the frenzied efforts of Edward III and Henry V to root out the French menace by taking over France itself, the year 1453 saw the final, irrevocable loss of the last fragment of the enormous southern realm which had been Henry II's. Yet the House of Plantagenet itself did not long survive the loss, and closely as its history was bound up with that of England, one may wonder whether there was not also a vital link with the warmer South.

To understand the inheritance of the Plantagenets, a sketch of feudal society and feudal kingship is an essential. In these days of state sovereignty, opposed only by the theory of supernational organizations, the spirit of feudal Europe of the twelfth to fifteenth centuries is completely foreign. Yet it offered a greater hope of universal peace and general prosperity than the earnest endeavours of present-day internationalists and planners of federal systems. It was of the essence of early feudalism that all its relations were personal. No impersonal abstractions, no departments of state, no imaginary entities such as England, France, or Germany, were present. "England" meant the human individual who was King of England; "France" likewise; "Germany", so far as it had a meaning, meant the Emperor of the German lands, the inheritor of the East Frankish Kingdom of Louis the German.

But with the exception of England, where William the Conqueror had introduced into the feudal system an innovation of immense importance by means of the "Oath at Salisbury", the "national" territories ruled by these Kings were made up of a diversity of smaller, often practically independent states. In England, the principle of the oath taken at Salisbury that feudal tenants owed direct loyalty to the King and not merely to their immediate overlord, had already in 1086 made a great and far-reaching difference between the position of England and that of any other western country. A united England was faced only by the problems of the semi-independent principality of Wales and the would-be independent kingdom of Scotland. France, on the other hand, where all the lesser nobility fell in behind their leaders if those greater feudal princes threw aside their loyalty, was rent in pieces. It was only at the close of the Middle Ages, and as a result of the policy of patience and cunning pursued by the French Kings, that the bulk of geographical France became politically French.

Feudal relations being personal, a breach of fealty was a personal dishonour; it is only by a survival of this notion that we speak of "nations" honouring or dishonouring their obligations. The men of the Middle Ages were both wiser and more fortunate than we, in that they knew precisely where to affix praise or blame. In spite of the frequency with which feudal ties were broken, the fealty once given did impose some check upon the turbulent vassal; if he were faced by his feudal sovereign in person he might very likely withdraw rather than assault the body of his overlord. In our century, which knows no ultimate restraints, in which abominations may not only be practised, but also defended and justified, it is well to consider those things which in another age did something to form a barrier against the tides of sub-human brutality which surge up and threaten to overwhelm the human race itself. The barrier was itself a part of humanity: the personal element; its links, sometimes strained, but never quite broken, were a personal and transcendent faith in God and a belief in personal loyalty between man and man.

In political loyalty the two beliefs blended together, for the King was not only a human personality, but also God's representative on earth; not merely a civil, secular power, for by his consecration and incoronation he received also the priestly function which, centuries before, the King had delegated to a special caste. The mediæval King, unlike the laity, took the Communion in both kinds, and the analogy of his consecration to that of a bishop was well understood. It was in virtue of this consecration, with its all-important ritual and formalities, that the King reigned. Even towards the close of the Middle Age, Henry VI could appeal to his coronation, approval, and anointing as proof of his right to reign. It was widely held that the solemn consecration, even of a usurper, must be a thing destined by God Himself.

In Saxon times no strict rule of legitimate succession had held in England; the King must certainly be one of the royal family, but his own birth need not necessarily be legitimate, for Athelstan, one of the greatest of the Saxon kings, was a royal bastard, and William the Conqueror's succession to the duchy of Normandy was similar. Gradually, owing to disputes over the succession, and more especially after the Saxon Witanagemot had passed away, with its power of final selection, there grew up the preference for a clear title by primogeniture. Probably Edward I, " the first-born son of King Henry ", was the first English King whose elder birth gave him undisputed title to the throne. The very long reign of Henry III and the crucial developments that had taken place in society during the thirteenth century thus consolidated into a fixed rule what was previously a matter of convenience. William the Conqueror divided Normandy and England by will; neither William Rufus nor Henry I had hereditary right; both were " elected " by the Witanagemot; Stephen also began his reign with " election " and coronation. At the death of Stephen, the hereditary right vested in the empress Maud, but the actual rights of her son Henry were covenanted by the treaty with Stephen. Owing to Henry's absence in Normandy, there was a period of six weeks from Stephen's death, when England was said to be "without a king ", until Henry's coronation.

Richard I was King by hereditary right, but his reign was dated from his coronation; John, who usurped the rights of his nephew Arthur of Brittany, claiming that as brother he was one degree closer to the dead King than a nephew, and therefore next-of-kin, owed his nominal title to " election ". Henry III began his reign with his coronation, nine days after John's death, the last instance of the coronation itself being regarded as the fountain of royal power. Edward I was absent when his father died, and his reign accordingly began from the day on which the nobles " recognized " him and had him proclaimed, four days later. From Edward II onwards, the new reign normally began on the day following the death of the previous King.

We may then conclude that the theory of kingship was undergoing gradual modification; before this change the King was regarded as such because he came of a certain family, because he was marked out by God, and because he actually succeeded in obtaining consecration. Afterwards he was King because he was the eldest legitimate son, even before his consecration; or failing a son, successor according to a definite system of inheritance: England followed one such system, France another. But by whatever method he became King, the sovereign was morally bound by an ideal, a theory of kingly government. In the coronation service he made oath with his people, but his obligations went much further than a mere legal compact: he was a father and maintainer as well as ruler and defender of his people. Inasmuch as he had been directed into this special position by God, and as God's own personal representative, the King could not surrender his rights to anyone, for they were less rights than a bounden religious duty.

Centuries before, the ideal of government had been described by the Roman Emperor and philosopher Marcus Aurelius: "The idea of a polity in which there is the same law for all, a polity administered with regard to equal rights and equal freedom of speech, and the idea of a kingly government which respects most of all the liberty of the governed." Falling short, as humans, from this noble ideal it can still be discerned as the guiding principle of the mediæval kings; the beyond their own human desires and ambitions, beyond the glories of their blood and state, they recognized this beacon light, and each, after his own fashion, was impelled towards it.

PART ONE: SPRING

CHAPTER I

HENRY II

Mediæval biography labours under one very heavy disadvantage when compared with the study of modern personalities or of those of classical Greece and Rome: genuine portraits are incomparably more difficult to discover, even if they exist. That this is a serious matter was realized by Carlyle, who seized upon the crucial importance of portraiture. Writing in 1854 on the subject of a proposed exhibition of Scottish portraits, he declared: " It has been, and always is, one of the most primary wants to procure a bodily likeness of the person inquired after; a good *portrait* if such exists; failing that, even an indifferent if sincere one. In short, *any* representation made by a faithful human creature, of that face and figure which *he* saw with his eyes, and which I can never see with mine, is now valuable to me, and much better than none at all. . . . Often I have found a portrait superior in real instruction to half a dozen written biographies. . . . I have found that the portrait was as a small lighted candle by which the biographies could for the first time be *read*, and some human interpretation be made of them."

On the question of portraiture in the Middle Ages a good deal of ink has been used, and more spilt, and it is commonly denied that there was any serious *attempt* at portraiture, let alone any genuine portraits, in Northern Europe before the opening of the sixteenth century. Exception might be made in favour of a few works by Jan van Eyck and Foucquet, but it is usual to regard effigies of stone, marble, or bronze, and figures in stained glass or in the margins of manuscripts as

35

King	Year	Principal Events	Year	Art and Literature
HENRY II	1146	Second Crusade preached	1140	Angers Cathedral begun; Jerusalem: Church of Holy Sepulchre begun
	1147	Lisbon freed from the Moors; Moscow founded	1154	Ripon Minster begun; Bristol Chapter House
	1154	Grant of Bull to annex Ireland	1159	John of Salisbury's "Polycraticus"
	1162	Thomas Becket, Archbishop of Canterbury	1163	Paris: Cathedral of Notre-Dame begun
	1164	Constitutions of Clarendon; Becket flees	1168	Santiago de Compostella: Cathedral Portico begun
	1169	Strongbow invades Ireland	c. 1170	Durham Cathedral: Galilee
	1170	Murder of Becket	1171	Newcastle-on-Tyne: Castle Keep
	1171	Henry II Lord of Ireland	1173	Layamon's "Brut" begun
	1173	Henry's Arbitration at Toulouse	1175	Canterbury Cathedral: rebuilding begun
	1174	Henry's Penance	1177	Angers: Great Hospital begun
	1179	Louis VII visits Canterbury	c. 1180	Wells Cathedral begun
	1183	Civil War between Henry's sons	1181	Portsmouth: Church of St. Thomas begun
	1185	John visits Ireland	1185	Dover Castle: Keep begun
	1187	War: France; Saladin takes Jerusalem	1185	Basle Cathedral begun
	1189	Third Crusade	1187	Chichester Cathedral: Retrochoir begun
RICHARD I	1190	Richard joins the Crusade	1192	Lincoln Cathedral: Choir begun
	1192	Richard's imprisonment	1193	Peterborough Abbey: West Front begun
	1194	Richard's release	c. 1195	Lichfield Cathedral: Choir begun
	1195	Great Famine; London rebellion	1195	St. Albans Abbey: West Front begun
	1196	Jaffa taken by Moslems	1198	Chateau-Gaillard built
			c. 1200	London: St. Paul's Cathedral central tower begun
JOHN	1199	Murder of Arthur	1202	Winchester Cathedral: Retrochoir begun
	1203	Fall of Byzantine Constantinople; John loses Normandy	1206	Rouen Cathedral begun
	1204			
	1206	Jinghiz Khan, Mongol Emperor; London granted right to elect a Mayor	c. 1208	Southwark Cathedral: Choir begun
	1208	Interdict on England	1210	Strasbourg Cathedral: Nave begun
	1213	John surrenders to the Pope	1211	Reims Cathedral begun
	1214	Battle of Bouvines		
	1215	Magna Carta granted; Crown offered to Louis of France		

King	Year	Principal Events	Year	Art and Literature
HENRY III	1216	Battle of Lincoln	1217	Hereford Cathedral: Lady Chapel begun
	1218	Western Invasion of Jinghiz Khan	1220	Amiens Cathedral begun; Salisbury Cathedral: Lady Chapel begun; Canterbury Cathedral: St. Thomas's Shrine
			1221	Dominicans arrive in England
			1222	Winchester Castle: Great Hall
	1224	Mongols enter Russia	1224	Franciscans arrive in England; Worcester Cathedral: Choir begun
	1225	Magna Carta ratified	1225	Salisbury Cathedral: Presbytery begun
	1227	Jinghiz Khan died	c. 1225	York Minster: North Transept
	1229	Emperor Frederick II occupies Jerusalem		
	1230	Teutonic Knights settle in Prussia	c. 1230	Ripon Minster: West Front begun; Wells Cathedral: West Front begun; York Minster: South Transept
			1231	Saint-Denis: new building begun
			1235	St. Albans Abbey: Sanctuary begun
	1241	Mongols overrun Eastern Europe	1239	Ely Cathedral: Presbytery begun
	1243	Henry III defeated at Taillebourg; Kharizmians take Jerusalem	1242	Durham Cathedral: Chapel of Nine Altars begun
			1245	Westminster Abbey begun; Siena Cathedral begun
			1246	Hayles Abbey founded
	1250	Emperor Frederick II died	1248	Cologne Cathedral: Choir begun; Paris: Sainte Chapelle
			1256	Lincoln Cathedral: Angel Choir begun
	1258	Mongols take Bagdad; the Mad Parliament	1258	Paris; South Transept of Notre-Dame begun; Salisbury Cathedral: West Front
	1261	Byzantines recover Constantinople	1260	Westminster Abbey: Choir begun; Pisa: Niccolo Pisano's Pulpit in Baptistery
	1264	Battle of Lewes	1264	Oxford: Merton College founded
	1265	Montfort's Parliament; Battle of Evesham	1265	Lichfield Cathedral: Nave begun
	1270	The Lord Edward goes on crusade; St. Louis died	1270	Hayles Abbey: Eastern Chapels begun
EDWARD I	1272		1272	Narbonne Cathedral begun

being no more than lay figures accoutred in the dress of their time and bearing the coat-armour of their house. It is unfortunate that this dogmatic, negative attitude should have received such wide circulation, for it has hindered the proper understanding of mediæval history by its support of the view that such understanding is impossible. Yet it is some thirty years since Lethaby went straight to the root of the matter when he wrote that "to say that a likeness was not intended, seems against both reason and record." The National Portrait Gallery, in bringing together electrotypes from the royal effigies, as well as a collection of early painted portraits, has performed an extremely valuable service, for the original effigies can seldom be studied with any comfort, if at all. Using the Gallery's collection as a basis, it is possible to find corroborative evidence for the portrait character of the effigies, and of the painted royal pictures as well.

A tentative search among surviving statues and corbelheads of royalty, supported by portraits in other media, has convinced me that actual likenesses were often intended, and that in the case of the Kings of England, and probably also the Queens and some few of the greater nobility, it would be possible to build up evidence of a cumulative character which would establish the personal appearance of the "sitters". Serious examination of the royal effigies alone makes it clear that the era of royal portraiture can be set back to the middle of the fourteenth century; the face of Queen Philippa, who died in 1369, not only agrees with descriptions, but is intrinsically a likeness, and not conceivably a vague representation of a queen. The various portraits of Richard II—that in Westminster Abbey, that of the Wilton Diptych, that of which a crude copy survives in the National Portrait Gallery, the stained glass figure from the east window of Winchester College Chapel and the illuminated initial reproduced by Mr. Anthony Steel as a frontispiece to his life—all agree with one another and with descriptions (7, 8a).

The problem in the twelfth and thirteenth centuries cannot be thus solved at first sight: the available material is much less in volume and has been subjected to far less detailed study. I can do no more than record my personal opinion that the existing heads often indicate at least the intention of producing a likeness, and that in the series of royal effigies, including those of the Angevins at Fontevrault and L'Espau, we have genuine, though not adequate, portraits. The small portrait heads of kings and queens carved on monuments, sedilia, or on each side of the chancel arch in churches are so similar to one another that one is tempted to carry back into the thirteenth century the royal censorship of the sovereign's portrait which was employed by Queen Elizabeth I. It is difficult to see how such similarity could be reached unless as a result of one or two processes: either the King sat for his likeness while on progress in different parts of the country; or else a " standard " portrait existed somewhere, which could be copied by provincial sculptors. Before leaving this subject I would add that I do not think the portraits were mainly the work of monkish or clerical artists, but normally of experimental lay craftsmen. And so far as possible portraits of the first two Plantagenet Kings are concerned, we depend upon the effigies executed by French carvers, and still remaining in France.

The descriptions of Henry II, added to the evidence of his effigy, give us a clear picture of the man: he was strongly built, with a large, leonine head, freckled fiery face, and red hair cut short. His eyes were grey, and we are told that his voice was harsh and cracked, possibly because of the amount of open-air exercise he took. He would walk or ride until his attendants and courtiers were worn out and his feet and legs covered with blisters and sores. This terrifying energy was the key-note of his whole character, and must have shone in his face, for it was said that men flocked to gaze upon him, though they had seen him a thousand times already. He could perform all athletic feats, but what was far more remarkable in his day was his knowledge of polite accomplishments and letters. He was a gifted linguist, for he had knowledge of all the languages " from the French sea to the Jordan ", though he spoke only Latin and French. His knowledge of law was very extensive, and he adhered to the ancient custom of sitting in judgment in person, though he instituted the legal circuits with their justices of assize able to decide cases remote from the King.

He was sparing in diet and frugal in personal expenditure; careless of his dress, though it was always made of fine materials. Walter Map praised his lack of pride: " . . . he does not take upon himself to think high thoughts; his tongue never swells with elated language; he does not magnify himself as more than man; but there is always in his speech that cleanness which is seen in his dress . . . he comes nearer to admitting himself to be despicable than to making himself a despiser." This was the more surprising in a man of such varied ability; his legal knowledge was not merely general: he was accustomed to settle questions of disputed charters, where forgery was suspected, by personal examination—dubious cases that came before his justiciars were referred to his more acute judgment. His memory was exceptional: he never failed to recognize a man he had once seen, nor to remember anything which might be of use. More deeply learned than any king of his time in the western world, he was appealed to from all quarters; the summit of his power was reached in 1173, when he was called in as arbitrator between Toulouse and Aragon, and in 1177, when at a council held at London he determined the ancient quarrel between Alfonso IX of Castile and Sancho VI of Navarre. That he was thus able to supplant the Court of Rome in international affairs is indeed an extraordinary tribute to his personality and his justice.

Map tells us that his mother taught him to prolong everybody's affairs and keep men dangling in hope while he filled his own purse, and that in respect to cases in his court, which went on " so that many die before they get their matters settled, or leave the court driven by hunger ", he followed this maternal counsel only too well. Yet Map's own statement that " whoever has a good case is anxious to try it before him; whoever has a bad one will not come to him unless he is dragged ", must be placed on the other side.

As to another of his failings, Map is inconsistent, for he
accuses Henry of shutting himself up, away from honest
men, accessible only to the unworthy; yet goes on to say
that whenever the King went out he was seized upon by the
crowds and buffeted hither and thither, even assaulted with
shouts and rough pullings and pushings, in spite of which
he never complained or showed anger, but listened to every
man patiently, and if mishandled beyond bearing, retreated
to some place out of reach.

The story of one of his judgments needs to be told in
full, as Map tells it. " It was the custom of our court that
sealed briefs containing their names and duties were drawn
up and delivered to the ministers of the court gratis. Now
the King's dispenser laid an information against a sealer,
that he had refused to deliver him a brief containing his name
and duties without payment. Turstin FitzSimon was the
dispenser, Adam of Yarmouth the sealer. The court after
hearing them was in doubt, and called in the King; he first
heard Turstin, and then Adam, who said: 'I had received
some guests, and I sent a man to beg the lord Turstin
to give me two cakes of your own royal sort. He answered,
" No." Afterwards, when he wanted his brief, I remembered
that " No ", and in like manner I said " No." ' The king
decided against him who had said ' No ' first. He made
Adam sit at the bench with the seal and Turstin's brief
placed before him; and he compelled Turstin to put off his
mantle, and on bended knee present Adam with two royal
cakes, decently wrapped in a white napkin, and when the
present had been received ordered Adam to deliver him the
brief, and so reconciled them; and he added that his officers
ought not only to help each other from their own stock or the
treasury, but also to help anyone of the household, and even
outsiders who were pressed by necessity."

His generosity was on a grand scale; but he kept the
secret of his " large and fat almsdeeds, lest it should be
known to his left hand what his right hand gave "; and
in the hope of reaching even those of the poor whose com-
plaints did not come to him personally, he appointed a

Templar as his almoner, to distribute a tenth of all the food and drink that came into the King's house to the destitute. In this respect Henry was the forerunner of vast and warm-hearted charity displayed by his whole line, all of whom were better fitted to bring a personal touch into the distribution of wealth than are the impersonal officials of the Treasury. Nor did his charity reflect a lavish outlook: his personal outlay was most moderate. Gerald the Welshman used to be fond of telling how the monks of St. Swithin at Winchester grovelled in the mud before the King, complaining to him even with tears that their Bishop, Richard Toclive, had deprived them of three dishes at their meals. Henry asked how many dishes they had left, and they answered "Ten." "In my court," said the King, "I am satisfied with three. Perish your Bishop, if he doesn't cut your dishes down to the same."

At other occasions he took pleasure in egging on the religious to mild dissipation, and travelling incognito was once entertained to a drinking bout by the Abbot of a Cistercian house, which should, of course, have most rigidly debarred such excesses. But even then Cistercian austerity was greatly relaxed, though within a few years of the death of St. Bernard, for the monks had their own private toasts of "Pril" and "Vril", answering to the "Washeil" and "Drinkheil" of the lay banqueter. Into all this the Abbot initiated his guest. Later on, the Abbot visited court and as he reached the presence was greeted with "Pril" by the King, who made him perform the whole ritual of the toast, to the amusement of everybody but the unfortunate ecclesiastic himself. Henry's respect for the cloth was not exaggerated: in 1157, long before the great quarrel with Becket over the rights of the Church, Bishop Hilary of Chichester, whose jurisdiction over the Abbots of Battle was on trial, objected that the secular authority could not deal with a spiritual jurisdiction, or depose any bishop or other ecclesiastic without leave from the Pope. The King's reply was "True enough, he cannot be 'deposed', but he can be quite shoved out with a push like this ", suiting the action to the word.

While attending church services the King used to spend his time " doodling " or sketching, or in whispered conversation; but he was not indifferent to the sanctity of such a man as Hugh of Avalon. One Brother Girard was once taking Henry to task for his sins, while Prior Hugh waited silently with his head bowed. Taking no notice of the monk, the King turned to Hugh and asked what he was thinking of: " Are you making ready to leave our kingdom?" Hugh answered gently that he did not despair of the King, but was rather sorry for the troubles and labours which hindered the care of his soul. " You are busy now, but some day, when the Lord helps, we will finish the good work begun." At this the King burst into tears and embraced Hugh, swearing that he should not depart from the kingdom while he lived: " With you I will hold wise counsel, and with you I will take heed for my soul!"

Hugh once excommunicated one of Henry's foresters, and was summoned to the royal presence at Woodstock, where he found Henry and his courtiers sitting on the grass in a circle. The King took no notice of Hugh's greeting but remained in a sulky silence. Hugh pushed aside an earl and sat down at the King's side; Henry, too restless to stay quiet, called for needle and thread and began to stitch a leather finger-stall which he was wearing on his left hand. After a minute Hugh said: " How like you are now to your cousins of Falaise ", alluding to William the Bastard's mother, the tanner's daughter. Overcome by the joke and the Prior's sly impudence, the King rocked with laughter, and then explained the allusion to those who had not grasped it. Not only could Henry take a joke in good part; he could also show remarkable delicacy. Map tells how he was riding at the head of a body of knights and clerks, talking with a distinguished monk, Dom Reric. There was a high wind at the time, and just as the cavalcade appeared a white monk who was walking along the street, looked round, and tried to get out of the way. "He dashed his foot against a stone, and as angels were not bearing him up at the moment, fell in front of the king's horse, the wind blowing his habit right over his neck, so that he was entirely exposed to the eyes of the lord King and Reric. The King feigned to see nothing and kept silence; but Reric muttered: 'Curse that religion that reveals the arse.'"

Henry's relations with Thomas Becket have overshadowed all his other dealings, not only concerning religion, but in his whole life and reign. Nothing could be more misleading than the notion of a saintly man of God ill-treated by a tyrannical potentate. It was said that Henry was never known to choose an unworthy friend, but Becket's worthiness is a matter of opinion. Extraordinary mixture of well-to-do man-about-town, witty and extravagant, and self-willed, self-torturing, and it must be said, self-advertising churchman, Thomas Becket won for himself an outstanding place in history by his genius for manœuvring other parties into the wrong.

As the child of wealthy parents, young Thomas was weighed by his mother against money, clothes, and food. This equipoise of commodities Rohesia, a Norman from Caen, not the Saracen of legend, gave away to the poor, just as at the present day Indian poor benefit from the birthday weighing in diamonds of the Aga Khan. In his roaring days, as Henry's boon companion, Becket was far from sharing the King's real charity towards the poor and outcast. Riding together through London in midwinter, they saw an old man shivering in his rags. Henry turned to his friend, asking: "Would it not be a meritorious act to give that poor old man a warm cloak?" Becket, then chancellor, agreed, whereupon the King called out "Yours be the merit, then!" and seized Becket's splendid furred cloak, which after a short struggle he wrested from Thomas's grasp and threw to the beggar.

Green remarked that Becket was not abreast of the highest level of thought of his own time. When Hugh of Avalon, as Bishop of Lincoln, forbade his archdeacons and their officials to take fines instead of inflicting penance, they defended themselves on the ground that the blessed martyr Thomas had done the same. " Believe me," said Hugh, " not for that was he a saint, he showed other marks of holiness, by another title he won the martyr's palm." In alms-giving also it is easy to see an element of vainglory in Becket's behaviour. Archbishop Theobald had doubled the amount of the regular archiepiscopal alms; Thomas on his accession doubled the amounts which had been given by Theobald. But when, the day after his consecration, some minstrels and jugglers who had performed before him when he was chancellor came to him for their usual rewards he refused them, saying that his possessions were a sacred trust from henceforward, not to be spent upon actors and jesters. About all this there is a sad atmosphere of cant.

The martyrdom of Thomas Becket was a martyrdom which he had repeatedly gone out of his way to seek, and while it is impossible to condone the savage folly of his murderers, one cannot but feel sympathy towards Henry, thus placed in a position of responsibility for the death of a man who in happier days had, after all, been his friend. Becket got what he asked for, but Henry, as generous and as just as he was free from petty spite, was left burdened with murder and sacrilege for the remaining twenty years of his life. It is a major irony of history that Becket should be regarded as a martyr for the cause of freedom from a state tyranny largely imaginary, and against which Henry and the like strong kings formed the greatest bulwark. The dubious character of Church interference in policy did not escape Henry: when in 1185 the Patriarch Heraclius visited him to launch a new crusade, Gerald the Welshman suggested that it was a great honour to the King that he should have been chosen out by the Patriarch above all the Kings of the earth. Henry retorted: " The clergy may well call us to arms and peril, seeing they will take no blows in the fray nor shoulder any burdens they can avoid." Even as regarded war against the infidel, the principle of pacifism was recognized, for Walter Map, writing of the Templars about 1186, says: "They take the sword and perish by the sword. But, say they, all laws and all codes permit the repelling of force by force. Yet He renounced that law who when Peter struck a blow, would not call out the legions of angels. It does seem as if these Templars had not chosen the better part, when we see that under their protection our boundaries in the Holy Land are always being narrowed, and those of our enemies enlarged."

Gerald, some fifteen years later, went further in accusing the Archbishop of Canterbury, Hubert Walter, of correspondence with the enemy (France), of sending food to the enemy for his own personal gain, and of making a corner in the grain market. "Moreover, knowing as well he might, since it was done by his advice, that owing to the war between the Kings an order had been issued that a search for arms should be made in England, he caused all arms that were anywhere for sale to be purchased, and collected a vast number in a very short time. Then as soon as a further order was made that arms should be procured throughout the realm, he forthwith offered his store of arms for sale and made a vast profit." It is clear that though kings were to blame in their almost incessant warfare, there were few, if any, others who could lay claim to a higher morality.

It is, however, easy to find fault, and Henry himself rebuked one who sought to curry favour by abusing the Bishop of Worcester, who had been criticizing the King for having his son crowned and for seizing Church sees into his own hands. "Do you think, you scoundrel, if I say what I choose to my kinsman and my bishop, that you or anyone else are free to dishonour him with words and persecute him with threats? Scarce can I keep my hands from thy eyes!" In such a scene we can sense Henry's sincerity, and his loathing of the carping critic and the toady. His fairness can also be seen in his unpopular refusal to join in persecution of the Jews, and his setting open his dominions as a refuge for the Albigenses when they were being harried in southern France.

In a positive sense, too, he mantained human rights; he put down the barbarous treatment of shipwrecked sailors, and repressed plunder and outrage. Even natural calamities he did what he could to mitigate: Map once crossed the Channel with him in a fleet of twenty-five ships which had the obligation of carrying over the King and his household free of charge. All but the ship in which Henry and Map were travelling were wrecked, though the crews were saved. In the morning the King called the wrecked sailors together and paid the estimated amount of their losses, coming to a large total, though he was not in any way responsible. His faithfulness to his pledged word was famous.

Born on 25 March 1133, the first day of the traditional year, Henry's life inaugurated a new age, and made of England a new country. Whether he himself attached any special importance to his birth-date is unknown, but like all men of the Middle Ages he would have been wise enough to allow due weight to astrological influences. He was not prone to superstition; though he accepted as a good omen the white hare which started up at his feet when he landed in Ireland in 1171, he displayed great shrewdness when the Welsh attempted to play upon his fears in the following year. In April 1172 he landed at St. Davids, and came to a stream spanned by a great stone known as Lechlavar. Merlin's prophecy ran that an English King, conqueror of Ireland, should die on Lechlavar, and as Henry came to the stream an old Welsh crone screamed out: "Avenge us to-day, Lechlavar! Avenge the people of this land!" Henry looked steadily at the stone for a moment, and then with firm steps crossed over. When he had reached the far side he exclaimed: "Who will ever again believe the lies of Merlin?" Two years later, when to the rebellion of his sons was added a Scottish invasion, Henry did penance at Canterbury for the death of Becket; at once God's forgiveness was signalized by a great victory at Alnwick, the Scottish King William the Lion being taken, while the Flemish invasion fleet in the Channel dispersed. At the close of this revolt Henry was left stronger than ever before, with

Scotland an absolute fief, and the rebel fortresses dismantled. No executions of captured traitors marred his triumph.

Henry's latter years were embittered by the bickering of his sons and the behaviour of his wife, Eleanor of Aquitaine, who aided and abetted them. Eleanor, apart from her magnificent heritage in lands, was an outstanding personage in her own right. One of the most conspicuous individuals of her time, even the lapse of centuries is unable to blur altogether the sharp outlines of her impetuosity. Born eight years before Henry of Anjou, she was the daughter of William X, Duke of Aquitaine. Her grandfather, William IX, had been famous both as a crusader and a poet. The House of Aquitaine was imbued with the richest culture of the South, and its members were accustomed to a high standard of material civilization also. Eleanor, its last representative, typified all its romantic qualities, filled with vitality and passion. About her memory legends linger, true indices of the force of the personality round whose wraith they centre. When only about thirteen she was married to Louis VII of France, a man so mild and ascetic in his habits that she flared out that she had " married a monk and not a King ". While Louis so reverenced the Church that he would humbly give precedence to the meanest clerk, Eleanor represented that pagan spirit of the South which found its final vivid expression among the Albigensian heretics. To her, such a husband was not " worth a rotten apple ", and even if we cannot credit the far-fetched story that she taunted her husband with her intention to elope to Saladin, of whom she had heard such glowing reports that she already loved him better than her cold spouse (Saladin was only ten years old), it is easy to see why such a story seemed plausible.

Little as Eleanor loved the Christianity practised by Louis, she fell a victim to Bernard's preaching of the Church Militant, and took the Cross after hearing his sermon at Vézelay on 31 March 1146, when she was some twenty-one years old. So violently did she embrace her new cause that another legend asserts that the ladies of her court sent spindles and distaffs, equivalent of white feathers, to men who refused to become crusaders. In 1147 she journeyed from Metz to Constantinople, and onwards to Jerusalem, in fulfilment of her vow. The meek Louis accompanied her. At the time of this, the Second Crusade, the new Church of the Holy Sepulchre was approaching completion, in the hands of its French architect, Maître Jourdain, who may well have come from Eleanor's duchy, so closely does the church resemble the great Roman-Gothic works of south-west France, such as the cathedral of Angoulême. This church, supreme artistic expression of the Crusades and central aspiration of Christendom, was dedicated in 1149. Out of the vortex of influences brought about by the first and second crusades in the half-century 1099-1149, from the interplay of Eastern and Western cultures, was born Europe's Gothic style, which, saving the perfection of harmonic music, is the greatest contribution of the West to the human achievement.

The sharing of adventure did nothing to bring Louis and Eleanor together. Violent quarrels with her husband during their absence from France led, stage by stage, to the annulment of the marriage in 1152, a step of inconceivable folly on the part of the French King, and direct cause of the bitter conflict between France and England which was to embroil the two countries for the next 300 years. In May 1152, two months after the annulment, Eleanor was quietly married to Henry of Anjou, then only nineteen, and "without the pomp or ceremony that befitted their rank". In spite of the storm of rage which the marriage let loose at the Court of France, the conjoined stars of Anjou and Aquitaine were in the ascendant. Henry, who ten years before had crossed over to England with Earl Robert of Gloucester, and received part of his education at Bristol from the famous Master Matthew during a stay of more than a year, already had his plans far advanced to gain the throne In the spring of 1147 he had again been in England with the ill-prepared and unsuccessful invasion that led to the Empress Maud's final retirement. In 1149-50 he paid another visit and was knighted at Carlisle by his great-uncle, David King of Scots, on 22 May 1149; now he was ready for the conclusive venture into the ill-governed land of promise.

At the beginning of January 1153, but a few months after his sudden wooing and passionate honeymoon, Henry crossed to England with 3,000 footmen and 140 horse in a fleet of 36 ships. Early on the morning of Epiphany, the sixth of January and Festival of the Three Kings who came from the East, he landed on the Hampshire or Dorset coast and entered a small church just as the Mass was beginning. The first words he heard, the introit for the feast, were the prophetic *Ecce advenit dominator Dominus, et regnum in manu ejus,* Behold the Lord the ruler cometh, and the kingdom in his hand. Before the year was out he had secured his rights of succession by treaty, and was in effective charge of the country; the death of Stephen in October 1154 gave him the crown itself. Since the time of Henry I the English nobility had worn long trailing cloaks, while the new fashion of Anjou was short; by bringing the fashion with him, Henry acquired the nickname of Curtmantel, and the swift sharp swing of his short cloak well symbolized the energy of the new age he introduced. He was crowned in Westminster Abbey on 19 December 1154.

Immediately the administration and national finances were reorganized: the unbroken series of fiscal records, the Pipe Rolls, now begins, and from them it has been calculated that the national income in 1155 was £22,000; in 1189, at the end of the reign, it was £48,000, a fair index, even though the rolls may be an incomplete guide, to the achievement of those thirty-five years. Within two years chaos had been reduced to order, anarchy was a thing of the past, men were able to go about their business in safety. "Business men went out safe to the markets from the towns and castles, and the Jews to their ready clients," as a contemporary put it. After three years of setting their house in order, Henry and Eleanor visited Worcester Cathedral at Easter 1158, and on Easter Day laid their crowns on the shrine of St. Wulfstan, solemnly vowing never again to wear them. In this manner they identified themselves with England and the English Kings, and devoted themselves to the continuation of their traditions.

Eleanor kept her splendid court, sometimes at London, sometimes elsewhere: at Marlborough Castle in 1164 she ruled over an English Christmas for the last time; thenceforward her relations with Henry deteriorated, and as her sons grew up she identified herself more and more with her own inheritance of Aquitaine. While Henry was having his quarrel with Becket she was holding court at Poitiers, and it was there that she presided over the fantastic Courts of Love. The artificial problems set for lovers, and her awards of the palm of amorous courtesy, are in keeping with the southern life of the troubadour courtiers amongst whom she had been brought up and of whose blood she was. While her husband busied himself with the institution of a new economy, administration, and legal system in his adopted country, encouraging foreign traders and seeing ramshackle timber houses give place to well-built mansions of squared stone, Eleanor was enjoying herself in the warm and mellow atmosphere of her own land, amid the sparkle and wit of a Mediterranean people. But she loved to play with fire, and to dabble in politics, and while Henry was granting to Bristol the right of colonizing Dublin and thus cementing by trade his recent victory in Ireland, his eldest son, the " young king " Henry, was being encouraged into rebellion by his foolish mother. In 1173 the revolt broke out, and at its collapse in the following year Eleanor was captured attempting to escape into the French King's domains, in a disguise variously stated as nun's attire, and that of a man riding astride. She paid the price of folly by spending the next fifteen years in honourable confinement, while Henry amused himself with fleeting amours, and a more serious liaison with Fair Rosamund Clifford, who could not in fact have been poisoned by the well-guarded Queen.

Unfortunately the sons had learnt their mother's lesson

only too well, and Geoffrey was able to answer a messenger sent by his father: "Dost thou not know that it is our proper nature, planted in us by inheritance from our ancestors, that none of us should love the other, but that ever brother should strive against brother, and son against father?" In 1182 the sons rent the Angevin dominions in France with a civil war amongst themselves; John, the youngest, who had pleaded with Henry to accept on his behalf the throne of Jerusalem proffered by the Patriarch Heraclius in 1185, was instead sent to Ireland as its sovereign, to keep him out of mischief. John's peculiar sense of humour got the better of him, and he permanently alienated the Irish princes by pulling their long beards in derision. After a few months the leagued Kings of Connaught, Desmond and Thomond, drove him from the country, never to wear the gay crown of gold and peacocks' feathers sent him by the Pope. In 1187 Richard again revolted from his father and joined Philip II of France, and war and family strife embittered Henry's last two years. Aged only fifty-six, but prematurely worn out by his immense exertions and by grief at the defection of his sons and, final blow, the treachery of his favourite, John, the great King died at Chinon, humiliated and friendless, on 6 July 1189.

The importance of Henry II does not end at his death; he was the making of England, and left his mark on every department of national life. Precursor of the unifying policy of Edward I, he refused to allow the patriotic Welshman Gerald to win the bishopric he desired, but " after the manner of the English tyrants " insisted upon the Chapter of St. Davids choosing as the bishop the Prior of Wenlock, which they did " with a very quavering hymn of praise, even in the king's chamber before his bed, the King himself being present with his guards." Yet he admired and encouraged Gerald, with whom he was on friendly terms. Meanwhile Gerald " kept vigil till dawn, working by candlelight and turning night to day ", writing treatises and histories " as though he were in the schools and set on nought save study." Walter Map referred scathingly to Henry's Court as more opposed to the Muses than all others, " since the worry of it would not allow an interval for rest sufficient for sleep, let alone study." Yet in spite of their restless life with Henry, Gerald and Map both owed him much, and the galaxy of English art and science which sprang from his entourage proves his immense significance in the world of culture and letters.

It was not alone " actors, singers, dicers, confectioners, huxters, gamblers, buffoons, barbers " who followed the Court; a great concourse of intellect centred about it. The twelfth century had opened brilliantly for England with Adelard of Bath's travels to Greece, Asia Minor, and the East; these remarkable journeys, with a purely scientific purpose, lasted for seven years, and enabled Adelard to refound Western science upon his Latin translation of the Arabic version of Euclid. He studied Arabian philosophy, and his greatest work, *Quaestiones Naturales*, pleads for the principle of free inquiry; he was encouraged by Henry I, and died about 1140. In a different field laboured his junior contemporary, Geoffrey of Monmouth, Bishop of St. Asaph and collector of scattered remnants of early chronology and legend into the *History of the Britons*, issued about 1139 and revised in 1147. The tone and prophetic character of the work encouraged a revival of English feeling and a benevolent British imperialism. Geoffrey's work is not pure history, and his more painstaking contemporaries only revealed their lack of humour in criticizing it as such, but as literature and as political pamphleteering it is brilliant, and its importance in the formation of a British national sentiment and a national cycle of Arthurian romance can hardly be overestimated.

Gerald the Welshman, half Norman, we have frequently met; his description of Ireland and his itinerary in Wales are far in advance of their time, both as examples of method and as literature. His autobiographical writings, though overcast by the thwarting of his life's ambitions, are full of wit and still fresh and true pictures of life. Walter Map, the other great literary pillar of the age, was a clerk in the royal household after spending several years in Paris about 1160. He became an itinerant justice, in 1179 was sent by Henry as representative to the Lateran Council, and after Henry's death became Archdeacon of Oxford. He was living in 1208, when Gerald dedicated the second edition of his Irish book to him, but died soon afterwards. His *Courtiers' Trifles* is filled with folk-lore and anecdote, and throws a great deal of light upon an age otherwise dark. Writing in 1182, but of about a century earlier, he refers to Edric Wild returning from a hunt through desolate country, and accompanied only by one page, finding a large building at the edge of a forest on the March of Wales. On looking in at the lighted windows, noble and page saw to their surprise a great dance of numbers of noble ladies, who later turned out to be phantoms; but the special interest of the story is that Map describes the building as " such as the English have as drinking-houses, one in each parish, called in English *ghildhus*." Here is direct information as to the prevalence, 800 years back, of the forerunners of the modern village hall.

On a wider canvas, Map sometimes strikes a modern note: speaking of the lack of contemporary appreciation, he says: "When I have begun to rot, the book will begin to gain savour . . . it will be an age of apes (as it now is), not men; they will scoff at their present, and have no patience for men of worth. Every century has disliked its own modernity; every age, from the first onwards, has preferred the previous one to itself." Map's supposed work, the *Confession of Bishop Goliath*, and some Latin poems, are among the choicest literary fruits of this " little Renaissance " of the twelfth century, but its riches of all kinds were amazing. Brilliant historians, writing from about 1170 on, were Richard FitzNigel, author of the *Gesta Henrici*, Bishop of London and Treasurer; and Ralf de Diceto, Archdeacon of Middlesex and then Dean of St. Paul's from 1180 to his death in 1193; others were Roger of Howden, clerk of the chapel royal and civil servant, and William of Newburgh, who among his historical work gives a brief account of Scar-

Becket and in the defeat and misery of his last years, there is something inevitable and noble in his failure. Through all his journeyings, restless unpackings late at night, frenzied repackings in the early morning, hither and thither through his vast empire, never still, we discern a human soul, a very real man and true King, who despite the faults of his temper and his passions was a loyal friend and pillar of justice, the greatest of his time.

CHAPTER II

RICHARD I

It is the common fate of sons to be misunderstood by their fathers, and of fathers to be unloved of their sons, but it has been the particular bane of the English throne that its successive holders should so seldom have resembled each other in their abilities or have been able to maintain a continuous policy. In this lies the most conspicuous difference between Plantagenet and Valois, and between the national policies of England and France, their descendants. It is this which accounts for the fact that England's fortunes rose and fell like a see-saw, while for 500 years until 1870 those of France, with only minor setbacks, steadily rose.

The family curse of Plantagenet, this internecine warfare of brother against brother, son against father, uncle against nephew, cousin against cousin, fell upon them from the start. Of Henry II's four sons, the young Henry, Richard, Geoffrey, and John, only John avoided an open breach with his father until that father was on his death-bed. Richard, the noblest and fiercest of them, his mother's favourite, had for years been alternating between bouts of open rebellion and fits of sullen discontent. The history of those years is far too complicated in detail and too devoid of matter of principle to be worth following out except by the serious student. What does concern us is that it was in these petty wars that Richard was first able to show himself a consummate master of warfare. By virtue of his behaviour in battle he won the name of Lion-Heart, a name already bestowed within less than ten years of his death, if not in his lifetime, and which will maintain his popular fame as long as history endures. He is the only member of the House of Plantagenet to be known rather by his personal nickname than by a mere number.

During his life he had another nickname, given him by

the troubadour Bertrand de Born: *Oc e No*, or Yea-and-Nay. This has been represented as meaning that he blew hot and cold and never knew his own mind; but exactly the opposite was its intention. He was famous for the fact that whatever he said, that he did, never breaking the word he gave. At least two independent contemporary observers described him as having a form worthy to occupy a place of high command, and from his effigy we may believe that his bodily appearance matched his high spirit and immense courage. Of great stature and with chin held high, he combined the athletic prowess of his father with the beauty of his grandfather and his mother. His hair, of the true Plantagenet hue, was "midway between red and yellow"; his legs were long, like those of his great-nephew Edward I, and he had an extremely long reach which stood him in good stead in personal combat. Altogether, his was a figure to inspire respect and admiration, even had he not been destined to such a commanding position and engaged in a meteoric career which was to startle the world before he fell in mid-flight at the age of forty-one.

Born at Oxford, probably in Beaumont Palace, on 8 September 1157, he was placed to nurse with a woman of St. Albans whose son had been born the same night. This foster-brother of Richard's was to become one of the greatest scientists of his time—Alexander Neckham, encyclopædist and first European student of magnetism. The surpassing fame of these two men, born almost at the same moment, goes far to support the main contention of astrology, that men's life and character are indicated by the positions of the stars and planets at their birth. Richard himself was no unlearned man, but was, on the contrary, a distinguished poet and musician. Of his Latin, as compared with that of his Archbishop of Canterbury—the same Hubert Walter whom we have seen accused of trading with the enemy and market-rigging—an amusing anecdote is told by Gerald the Welshman. The King had occasion to pronounce the Latin formula "volumus quod istud fiat coram nobis", whereon the Archbishop sought to correct Richard, saying "coram nos,

Domine, coram nos." "And when he heard this the King looked round at Hugh, Bishop of Coventry, a learned and eloquent man, who at once replied: 'Stick to your own grammar, my lord, for it is much better,' and his words were followed by loud laughter from all who were present."

Richard's fondness for music led him to conduct his own private chapel, walking up and down the choir beating time and coaching the choristers, while he also entered into poetic combats with such troubadours as Bertrand de Born, his one-time enemy and later friend. De Born had reason to admire Richard as an ideal prince, for in one of Bertrand's poems he tells us that his wish was "that great men should be always quarrelling among themselves"; in order that Bertrand might celebrate their exploits. Unluckily, this constant quarrelling brought out not only Richard's noble qualities, but others less lovable. His constancy to his word and to his purpose became an obsession and led him into excesses of cruelty from which his father had been free. After his victory over conspirators who invaded his duchy of Aquitaine in 1183, he had some drowned, others slain with the sword, and yet others blinded, by way of example.

Yet we must not forget that his daring and courage were not solely employed for political ends; he had also generosity and a strain of quixotic altruism. Even his severity was explained by the unmitigated treachery and ferocity of his opponents and the fact that his aim was "to make innocence secure amid evildoers" as Gerald expressed it. His working life had begun before he was fifteen, when on 11 June 1172 he was installed as duke of Aquitaine at Poitiers. Seated in the abbot's chair in the Church of St. Hilary he was invested by the Archbishop of Bordeaux and Bishop of Poitiers, while later at Limoges he received the ring of St. Valeria, protomartyr of Aquitaine, and was publicly proclaimed as duke. Seven years later he first showed himself as the great captain of the age by his siege and capture of Taillebourg in Saintonge from Geoffrey of Rancogne, lord of Pons. Taillebourg, considered impregnable, was razed to the ground. From this ten-days' siege at the beginning

of May 1179, we may date Richard's surpassing interest
in the art of fortification. It is interesting to recall that
at this time his father's engineer, Maurice, had just completed the great stone keep of Newcastle, and was about
to begin that of Dover. By 1185, though in title but a duke,
Richard was given a paragraph in the description of the
reigning kings of the time, written by Geoffrey of Vigeois.
Richard, he declared, had never been slow to deeds of prowess,
and his youth had been marked by the strenuousness of his
life.

The turning-point of Richard's life was in 1187, when
news came of the crushing defeat of the Christians by Saladin
at the Battle of Hattin, fought on 7 July. Richard heard
of the catastrophe about the end of October, and on the following day took the Cross; the rest of his life was devoted to
the reconquest of Jerusalem and the rehabilitation of a
Christian Palestine. To the European, even when his Christianity has been superseded by indifference, the Crusades
appear as a great western Cause with which he is personally
identified. Irrespective of religious factors the Crusades are
seen as a " good " thing, and the Arab world of Saladin
as the mortal enemy. What is seldom realized is that from
the point of view of eastern Christians the advent of their
western co-religionists was sheer disaster. It was only when
the West had shown its own incompetence, vice, and greed,
and its total incapacity to unite, even for the highest causes,
that the permanent victory of Islam was assured. The most
profound practical distinction between the peaceful doctrines
of Jesus, and the warlike creed of Mohammed, lies in the
boundless possibilities of fission and internecine strife found in
Christianity, notwithstanding its Catholic claims on the
one hand; and on the other, in spite of the wars of jarring
sects, the deep underlying unity of Islam. That this has
made of Islam incomparably the more formidable opponent
of the tolerance of the ancient world is another matter.

Bearing in mind that the motives behind the Crusades
were mixed, it is still possible to see that Richard's intentions were noble and whole-hearted. He could not quite

put aside those personal quarrels which were the curse of the age: only a year after he had taken the Cross and before he had made any substantial move to leave Europe, took place the wretched meeting, fraught with tragic consequences, of Richard, his father, and Philip Augustus, King of France, at Bonmoulins. Richard, his elder brothers being now dead, claimed immediate recognition as Henry's heir, and the fulfilment of his long-deferred marriage to Aloysia, the French King's sister, who had long been in Henry's keeping. It was whispered that Henry had taken advantage of his ward; at any rate he refused both demands. Richard immediately did homage to the King of France for all his continental possessions, and so began the last rebellion that was to end only with his father's life in the following year.

No sooner was Henry dead than Richard showed himself in a better light; clearly he felt some remorse, for he went out of his way to reassure all his father's faithful supporters, and turned away the traitors who had deserted to his own cause. He made one exception: his young brother John, for whose fickleness he was always ready to find an excuse. On 20 July 1189 Richard was invested with the ducal sword and banner of Normandy in Rouen Cathedral, and received the fealty of his Norman barons. After this he proceeded to England and declared a general amnesty, whereat the chronicler William Newburgh was shocked. "Through the King's clemency, these pests came forth from prison, perhaps to become bolder thieves in the future." Finally, in Westminster Abbey on 3 September, he was crowned and consecrated King of England in a ceremony which has remained the prototype and model for all its successors. Now that all obstacles had been removed from his path a lesser man might have contented himself with the promise of a Crusade later on. Not so Richard.

From the first his one anxiety was to raise money; not for personal gratification, but to equip an army of devotees worthy of the head of the House from which sprang the Kings of Jerusalem. He put up for sale everything that he had, and declared that he would sell London if he could find a buyer. Seldom has the world seen a man so completely romantic in his devotion, so utterly possessed by an ideal, as Richard at this time. Not for self-glorification, but from personal loyalty to his Saviour, the Feudal Sovereign of a Higher Realm, he would win back the Birthplace and the Sepulchre, or die in the attempt. Richard was assisted by the knowledge that he was also fulfilling his father's intentions: Henry's will, made in 1182, is almost entirely concerned with bequests to religious orders and causes, and at the head stand three sums of 5,000 silver marks each to the Templars, to the Hospitallers, and to the common defence of the Holy Land. Further sums totalling almost 25,000 silver marks were left to religious orders, to lepers, anchorites and hermits, in Palestine, England, Normandy, and Anjou. It has to be remembered that the mark was a measure of two-thirds of the Tower moneyer's pound at 5,400 grains of silver, and that the purchasing power of the monetary pound in the twelfth century was quite sixty times as great as now—thus we should multiply these marks by forty to get an approximation in pounds sterling. Henry also left legacies of 300 gold marks (which have further to be multiplied by a variable gold-silver ratio, in mediæval England about eleven to one) to poor Englishwomen of free condition as dowry to help them to marry, and of 100 gold marks each to Normandy and Anjou for the same purpose.

Richard also carried out his father's wishes in giving to his brother John the administration and profits of six counties; a gift more generous than wise, in view of the state of the exchequer and John's unreliable temperament. An incident at the coronation had been the occasion of a terrific outburst against the London Jews, while the next few months saw equally violent rioting directed against their congeners in Lincoln, Norwich, and York. Too much engrossed in his Crusade to concern himself with such matters, so soon as John had been put in charge of his new lands, the King left England and spent Christmas in Normandy. But the solemnity of the venture damped down the merry-making, and there "was little singing of *gestes*". Richard founded a house of Austin Canons in Poitou, a spiritual insurance policy, and then set out to join the French King at Vézelay. An ill omen marred his start, for the first time Richard leaned upon his pilgrim's staff it broke beneath him; however, early in July 1190 the great Franco-English host set out, the two Kings riding together discussing their plans.

Every mediæval pilgrimage—and a crusade was but a special sort of pilgrimage—had about it a good deal of the atmosphere now associated with conducted tours and the arrangements of the late Mr. Thomas Cook. Like these modern counterparts, pilgrimages were an excuse for the ordinary man to break away from routine and to acquire a stock of stories whose retailing would be likely to bring him in a steady supply of refreshment, if not of hard cash, after his (admittedly problematical) return. So we need not be surprised to learn that Richard and his knights on the progress through Italy managed to do some sightseeing around Ostia and Naples, and to visit Salerno with its great university and medical school. Riding with one knight through Calabria, Richard saw a beautiful falcon in a remote village, and insisted on taking it away with him. This caused a pitched battle of stones and knives, from which the King and his retainer narrowly escaped with their lives. Such an incident, recalling the rape of Naboth's vineyard and the far earlier provision of the wise King Uruka-gina of Lagash, that a noble might not insist upon the purchase of any man's land or animals, comes to us with a sense of personal outrage. In the case of a hero such as Richard this shock is the greater; but is such a high-handed action as bad as the countless acts of official commandeering and intimidation which burden the modern citizen of bureaucracy?

By October 1190 the Crusaders reached Messina, where they had to cope with local opposition. The Lombards who controlled the catering supplies refused to sell even necessities, "and but for God and the navy many would have led a poor life." Among the incidents of this trying time was

26

a quarrel between Richard and a French knight, William des Barres, who in 1188 at Mantes had broken his parole. On this occasion he was one of the French ringleaders in a mock battle with lances of cane or reed, which turned into a serious affray between members of the French and English forces. Richard was so enraged by this second fault of his old enemy that he declared perpetual hostility: to his lasting honour this enmity gave place to forgiveness and friendship when des Barres, later on in Palestine, had saved the forces of the Crusade by bravely counter-attacking the Saracens on the line of march between Acre and Haifa.

At Messina also took place another occurrence which opens up a darker side of Richard's character. In December he did penance for vice, and after receiving absolution from the bishop was said to have returned to his iniquity no more. Yet four or five years later, in the spring of 1195, a hermit warned him to be mindful of the fate of Sodom and put away his unlawful deeds, lest he be visited by the vengeance of God. On the Easter Tuesday the King became violently ill, confessed, and again did penance, and recalled his wife to his side. After this his mysterious ailment was cured. The evidence is clear that Richard, like many other warriors and also some most unwarlike men, was the victim of homosexuality. In this his case differs from those of William Rufus, Edward II, and James I, where volumes of rumour seem to be unsubstantiated by any real proof.

It is a pity that the modern world should have shown itself, especially in England, so susceptible to this frighteningly easy method of blackening reputations. No other slander can be so damaging; none so difficult to disprove. But apart from false allegations the true history of " unnatural " vice does deserve serious consideration, the more so as it is in recent England the subject of intense persecution and of penalties so ferocious as to seem incredible. So ill-informed is the public on this question that as enlightened a writer and historian as Chesterton (in his life of St. Francis of Assisi) could allege wholesale sodomy as the besetting sin of the pre-Christian paganism of Greece and

P.   C

Rome. Obviously Christianity has done little or nothing to deal with the problem, and Chesterton and many others seem unable to distinguish between the quite small proportion of actual vice and the much wider question of that large minority of human beings whose erotic emotions, though without becoming vicious, are centred upon members of their own rather than the opposite sex. The prevalent life-and-death friendships between the warriors of ancient Greece undoubtedly belonged for the most part to the latter and not to the former class of subject. This profound psychological problem demands radically new treatment; it can never be solved by such indefensible cruelty as the martyrdom of Oscar Wilde and his fellow-sufferers. It is easy to class the unpopular and unsuccessful, such as Edward II and James I, as " degenerates ", but a change of heart may be induced by breaking the conspiracy of silence surrounding the popular hero Richard.

In February 1191 the King's mother, Eleanor, came out to Naples, bringing with her the young Princess Berengaria of Navarre. They met Richard at Reggio on the Straits of Messina at the beginning of April, but Queen Eleanor stayed only four days. Berengaria stayed with the crusaders, and a few weeks later, in Cyprus on 12 May, she was married to Richard and crowned Queen of England at Limasol, where a chapel is still shown to visitors as the site. This sudden and romantic marriage while on Crusade suggests a case of love at first sight, and so it probably was. Richard had been disappointed of his intended wife, Aloysia of France, and his impetuous character could not be expected to consider further prolonged negotiations with a view to an arranged political marriage.

Before leaving Sicily, Richard had met King Tancred at Catania early in March 1191, was presented with a ring and in return gave to Tancred a sword believed to be the Excalibur of King Arthur. Two months later, while sailing towards Cyprus, the fleet was caught in one of the notorious storms of the Gulf of Adalia, and was saved only by Richard's fine seamanship. Thus, while his younger brother John has been regarded by some as the founder, after Alfred, of the British Navy, it may be that it was Richard who was our first royal seaman. On landing in Cyprus his first concern was to settle the problem of the Byzantine ruler, the Emperor Isaac Comnenus, who was suspected of a hostile understanding with the Saracen enemy. Isaac in person watched the disembarkation of the crusaders from a little distance, but Richard caught sight of him and shouted to him to come and joust; Isaac rode off, pursued by Richard, who commandeered a passing country horse with a saddle of sacking and rope stirrups. But on such a mount he was not able to come up with his enemy. During the later pursuit of the Greeks up-country, one of Richard's clerks, Hugh de la Mare, feeling that the King was running into danger, begged him to retreat from the disproportionate numbers of the Greeks, but Richard told him to "get back to his writing business" and leave matters of chivalry to his sovereign, a sound piece of advice capable of wider application.

On 11 May three galleys were seen in the offing, steering in towards Limasol, and it was found that they carried King Guy of Jerusalem. Guy of Lusignan had acquired the throne by marriage to Sibylla, the widowed queen; he was himself one of Richard's vassals from Poitou. Taken prisoner at Hattin by Saladin, he had given his parole and obtained his release, but immediately breaking his word attacked Acre. His reign, including as it did the fatal Battle of Hattin and the loss of Jerusalem, gained for him the reputation of feebleness and ineffectuality. This was attributed to the one blot upon his otherwise excellent character: "he knew no evil". One may suspect that this reason for his simplicity was advanced, not without a trace of humorous intention.

The remaining fortnight of May 1191 was filled with negotiations leading to the final surrender of Cyprus by Isaac to Richard. When the King went to meet the Emperor in a garden of fig-trees near the coast not far from Limasol, he wore a gorgeous costume calculated to show that he was not inferior to the Byzantine in culture any more than he was in force of arms. His tunic was of rose-coloured samite and his mantle was spangled with small half-moons of solid silver set in rows, interspersed with shining orbs like suns; on his head he wore a scarlet cap, while his golden-hilted sword was girt on with a silken belt and provided with a chased scabbard of silver. He was mounted on a splendid Spanish charger, with a red saddle studded with golden and bright-coloured stars, having on its hinder part two lion cubs rampant and "as if snarling at each other"; golden spurs completed his outfit. Seeing that prolonged struggle would not save his island the Emperor finally capitulated on 31 May.

It is not my purpose to follow the Crusade, with its quarrels, disappointments, and ultimate failure. It yields a sufficient crop of personal incidents, however, some of which are worthy of record. While besieging Acre, surrounded with its low-lying marshes, both Richard and King Philip of France caught malarial fever, and accepted presents of fruit and delicacies from their chivalrous enemy, Saladin. Richard returned a Negro slave in recompense, and there was certainly no thought of slackening the conflict upon either side, but these courtesies were fastened upon as marks of treachery on Richard's part. In his letter to the Emperor of Germany, while a prisoner there some five years later, Richard refers to these incidents and sufficiently explains their character. "Acre taken, two battles won . . . abundance of rich spoils (with which the world is witness I have not enriched myself) indicate sufficiently, without my saying so, that I have never spared Saladin. I have received from him small presents, as fruits and similar things, which this Saracen, no less commendable for his politeness and generosity than for his valour and conduct, hath sent to me from time to time. The King of France received some as well as myself; and these are the civilities which brave men during war perform one towards another without ill consequences."

It is sad that this chivalrous courtesy should have been stained by deeds of savagery. After Hattin, in 1187, Saladin had massacred all the Templars and Hospitallers who had been captured, and now, after the taking of Acre by the crusaders, the same fate befell their Saracen prisoners. In extenuation it has to be admitted that a delay of over a week had taken place, in which Saladin had warning of the proposed treatment of the Saracens unless he fulfilled an agreement made at the fall of the town. Saladin's procrastination took fatal effect, and Richard and the western commanders perpetrated their greatest crime, a disgrace to Europe which the East has neither forgotten nor forgiven. Not even the nightly prayers and tears of the crusaders could succeed in their purpose. In spite of the great victory of Arsouf, on 11 September 1191 and subtle diplomatic negotiations with Saladin, the army never reached Jerusalem, and Richard, who from the heights of Nebi Samwil could have at least had a sight of the Holy City, covered his eyes and refused to see what he was unable to deliver from its oppressors.

This renunciation did not take place until July 1192, the intervening year being filled with marches and countermarches, successes, failures and the discomfort and disease of a campaign in a hot country with only rare supplies of water. That a western army could keep the field so long was mainly due to the very considerable degree of science, skill, and organization of the Order of Hospitallers, in charge of the medical arrangements. It may be a salutary smack in the face for twentieth-century self-sufficiency to learn that these dark-age practitioners were using anæsthetics for their operations and provided an efficient health service. In spite of the conflict between Christendom and Islam men of science were able to enjoy contacts with both cultural worlds, and to benefit from two great reservoirs of tradition and garnered knowledge. All the science of the ancient East and rather more of that of Greece and Rome than we now know, was available to the students of the twelfth-century Levant. Neither Arabic nor European universities were then in a moribund or fossilized condition, everywhere was keen study and inquiry. Only the barren revival of scholasticism during the thirteenth century frustrated the European development of this movement of renascent culture, emerging from the dark age of barbarian invasion and warfare.

Of the rest of Richard's stay in Palestine there are detailed accounts by contemporaries, from which we must take a few vivid scenes. His care for his men was remarked on; during a retreat upon Ramleh, when many of the rank and file would have been left to fall into the enemy's hands, King Richard took personal steps to see that such men were found and brought away to safety. In every engagement his own activity was outstanding, and in the less glorious but equally arduous fatigue duties he was constantly busy. At the rebuilding of demolished Ascalon he worked as a stonemason with his own hands; by a strange coincidence Saladin was doing similar work on the defences of Jerusalem at about the same time; at the siege of Darum in May 1192 "the valiant king of England himself, and his nobles" were seen "sweating under the burden of the various parts of the catapults, which like pack-horses they carried nearly a mile across the sand." On 1 August he relieved Jaffa at the last moment, leaping into the sea from his ship only half armed, to reach the shore and put heart into the hard-pressed garrison. During the last months of the Crusade he would ride up and down before the ranks of the enemy, challenging any infidel to fight him in single combat, but no one had the temerity to accept. Indifferent to danger or glorying in it, he took no precautions against becoming separated from his staff, and returning to Ascalon from one foray he was alone when attacked by a wild boar, which he overcame only with difficulty.

During the campaign the western forces had been split by hidden and open quarrels and faction-fights; rival candidates for the throne of lost Jerusalem, Guy of Lusignan and Conrad of Montferrat, manœuvred for advantage by secret diplomacy, profiting from the deep rivalry between the French and English courts and contingents. Conrad succeeded in his claim, but was assassinated; inspired slander promptly insinuated that behind this murder lay Richard's hand; but we may surely believe his own declaration that "the assassination of the Marquis de Montferrat is foreign to my character. . . . I have not hitherto evinced such a dread of my enemies as men should believe me capable of attacking their lives otherwise than sword in hand." A third party, the crusaders led by Hugh of Burgundy, added to the confusion, and their duke set the keystone on the dissension in the camp by inspiring a vile and scurrilous song to be made and sung against King Richard throughout the army. Richard, poet and composer as he was, retorted in kind, and was not considered blameworthy for doing so. Such "flytings", serious as well as comic, were a feature of court life of the age.

In the midsummer of 1192 Richard answered the prayers of his chaplain, William of Poitiers, not to desert the Christian cause as the French King had done, by causing his herald to proclaim that he would stay until the next Easter; but all hopes of a complete military victory had left him, and he offered to do Saladin fealty and personal service "whose value you, Saladin, well know", for the fiefs of Ascalon and Jaffa. In August, Richard was again seriously ill, and sent to Saladin to ask for fruit and snow, which his great opponent generously and courteously returned. Such incidents recall the story of the Maoris in the war of 1861-71 in New Zealand, who, noticing that the small British party of soldiers whose position they were besieging, had ceased fire, sent in a flag of truce with half their own ammunition that the fight might be fairly continued. Richard, worn down by the defection of his allies, disease, disappointment, and the climate, at last took ship and sailed away from Palestine on 9 October; only five months later, on 4 March 1193, his enemy Saladin died of typhoid. But before his death Saladin had assured for seven centuries the supremacy of Islam in the Holy Land, though the mighty deeds of Richard left their mark, and for years Arab mothers quietened their restless children with the words "England is coming!"

It was on his homeward journey that one of Richard's most ill-advised exhibitions of anger " came home to roost ". At the taking of Acre, duke Leopold of Austria disobeyed the orders of Richard and the King of France, whereon Richard ordered the duke's banner to be pulled down and trampled in the dirt. Now, returning by way of Corfu, Richard for some reason determined to touch at Ragusa in the Adriatic. Trusting to his reputation to keep him safe, he struck a bargain with a galley of pirates to take him to Ragusa for 200 marks of silver. Having made a vow during a storm at sea he paid for the rebuilding of Ragusa Cathedral when he reached that port, and then sailed on for the head of the Adriatic. He was caught in another storm and wrecked in mid-winter between Aquileia and Venice, and trying to make his way overland across Europe rashly entered the Austrian duchy, was recognized, and clapped into prison by the vengeful duke. Though he did his best to play off the duke against the Emperor of Germany, Richard was forced, after fifteen months of imprisonment, to give securities for an enormous ransom. There seems also to be some truth in the rumour that in doing homage to the Emperor for Burgundy, to which he laid claim, Richard had also admitted the Emperor's suzerainty over England. This had repercussions as late as the fifteenth century, when Humphrey duke of Gloucester met the Emperor Sigismund with a drawn sword in the tide-water at Dover and refused to let him set foot ashore until he renounced all claims on England. Richard made a triumphal entry into London on 16 March 1194, and a month later solemnly wore his crown in Winchester Cathedral, supposedly to reassert his full sovereignty.

While a captive Richard had written his famous song " Ja nus hons pris ", addressed to his half-sister the Countess Mary of Champagne. To while away the time, after producing the poem in French, he wrote a second version in Provençal, and set them to music. This much is true, and the poems and music survive; of the romantic legend of the faithful squire Blondel, who sought his master across

Europe, singing the songs of their Aquitanian countryside, until he obtained a reply from a barred window, we cannot be so certain. There is nothing inherently improbable in the story, for of such stuff were the troubadours made, and it was in the spirit of such romance that Richard lived and breathed. During his lifetime he had become a figure of portent, so that when he reached home a party of rebels who were holding St. Michael's Mount in Cornwall immediately surrendered, their leader having died of fright when he heard of the King's return. The less impressionable Germans who accompanied him were startled in another manner: their practical minds were amazed by the riches of the City of London and the fertile country of south-east England which they passed through.

John, who had been feathering his nest during his brother's absence and even intriguing to keep Richard in captivity, was promptly forgiven. Though twenty-seven years of age he was smilingly told by Richard: " You are a child ", while his epicurean temperament was invoked by Richard's special order to have an excellent salmon prepared for him. John, so unlike his brother in spirit, does not seem to have resented this contemptuous forgiveness. Other traitors were not so fortunate, and in 1196 Richard was specially blamed in that in punishing the rebellion in Brittany he spared neither grown man nor child, not even upon Good Friday itself. About the same time, while he was building his famous Château-Gaillard, Saucy Castle, at Les Andelys, to guard the French frontier of Normandy, he and King Philip vied with each other in the cruelty of their treatment of bands of captured prisoners. Both seem to have been equally to blame, though the English and French chroniclers differ as to who first began to practise these savageries. This great castle, the first of a type new to Europe, is said to have been designed by Richard himself; it was, at any rate, the outcome of his experiences in the East, but like more recent experiments in lines of static defence, it proved useless in the hands of a defender lacking Richard's resolution. Richard boasted that he would hold it if it were made of butter, but does not seem to have realized the inverted implications of such a boast.

The blame lay with King Philip, who not only deserted the Crusade, but utilized Richard's captivity to undermine his position in France. Here was the French royal policy of steady aggression against the feudal nobles, a policy destined to be crowned with success after 300 years of bloody struggles. Philip at one point in their negotiations suggested to Richard that their quarrel might be decided by a judicial combat between teams of five knights on each side; Richard replied that he would consent to the proposal of judicial combat, providing it was between the two Kings in person —whereat King Philip withdrew. We shall see later that Edward III and Henry V also proposed to avoid war by personal single combat, with a similar lack of success. To the threat of war was added the ghastly reality of famine, which had been spreading across Europe for several years; by 1195 it reached Normandy, where Richard took steps to serve out sufficient food to the poor every day, not only at his own court, but throughout the countryside. On the whole his measures seem to have been successful.

Unfortunately, the Crusade, rebellion, war in France, the famine, and his appalling ransom to Germany, brought about a complete financial breakdown. Still able to see stern realities as a poet and humorist, Richard wrote a *sirventes* on the subject, containing the lines:

> Saviez qu' à Chinon,
> Non a argent ni denier

and raised money by the ingenious expedient of having a new seal cut and repudiating grants made under the old one. The new seal, first used in May 1198, is important heraldically, for upon it the three lions, *passant gardant* of England, first appear. But Richard was not to live long to use it, nor to show whether he could have retrieved the difficult position in which he and his countries were placed. Less than a year after the making of his new seal he was dead.

Near Châlus, a little town in the Limousin, a peasant was ploughing at the opening of the year 1199. To his amazement his plough revealed the seated figures of an emperor, with his wife, sons, and daughter, all of pure gold and set about a golden table with golden coins. His lord, Achard, the holder of Châlus, claimed this remarkable treasure-trove, which was in turn demanded from him by viscount Aimar of Limoges as overlord. Richard, as the viscount's overlord, made claim in his turn, a claim well founded according to the customary laws of the time. But such a valuable treasure was not to be had for the mere asking, and on 4 March 1199 Richard began to lay siege to Châlus in the hope of obtaining it. During the siege, sustained with great obstinacy by the townsmen, Richard exposed himself with more than his usual bravado. Seeing a crossbowman loosing at him an exceptionally well-aimed bolt he stopped to shout applause before leaping out of its flight. His move came too late, and the quarrel struck him in the shoulder. For more than ten days Richard continued the siege, and succeeded in taking the town, but his refusal to submit to treatment cost him his life. When the head of the weapon was at last extracted the wound had gangrened, and the King died of blood poisoning on the evening of 6 April. With him during his last hours was his aged mother. On Palm Sunday his body was buried in the abbey church at Fontevraud, and his lion heart among the relics in Rouen Cathedral. Nothing but his memory remained to England, where he became a national hero.

Perhaps the people's estimate is a just one after all; that he was almost wholly a foreigner, when such is generally the nature of kings, is insignificant; to blame him for failure in bringing material prosperity to England would be unfair and irrelevant. But in what goes to make a hero his vices, his anger, his vengeful cruelty even, count for as much as his chivalric virtues and his skill as a poet, the last of an epoch: his qualities were more than life-size. It is here that his secret lay, and that the secret of his lasting fame still lies—he would not be bound down by the chains of the average, the mediocre, and the reasonable, and died because the merely possible was not enough for him.

CHAPTER III

JOHN

With Richard Cœur-de-Lion we have trodden the lofty stage of tragedy; his brother John (whose vice and mischief were so like those of the fabled satyrs) provides comic relief. John has so often been painted as the bad King, a monster of wickedness, a murderer, a lecher, irreligious, inefficient, inglorious, that he has become a historical Guy Fawkes, stuffed with paper. If one must take one's history in literal doses, all this is true, but it gives a picture of the seriousness of an evil character, that was never wholly true of anybody. Writing a generation ago, Chesterton remarked of this very point that he sympathized with the whitewashing of King John, "merely because it is a protest against our wax-work style of history." King John is always "pulling out Jews' teeth with the celerity and industry of an American dentist", just as Alfred was always spoiling cakes and Henry VIII marrying. No amount of whitewash would make John into a moral exemplar, but it is unnecessary to whiten his character to find in it some attractive points.

At the root of John's wickedness, and also of his comic side, lay the fact that in an age of believers he was both a sceptic and a cynic. The cure for evils lies far more in laughter than in censure, and many childish characters who would be quite prepared to earn a reputation for serious wickedness by imitating John would be shy of getting themselves laughed at. But it is possible sometimes to laugh with John, as well as at him. When Gerald de Barri suggested that he should go to Ireland he neatly retorted that as he had not so many relatives in that country as had Archdeacon Gerald he was not so keen on going there. In fact he was not prepared to relinquish his English life of comfort for the dangers of the sister island. He had the good quality

76

of being accessible to everybody, with that easy flow of conversation that even in defect of other qualities can soon lead to popularity. It is evidence of this popularity that Richard should have changed his mind about making Arthur of Brittany his heir, and on his death-bed left the throne to John; Richard must have felt that John was at least a safer King than Arthur. That John would be so foolish as to murder Arthur in cold blood and thus ruin his own cause, never crossed his great brother's mind.

Though John's effigy in Worcester Cathedral is not contemporary we cannot doubt that it represents his features as preserved by likenesses made in his life and in the memories of the elder generation. The face has a sly, wolfish cast, with slanting eyes faintly amused at the righteousness of better men, and a sensual mouth slightly drawn into the dog-like grin distinctive of the cynic born. Like his father he was plumpish and strongly built, not tall. When his tomb was opened his skeleton was found to measure just 5 feet 6 inches. In his younger days he had thick curly hair, but later became bald and ran to fat. His temperament would have been called " French " in Victorian times; he loved to saunter through life, seeing and enjoying the surface of things; the best food, expensive drink, fine clothes, pretty women, amusing companions with whom he could while away the hours in chatter and eternal games of backgammon. As an infant he had been entered as an oblate at Fontevrault Abbey, and it was probably this early religious training that, as has often happened, made a sceptic of him.

The cloistered round of his childhood, the apparently senseless ritual, and the compulsory prayers which to him had had no inner meaning, were never forgotten. Seeing a buck broken up at the end of one of his hunts he remarked: " You happy beast, never forced to patter prayers nor dragged to the sacrament." He had been born on Christmas Eve, 1167, at Beaumont by Oxford, and as the youngest son received no share of the family inheritance which had already been allotted to Henry, Richard, and Geoffrey. His father called him " John Lackland " in jest, and the name stuck;

it was so appropriate to the whole of his career, with its loss of Normandy, and loss of England only prevented, in a literal sense, by his death. When he was six years old his brothers' rebellion led to his return to England, with his captive mother. In July 1174 they landed at Southampton, and Eleanor was sent a prisoner to Salisbury—Old Sarum on its lonely mound, not the modern city of the plain.

When he was eighteen the visit of the Patriarch Heraclius to seek help and to offer the throne of Jerusalem to Henry II seemed to John to open up for him the chance of fortune which he had missed at birth. He set his heart on the position and prospective riches of King of Jerusalem, and grovelled at his father's feet in the vain hope of persuading him to accept the proffered gift on his behalf. But Henry was too shrewd, and instead sent him to Ireland to show his mettle. As we know, his dandified rudeness to the Irish princes, whose trailing beards struck him as funny, put a prompt end to his stay. He was not cut out to be a pioneer. For the next few years he hung about his father, hoping that his assiduity would be rewarded by the share of his rebellious brother Richard. He had backed the wrong horse again: Henry's star was declining, and John, completely devoid of principles and of any belief in them, deserted to Richard at the last moment. He was saved by Richard's generosity and good nature.

Before setting out for the Crusade, Richard gave his brother the administration of six English counties, but knowing him too well, would have made him undertake non-residence had not their mother pleaded for her youngest. So long as his parents were either of them living, John enjoyed the position of the spoiled Benjamin, and as no one took him seriously enough to be angry with him, his waywardness became habitual. So when Richard had gone he had a free field for the exercise of his considerable fund of intrigue. He had been married to the heiress Hadwisa of Gloucester, taking his place in English baronial circles. Since his wife was a distant cousin, the Archbishop of Canterbury, Baldwin,

pronounced the marriage void and laid the couple's lands
under an interdict. John appealed to the Court of Rome,
and the ban was lifted. When it suited his purpose John was
prepared to make use of the complicated machinery of the
Church, and felt no shame in doing so with the utmost consistency.

Although richly married and endowed with lands of his
own, John had not been sufficiently trusted by Richard to
be given any share in the council of regency. The principal
regent was the chancellor, the Norman William Longchamp.
Longchamp, like so many clever men from the southern side
of the Channel, both before and since his time, made the
mistake of despising the English. He went so far as to intro-
duce the French fashion of being served kneeling by his
English servants. John, with little haughtiness in his own
disposition, and who found it convenient to identify himself
with the English, was violently annoyed. Without regard
to the undertakings he had made to his brother he determined
to drive Longchamp out of the Regency, and was supported
in his aim by his bastard brother, Geoffrey Archbishop of
York. John's forces occupied London and conciliated the
citizens by granting them the coveted right to choose a mayor.
Longchamp, thoroughly frightened, disguised himself as a
woman and tried to leave England, but was discovered as
a result of attempted flirtation by a Dover fisherman, and
arrested. Luckily for him, John was put in merry mood
at the report, and gave orders that he should be allowed
to leave for France, which the chancellor did upon 29
October 1191.

From this date John increased his grip until his brother's
return two and a half years later, when his pretence at government collapsed like a house of cards in spite of his secret
alliance with Philip Augustus of France to keep Richard
quietly in prison and share the spoils. In January 1194
John had actually ceded to Philip by treaty most of Upper
Normandy except Rouen and several other frontier districts
and towns. Such shortsighted folly met its due reward
before ten years were out, when John was King, and Philip

overran his possessions in northern France. Notwithstanding his repeated treachery he was received back into Richard's favour, and continued to make the best of life during the remaining five years of his brother's reign. When Richard was dying it was his fickle, faithless young brother that he declared his heir, and there must have been something singularly attractive about this idle young man, so well loved by his father, his mother, and his oft-betrayed brother.

The ghost of his whimsical charm still clings about some of the stories told of him; on Easter Sunday, just after his accession, he refused to communicate at the Easter Mass. Hugh of Avalon, now Bishop of Lincoln, severely rebuked him, and treated him to a sermon of extra length. At about the same time, possibly outside the portals of the abbey church of Fontevrault, Hugh drew his attention to a sculpture of the Last Judgment, pointing towards the damned souls dragged down by devils into the mouth of Hell. John took him by the arm and pulled him to the other side, saying: " Show me rather these, whose good example I mean to follow." On 25 April 1199 he was invested duke of Normandy in Rouen Cathedral, but his early loss of the duchy was presaged by his dropping the ducal spear when he heard the chuckles of the young nobles; the idea of their boon companion John being the hero of a solemn ceremony had been too much for them. For all this, the first years of his reign passed without more serious consequences than a ding-dong civil war with the provinces of Anjou and Maine, which had recognized Arthur of Brittany as Richard's heir. During these few years John was counselled and supported by his mother, now over seventy-five, and by mediæval standards a very old woman.

No amount of good advice could have postponed the evil day indefinitely; John had a genius for doing the wrong thing. One of the first of his big mistakes was his divorce of Hadwisa; this created as great an adverse public opinion as did George IV's treatment of Queen Caroline. But nothing suggests that Hadwisa was as foolish as Caroline; John was simply tired of her, ready to move on to other pleasures, and glad of the old consanguinity dispute to provide him with regained freedom. Envoys came from King Sancho of Portugal to propose John's marriage to a Lusitanian princess, but diplomacy was far from John's thoughts. In the summer of 1200, while campaigning against the Lusignans who had captured his mother, he met the betrothed of Hugh de Lusignan, Isabella of Angoulême, a girl of twelve years. John was immediately infatuated, Isabella not unwilling, and a marriage was rushed through. After a honeymoon spent in Normandy the royal pair crossed to England at the end of September, and on 8 October 1200 Isabella was crowned Queen of England at Westminster.

Next year John and Isabella visited Paris, and though it may not have been a reflection upon the English King's personal tastes, the French are recorded to have said that their visitors were not able to pick good wine from bad. This was before the Bordeaux wine trade had grown to full measure, and England was still accustomed to taking ale and mead with its food; but John, who was a good deal of an epicure, must have had an extensive knowledge of the wines of France. The pretences of friendship over, the great struggle began once more, and in 1202 the old Queen Eleanor was besieged at Mirebeau, twenty miles north-west of Poitiers, by Hugh de Lusignan and his uncle Geoffrey. The outer defences had actually been forced, when the tables were turned by the arrival of John, who had covered the eighty miles from Le Mans in a forced march of only forty-eight hours. On 1 August he not only raised the siege and delivered his mother, but took many prisoners, among them his nephew and rival, Arthur. This relief of Mirebeau was the one great exploit of John's career, and the fact that it was performed on his mother's behalf is suggestive of the moral ascendancy of the old lady, over a man otherwise so disinclined to exertion.

John and his young bride made up for this warlike energy by spending the long Christmas holidays at Caen, banqueting richly by day and keeping their bed until midday dinner. The King's complete enslavement to his second wife was such that men said she had put a spell upon him; in 1203 his only energetic action was the cold-blooded murder of Arthur. No one will ever know the truth of this deed; it is almost certain that John was guilty; at least the killing was directly inspired by him. Here again John showed himself abnormal: ferocious energy in open battle was admired—in this John was backward. But stealthy murder was genuinely shocking to the conscience of royal and noble Europe. No better way of delivering himself into his enemies' hands could have been devised—John's own act joined righteousness to the motives of self-interest which were already gnashing their teeth all around him.

Philip Augustus was not the man to lose such an opportunity; declaring John's holdings forfeit, he invaded Normandy in force, and on 6 March 1204 captured the great keystone of Norman defence, Château-Gaillard. John repeatedly put off any attempt to take the field seriously, saying he could easily win everything back later on. His reluctance to leave the Queen was very marked, and led to the gibe that he was chained to the marriage-bed; whatever the true cause, his lack of any policy led swiftly to the loss of Normandy, the Channel Islands only excepted. Within a month of the fatal loss of Château-Gaillard, on 31 March 1204, his old mother Eleanor breathed her last at Poitiers; she had been a Queen for over sixty-six years. On 24 June King Philip captured Rouen, and soon afterwards Poitiers fell; in very truth was John now John Lackland, and men sneered "Yes, and Bluntsword too!" But the word used might have several meanings, and if we translated it " Slapstick " it might best convey that curious unreal air of pathetic farce that is wreathed about John's ineffectual efforts to stem the tide of defeat. He cuts so fantastically poor a figure that it is impossible to see in him the murderer of Arthur meeting with a just retribution; it is easier to think of him as pixy-led to his doom.

The loss of the whole keystone of the great Angevin Empire, the provinces of Normandy, Maine, and Anjou, was indeed fated; but the union of France was not yet to be. Although John was incapable of retaliation on a grand scale he was well served by some of his subordinates, and in particular by the ruffianly land buccaneer, Savary de Mauléon. De Mauléon had been taken prisoner and shipped to England at an earlier stage of the French war; in 1203 he had been captive at Corfe Castle in Dorset, when by making his jailers drunk and then cracking their skulls he seized the castle single-handed. An exploit of this kind marked him out as a man whose services were worth having, and Hubert de Burgh, on John's behalf, induced him to change sides. With a small band of his personal friends, likewise imprisoned in England, Savary was dispatched to Normandy, where John was ready to make use of a handy turncoat. Two years later it was De Mauléon who saved the situation. The French had broken through at Poitiers and pushed on to the sea, taking Niort on their way. Guienne and Gascony were directly threatened, and Niort was the spearhead of the French advance. Savary, who knew well the customs of the countryside, dressed his men in green branches and may-blossom on the eve of May Day, and lay concealed around Niort until the citizens had come out for their annual picnic in the woods. Masquerading as May revellers, the free company entered the town and succeeded in retaking it for John. From this moment the English cause was able to regain breath and a faint hope of survival.

At last, thanks to De Mauléon's unscrupulous tactics, John was able to make a counter-offensive, and by September 1206 his success was sufficient to breed miraculous intervention. Reaching the Loire near Angers in September 1206, his expedition found that all boats had been removed or destroyed. Nothing daunted, John made the sign of the Cross and led the way into the river, which he succeeded in fording with the whole of his army. What are we to think of such an event, related of a man notoriously evil, by ecclesiastics who were among his strongest opponents? Some remarkable occurrence must have taken place, and it throws a curious light upon the moral judgments of the time that a miracle should be credited even to a man of notorious irreligion and crime.

Before the disastrous campaign in Normandy, John had shown himself notably interested in affairs of architecture and town-planning. In 1202 he specially recommended to the Mayor and Citizens of London, then engaged in building London Bridge, the services of the noted French scholar, Isambert of Xaintes (Saintes). Master Isambert had already gained a high reputation as designer of the important bridges at Saintes and La Rochelle, in Saintonge. Here, from the least promising of kings, we see that lively personal interest in affairs which was so typical of his whole family. Even more striking is the case of Liverpool, which John visited early in 1260, after the loss of Normandy. He appreciated its natural situation, and its potential importance as a port, and on 28 August of the following year granted it a charter. Liverpool was perhaps the first piece of conscious planning in England since Roman times. Whether we see in this the hand of Master Isambert or of some other foreigner acquainted with the relics of Roman civilization, or the personal activity of the King, the initiative was due to John in person. Not only at Liverpool, but in the case of many other towns John granted charters, and his importance as a founder of municipal privileges may even have been exaggerated by some writers. Yet his keen interest is beyond question, and it is paradoxically to John that English civic life owes much of its importance.

The year 1207 saw the founding of Liverpool, and some two months later another event of considerable importance: the birth of John and Isabella's first son, Henry, afterwards King Henry III. Born at Winchester on 1 October and just when the loss of Normandy had vastly increased the prestige of the English kingdom in the eyes of its sovereign, Henry was to be the first English King by birth and inclination since the Norman Conquest. It was to an impoverished country that the heir was born: John always found great difficulty in collecting taxes, and it may be suspected that large payments in ready cash were a principal motive in his granting of municipal charters. Though chronically hard up, John was not stingy, but always too ready to lend to others; so the vicious circle of his finances went on. To this depletion of his pocket we owe the notorious stories of his victimization of wealthy Jews, whose teeth he had extracted one by one, until they should reveal the hiding-place of their hoarded gold. Some of these may be fables, but there is an interesting flavour of consistency about most of the stories told of John: a cynical and slightly macabre sense of humour.

One story, however, shows John in a pleasantly romantic light: in 1209 he came to terms with William the Lion, King of Scotland, who did homage and gave hostages, among them his daughters Margaret and Isabella. At mid-summer John provided the Scottish princesses with new dresses of dark green, with others of light green for their attendant ladies, and gave them, among other rare foods, one hundred pounds of figs. Possibly the gifts were the result of policy, calculated to display the riches and foreign trade of England to these visitors from the thrifty North, but John was not altogether a bad fellow and took pleasure in doing what he could to cheer up his young guests, captive for no fault of their own.

The first half of the reign had seen most of John's over-seas possessions shorn away; the second was to see him excommunicated, deprived of all he had left by the Pope's decree, alternately defiant, savagely anti-clerical; and meekly subservient, anxious to save what he could from the wreck by obedience to the will of Rome. The complicated plot and counterplot of policy are best left alone; in themselves they have little to tell on the subject of the King's character. Trouble arose over the appointment of a new Archbishop of Canterbury: John wanted to promote his personal friend and creditor, John, Bishop of Norwich, an amusing and pleasant companion. This personal nomination was countered by the Pope, Innocent III, who was careful to rig the election of a rival candidate, Stephen Langton, a prolific writer on behalf of clerical privilege and against royal absolutism: the old story of Henry II and Becket, with the personal element left out. It was a major tragedy for the future relations of Church and State in England that John was neither clever enough, nor sufficiently interested, to play to best advantage the hand he held.

Innocent III, in pushing in Langton, had gone absolutely beyond his rights, and John's indignation was justified. It was not the King who had gone out of his way to provoke this quarrel. But his methods of conducting the struggle, though they must have tickled his palate and still tickle ours, were not consistent enough to win. On 23 March 1208 Pope Innocent laid England under the ban of an Interdict; the English people were placed beyond the pale of the Church and its beneficent offices. John declared that if the clergy obeyed the Pope and ceased to perform their religious duties their property would be confiscated by the Crown; and it was so. Just to show that there was no ill-feeling towards the clergy as individuals, the King granted them adequate allowances to live upon; on the other hand, he amused himself by ordering the sheriff's officers to raid the parsonages and take into custody the females euphemistically termed " housekeepers " and hold them to ransom. Further, to demonstrate his impartiality, he decreed that anyone found guilty of insult or injury to a monk or priest should be hanged. As time went on his exasperation would not permit him to adhere to this order, for he met by the road some officers leading a man who had robbed and murdered a priest. Hearing the man's crime he ordered him to be unbound and let go, for " he has killed one of my enemies."

The Great Interdict lasted until 13 May 1213 and ended when the Pope's deposition of John and declaration of the forfeiture of his lands to the King of France, forced him to submit rather than fight another losing campaign. But he had not lost all his old spirit, for when a hermit, one

Peter of Pontefract, prophesied that his reign would not last longer than fourteen years, John waited only for the anniversary in order to hold a great open-air festival in honour of the fanatic's discomfiture. This was in 1213; next year the King engaged in another fruitless campaign in France and found his public embarrassments crowned by the defection and infidelity of his Queen. Returning to England he met the conspiracy of the baronage who took advantage of the catastrophe of Bouvines, where the French defeated the forces of Flanders, leagued with troops sent by John and by the Emperor, to press upon him their scheme of " reform ", embodied in the document afterwards famous as Magna Charta. Time has shown that this document, whatever the motives of its drafters, was at best but a poor defence for the liberties of the subject, just as Château-Gaillard, lacking human spirit behind its walls, had proved a poor defence for Normandy.

It is hardly surprising that John, who was an Angevin and son to Eleanor of Aquitaine, did not feel bound by the Charter wrung from him under duress, and obtained absolution from the Pope, now his ally. The barons promptly showed their patriotism in its true colours by calling in Louis the Dauphin of France, and a year's civil war with no marked success on either side terminated only when John died. In more or less haphazard journeying around England he had crossed the Wash from Norfolk into Lincolnshire, but with his fatal knack of mistiming and unaided by providential intervention he lost the whole of his baggage train, with the crown of England and a great treasure, in the treacherous sands covered by an advancing tide. Too much of a materialist and sceptic to be buoyed up by faith or hope, John tried to console himself with the pleasures of the table. Copious feasting, followed by peaches washed down with wine and fresh cider, brought on a dysentery which was too much for a frame exhausted by high living and disappointment bordering on frenzy. He bravely insisted on mounting his palfrey and pushing on to Sleaford Castle, and next day, though too ill to ride, had himself borne to

Newark-on-Trent. There, on the night of 18 October 1216, he died, in his forty-ninth year. It may be that only his death could have saved the throne for his son, and he himself would have rejected any sympathy. We need not feel any, except that inevitable pang for the loss of a strange and vital human being, one of the uncommon personages of our history, and then, as now, a psychological enigma.

CHAPTER IV

HENRY III

At John's death, his heir was a boy of nine, and for the next ten years the King was under the tutelage of Hubert de Burgh and his rival, Peter des Roches. It is those ten years from 1217 to 1227 that mark the significant cleavage between the twelfth and the thirteenth century outlook. The thirteenth century was an extraordinary epoch, compounded of advance and retrogression in almost equal proportions. Whereas the twelfth century had been a great age of scientific discovery, in which the realms of thought and of art were widened out, the thirteenth was to witness the first riveting of the bands forged by scholasticism upon the minds of scholars, and the barren substitution of authority for empiricism. On the other hand, in the manual arts such as architecture, sculpture, and painting, great strides were made by lay craftsmen sufficiently beneath the notice of the learned world of the schools to be able to carry on a living empiricism of their own. In other fields, notably those of law and administration, advances were made in the direction of unity by a process of codification and the hardening of earlier tentative formulae into settled rules.

John, with his free thinking and his curiously modern outlook, had been a true child of the twelfth century, and he had been surrounded during his career by great twelfth-century figures. The men whose stores of knowledge and wit had been the glory of his father's court, in many cases survived through the reign of Richard into his own. Walter Map lived until after 1208; the great Gerald de Barri, the Welshman, Archdeacon of Brecknock, until about 1220: so long as such men were living, the spirit of their century continued. But now, as their generation was extinguished and the catastrophes of John's reign gave place to an uneasy peace, a boy was on the throne, and the country contained no one of sufficient standing to maintain continuity with the past age. On the continent of Europe too there was a pause, while Dominic and Francis were busy in founding the orders of friars who were to carry their names and fame to posterity. The astringent qualities of Dominic and the sweet reasonableness of Francis were the two faces of a medal, and the type of a new movement symbolizing a new age: the orders of friars were a manifestation of humanism, an attempt by spiritual conversion of the masses to bring Christendom into that unity which this newer age demanded.

At the threshold stood Dominic and Francis, but the key to the age lies in the enormous work of Thomas Aquinas, who was born about 1227 and died in 1274. His studies covered the whole of theology and philosophy, as then known, and he produced in meticulous detail a system combining revelation with knowledge, in the main still valid for the catholic world of faith. Of all works of unification carried out by a single human brain, his was possibly the greatest, and in this he symbolizes the tendencies of his century. This all-pervading unity, so often sought in human history and so seldom attained, was not to be found in the arts until a century after Thomas's death; while in the realm of science his own lifetime was to throw up another, in a different realm as great as Aquinas, who was to show that the experimental knowledge of Aristotle himself (the great philosophic pillar of Aquinas) was not beyond the reach of criticism founded upon fresh experiment. This voice of experiment in an age of authority was an English voice, that of Roger Bacon, who died in 1293 at the age of eighty. To Bacon, one of the grandest prophetic figures, we shall return.

Outside this realm of scholastic disputation and learning for learning's sake, lay the very different world of the layman with his everyday work and his habit of steady and cumulative experiment in the many handicrafts by whose practice the life of the time was carried on. The combination of wide learning with wide travel, which in the previous century had brought to Western Europe a new manner of life and

with it a new style in art, now bore fruit. The tentative
Gothic architecture, mixed with dying Romanesque forms,
which had been gaining ground through the reigns of Henry
II, Richard I, and John, was now reaching its first springtime beauty in England. In general, the other arts practised by laymen took their cue from architecture, and in
discussing the progress of architecture we discuss them all.
The first pure Gothic found in England arose within a few
years of 1190, and the choir of Lincoln Cathedral, built by
Geoffrey de Noiers for Hugh of Avalon between 1192 and
1200, was perhaps the first Gothic building in the world
to cast aside completely the vestiges of ancient forms. At
Wells, also, there grew up a new and gracious church, different in type, but also purely Gothic. It was from these
beginnings that the new cycle of art forms took its rise, only
to die away after some four centuries of persistent growth,
before the withering blasts of the so-called Renaissance.

The secret of Gothic art, that in which it differs from the
arts of other places and ages, seems to reside in its nervous
tension, in the fact that it is instinct with life. Chesterton
was led to this discovery by an optical delusion, in the
evening light, that Lincoln Cathedral had begun to stride away
across the plain, when in actual fact it was some furniture
vans, whose silhouettes he had mistaken for cottages, that
had started in the opposite direction. "The truth about
Gothic is, first, that it is alive, and second, that it is on
the march. It is the Church Militant; it is the only fighting
architecture. All its spires are spears at rest; and all its
stones are stones asleep in a catapult. In that instant of
illusion, I could hear the arches clash like swords as they
crossed each other. The mighty and numberless columns
seemed to go swinging by like the huge feet of imperial ele-
phants. The graven foliage wreathed and blew like banners
going into battle; the silence was deafening with all the
mingled noises of a military march. . . . And amid all the
noises I seemed to hear the voice of a man shouting in the
midst like one ordering regiments hither and thither in
the fight; the voice of the great half-military master-builder;

the architect of spears." Here the combination of happy accident and imaginative insight go far to reveal the nature, not of the architecture alone, but of the whole complex which made up mediæval civilization.

Born in the twelfth century, this civilization reached its springtime in the thirteenth, and in England its specially national characteristics are first seen in the reign of Henry III. The first of the great opportunities came with the planning of a new cathedral for the city of New Sarum. Salisbury Cathedral was, like all works of Gothic architecture, an experiment, but as the first of a new phase of arts its experimentalism is of more vital interest than the matured æsthetic qualities of many of its successors. In the mistakes of composition and proportion which mar the total effect of Salisbury we can see just how tentative its building was. We should be more conscious of these imperfections, were we not mentally overwhelmed by the skill and daring of Master Richard of Farleigh, who in the middle of the fourteenth century used all the resources of his more advanced age, including concealed metal reinforcement, to set a great tower and spire upon the truncated building, and so complete its pyramidical composition. But at the first building of Salisbury, begun with the construction of the Lady Chapel between 1220 and 1225, we can see a high degree of sophistication of mind; the extraordinary slenderness of the Lady Chapel's shafts of Purbeck Marble, suggesting the unexpected strength of the rolled steel stanchion, and its air of exaggerated attenuation, clearly mark the efforts of an individual mind to find not only self-expression, but expression also of an overmastering idea: the service of God through His temples. Both the high degree of this sophistication and the impracticability of its constructive expedients are explained by the works having been carried out under the artist-cleric, Master Elias of Derham.

This Master Elias was an unusual character, a clerk by training and yet not devoid of manual skill, which he employed upon the making of shrines and tombs. He is thus one of the very few figures of the Middle Ages to partake of the diverse qualities of lay and clerical art, and his appearance at this crucial moment in the development of English art was doubly fortunate. The Gothic tradition of building had not yet found its feet: once the tradition had hardened into a routine training for the budding master masons, no startling innovations were to be looked for; but in the time of Master Elias the art was still semi-fluid. It was still possible for a man possessed of wider learning and more academic views than the building masters to mould the current output of the time into a new shape, to force the tide into a new channel. It was inevitable that in the thirteenth, of all centuries, such a personal, individual approach would have only a limited chance of survival, and Salisbury Cathedral stands apart from its successors as well as from its forerunners. It is one of the few works dated before the sixteenth century with a self-conscious and stylized personality—a sort of mannerism. But though its singularities were discarded, it played a considerable part in shaping English style, not least by the effect it had upon the youthful mind of Henry III, who saw it rising from his favourite country seat at Clarendon, less than three miles away.

Henry had been crowned at Gloucester on 28 October 1216, aged nine years and twenty-seven days, but his career begins in January 1227 when he was declared of age by Hubert de Burgh, who was able by this means to get rid of his rival, des Roches. It is not easy to picture what Henry was like as a young man; we know that later on he was rather plump, like his father, and also like him in his middling height, so different from the commanding stature of his uncle Richard or his own son, Edward. He had one personal peculiarity, a drooping left eyelid which covered half the eye, but in other respects was good-looking and even handsome. His famous effigy, made nearly twenty years after his death, but almost certainly copied from the wax figure made to be carried at his funeral, is somewhat smoothed and perhaps slightly idealized, but there are no grounds for supposing that it has no resemblance to the dead king, and it does resemble a large number of carved royal heads which appear on buildings erected in his reign.

In the face of gilt bronze there is petulance and self-will and some weakness and that kind of narrow-mindedness which is incapable of seeing more than one object or more than one point of view at a time. All his life long, Henry remained as single-hearted, and as narrow, as a schoolboy. But we must not judge him: he was never cruel or bigoted in his narrowness, and his single-mindedness had about it a good deal of that quality which sheds a blessing upon the pure in heart. Where his father's passions had been directed promiscuously, Henry's emotions were centred upon the happiness of his household and of the many individuals with whom he came in contact, and in especial upon the pursuit of beauty in all the forms of art. He has been described as a royal connoisseur, but the word has come to imply a preciosity and artificiality foreign to Henry. He knew what he wanted, and was prepared to go to any lengths to get it; as the contemporary satirist sang, he was so enamoured of the Sainte Chapelle, built in Paris by his brother-in-law, St. Louis, that he would have liked to take it off in a cart. He surrounded himself to an extent that no later English King, save perhaps Richard II, ever did, with individual craftsmen and artists of every kind. Nor was he content with their remaining anonymous members of a vast civil service; they were known to him by name, and with them their wives and families, and he took good care to notice their private occasions of joy and sorrow.

Of all the Kings of England, Henry most conspicuously exemplifies the distinction between the political career seen by the average historian, and the temperamental aspects of character seen by the biographer. It is singular how pamphleteers among the King's opponents have continued to hold the stage to the exclusion of the vast quantity of evidence derivable from the state records of his reign. Every one of Henry's actions is viewed from a hostile stand-point, and the very matters in which he showed his wisdom, and even a sense of humour, are made into articles of accusation. Stubbs, referring to his want of money in 1248, when the barons suggested that the King should sell his jewels to the wealthy citizens of his capital, described as "tyranny" Henry's view that if the Londoners were rich enough to buy his jewels they were well enough off to give him something freely! Historians of England have ever loved to paint tax-resisters indiscriminately in rosy colours, and it is surprising that the twentieth-century Englishman should meekly submit to the most preposterous burden of imposts, when he is taught to revere the selfish and insubordinate barons of Henry III and the iniquitous opponents of Charles I and his sons.

The upholders of the usurped prerogatives of Parliament, and particularly of the lower House of Parliament, look to the unattractive Simon de Montfort, earl of Leicester, as their patron saint, and love to point out that as husband of the King's sister, De Montfort would have been the greatest prop of the Crown, had it not been for the King's extravagance and folly. But the cause of Earl Simon's revolt from his master lay in his own tyranny and extortion. De Montfort, as administrator of Gascony, had feathered his own nest to such a tune that the Gascons complained to their King, who inquired into the facts and took their part; thus truly securing his subjects from oppression. It is unnecessary here to follow the sordid story of intrigue and rebellion which will be found in the standard works; but it is worth remarking that Henry's son Edward, himself a great and independent character, had for his father the utmost love and respect; a testimony which, considering the common opposition of royal sons, deserves to be set against the gibes and sneers of lesser men.

Like his grandfather Henry II, Henry III married a princess of the warm south, Eleanor, one of the four daughters of Raymond Berenger, count of Provence. Of the other three sisters, Sanchia married Henry's young brother, Richard, earl of Cornwall and King of the Romans; Margaret married Louis IX (St. Louis), and Beatrice, the youngest, Louis's younger brother, Charles, afterwards King of Sicily. Their father was one of the last of the great Provençal poets, and the daughters took with them both the less tangible culture denoted by the fine arts and the material benefits of a highly organized civilization. In England, Eleanor's arrival was followed by great activity in the royal palaces and manor-houses, which began to be fitted with window-glass, wood-panelled walls, fitted baths, and improved plumbing and sanitation. The royal marriage took place at Canterbury in January 1236, and three and a half years later, on 17 June 1239, the eldest child Edward was born at Westminster. Through thirty-six years of married life, until Henry's death, he and his Queen remained devoted to one another, and the family life led by them with their two sons, Edward and Edmund, and three daughters, was idyllic.

Henry's rule extended for forty years, from his assumption of the regality in 1227 to the delegation of actual power to Edward in 1267; only thorough combing of the records could give a balanced picture of the reign. Here I propose to give, mainly from the Liberate Rolls, a mere selection of interesting and revealing facts, which may well give a lopsided view, but not more so than do the customary libels. Upon the Liberate Rolls (so called from the Latin writ of " Liberate "—Deliver ye . . .) were entered the King's personal orders to sheriffs, bailiffs, exchequer officials, and others, against which they were to make payments for given commodities or to named servants of the Crown. In Henry's time, owing to his extraordinary degree of individual interest in every department of the Household and every aspect of the lives of those around him, these rolls contain an exceptional amount of detail, and in the case of many of the architectural works of the King, exact specifications of what was to be done. As a series of documents revealing the ambitions and tastes of one man, the English Liberate Rolls of Henry III are probably without rival in the world.

Many of the payments recorded in the rolls are regular; the King would grant a yearly fee and a yearly livery of robes to a given officer, and writs of Liberate would issue for the payment of each instalment. Thus from the begin-

ning of his personal rule we find that the clerks of the
King's Chapel, three in number, were paid three times a
year, and sometimes on other occasions, a sum of 25s. for
singing " Christus vincit ". The occasions on which they
sang this anthem are specified: at Westminster on Whit-
Sunday 1227; at Oxford on Christmas Day 1228; in 1232
at Worcester on Christmas Day, and at Westminster on the
Feast of Purification following; at Woodstock on Midsummer
Day 1233; a special payment of 100s. was made in 1237
for singing on the day of the King's and Queen's coronation
in the previous year. Later the three clerks were granted £5
per year each; their names were Walter de Lenches, Robert
of Canterbury, and Peter of Beddington. As time went on,
this ceremony became more frequent; in the King's twenty-
fourth year the clerks sang on twelve occasions. Robert of
Canterbury was a married clerk; in January 1237 the
King ordered the sheriffs of London to provide for Isabel,
wife of Robert of Canterbury, a robe consisting of a supertunic and cloak of green or burnet cloth, priced at 2s. a yard,
with trimmings of rabbit and lined with lambskin; towards
the end of the same year Robert was given 40s. for his own
expenses. Further gifts to his family occur later.

The care taken by the King is shown by a meticulous list
drawn up in October 1227 for the clothing of the staff at
Bristol Castle. The master janitor and cook were each to
have a tunic and supertunic of cloth priced at 14d. a yard,
with lambskin linings; three other janitors were to have
tunics and supertunics, without fur linings; two carters and
seven watchmen the same, without linings, and of material
at 1s. a yard; the clerk and the spenser the same with
fur linings and at 15d. a yard, while the recluse who dwelt
in the castle had a tunic and cloak with a lining of coarse
lambskin and at the price of 12d. a yard. Not only household
staff were so rewarded; in 1226 William and Walter, the
King's miners, were given robes priced 16d. the ell with
fur of lambskin, and three years later Adam and Richard,
the King's miners of Cumberland, had 5s. of the King's gift.
One can sense a refined yet rather childish delight in the

compilation of these "shopping lists"; the King's cousin, Eleanor, living at Bristol in 1227, was to be sent 50 pounds of almonds, the like of raisins, and a frail of figs, and also 50 ells of linen cloth and 3 wimples.* In the same year the King ordered the bailiffs of Wilton to provide him with 500 ells of coarser cloth of lower price "to be carried to the King at London so that it be there by Friday the morrow of the octaves of the Ascension." Later they were allowed to reckon the sum of £12 5s. 10d. "that they spent in 800 ells of linen for tablecloths against Whitsuntide."

Rich presents to ambassadors from abroad and gifts to his own departing envoys often figure in the rolls; between 1226 and 1240 envoys were received from the Emperor, Cologne, Brunswick, Flanders, Spires, Bohemia, Denmark, Norway, Scotland, France, Béarn, Toulouse, Milan, the Pope, Castile, Portugal, Constantinople, the Sultan of Damascus, and the Old Man of the Mountain in Syria. A sum of 100 marks was paid for scarlet and linen cloth in 1228 to be sent to the Sultan of Damascus. Ten years later order was given to the Sheriff of Kent to make provision of all necessaries for the Saracen who had come "from the parts of France on a message from the Old Man of the Mountain" with his staff. In 1227, when Philip D'Aubigny left England as Henry's envoy (he died in Jerusalem during the short period of western supremacy under the Emperor Frederick II, and lies buried before the portals of the Church of the Holy Sepulchre), his servant, Richeman, was given 20s. by the King for his expenses. In 1247 Henry was visited by Baldwin II, the poverty-stricken Emperor of Constantinople, and besides entertainment, gave him "500 marks of the best money" and £20 for his expenses, while the constable of Dover Castle was ordered to see that the Emperor was well housed while waiting for his ship, and to pay the cost of his return passage across the Channel.

The King's own purchases are full of interest: in 1228 he laid out 10 marks on "a stomachic and ginger and balsam"

* Is it too fanciful to imagine Henry savouring the fineness of the linen with lingering touches of his long, delicate fingers?

for his own use; in 1236 provisions sent to Marlborough Castle included 40 pounds of dates, 6 frails of figs, 4 boxes of pressed grapes, 4 dozen towels, 4 pieces of "leyre" cloth, and 5 or 6 packets of good ginger—all these for Christmas use. In 1229 John the King's cook was sent to Gloucester to buy lampreys for the King's table, to be salted down, while the Sheriff of Gloucester was to order that no one should buy or sell lampreys until John had obtained the royal quota. In 1239 the bailiffs of Southampton provided large quantities of almonds, rice, ginger, cinnamon, dates, and 100 pounds of gingerbread. Three years after this the Sheriff of Norfolk "as he loves the King and his honour and his own safety" was to seek 15 lasts of the best and most "exquisite" herrings "for the King's own eating" in addition to 60 lasts for the King's alms, to be placed on board a good ship and sent to Portsmouth by a fortnight after St. Hilary, to be carried to the King in Gascony. It is pleasant to reflect that a King of England has shared with many of his humbler compatriots abroad a longing for the accustomed kipper.

Fish was a staple food of the Middle Ages, not merely because of Friday abstinence, but because meat was scarce in the winter months, owing to lack of fodder. In addition to herrings Henry had a fondness for salmon pasties, specially made for him. He also took considerable trouble over his cellar: a typical order in 1233 was for 15 tuns of Gascony wine and 5 tuns of Anjou to be taken to Woodstock; 5 tuns of Gascony and 3 of Anjou to Oxford, and to Reading 3 tuns of Gascony and 2 tuns of Anjou. Mulberry-flavoured and raspberry flavoured wines were also bought (30s. 4d. being the price of a small butt of either), while an English tonic-wine seems to have been made in Wiltshire, 3 tuns of it, iron-flavoured (*ferratum*), being presented to the King by the Prior of Ogbourne St. George in 1241; 1 tun was sent to Westminster, 1 to Windsor, and 1 to Winchester. In the same year Henry paid 28s. for a tun of wine which he presented to Wilhelma the Queen's damsel.

The King's clothing was also given special consideration; in 1228 William, the royal tailor, was entrusted with £100 to take to St. Edmund's fair to buy the King's Christmas robes, and in 1233 the sheriffs of London were to cause eight fur trimmings of miniver and one of lettice for the King's own use to be made and carried with the greatest possible speed to Gloucester, so that "they shall be there on Friday before Whit-Sunday in good time, as the sheriffs love their goods." At the same time the bailiffs of Bristol were to provide for Eleanor, Henry's cousin, 14 ells of good scarlet cloth to make her a robe for Whitsuntide, with four good and large trimmings of hindskin, and two fur trimmings of rabbit for the use of her two chamber-women. A month later we get a grim reminder of the constant guerilla warfare on the Welsh border in the order to the Sheriff of Shropshire to pay Richard de Muneton and his fellows 57s. for 57 heads of Welshmen whom they had lately slain at "Strattondal", the valley of Church Stretton by the Long Mynd.

A few more of the officers of the household must be mentioned; Master Ralph de Neketon, the King's physician, procured a large quantity of spices in 1236; four years later it was Master Peter "medicus" who was receiving a fee of £5 a year, as well as a further gift of the same amount. In 1246 Master Richard the harper was to have a tun of good wine of the King's gift to keep the feast of his wife's purification; the King's joy at the birth of his harper's child and the mother's recovery may seem a trifle exaggerated when we consider that some 250 gallons of wine go to the tun, but such reckless generosity and the caution that it was to be good wine have a pleasant ring. In 1240 Henry had given 20s. each to Philip, son of Richard the tailor, and to Peter, son of Emma, to be used for their maintenance, because they had been baptized immediately after the King's eldest son, Edward, on the same day and from the same font. In that same year, 1240, the sum of 28s. 6d. was spent on a tunic, supertunic and cloak, with lining and trimming of rabbit skin, for the wife of John de Mech, the King's fiddler, of the King's gift, by the King's order. In 1248 two players or minstrels of the King's half-brother,

Guy de Lusignan, named Clarin and Lancelot, were given
33s. 4d.; and in 1251 Master Henry de Avranches, the
King's versifier and earliest predecessor of the Poets Laureate,
was to be paid 100s. arrears of his wages "without delay
or objection", and the further stipulation has been added
between the lines of the roll "even if the Exchequer is
closed."

In 1245 a number of carcases of bacon which were being
sent to the King in Gascony during his disastrous campaign
against Louis IX were stored at Portsmouth in the house
of one Hugh de Stoke; the house fell through overloading,
and Hugh was ordered to have 20s. compensation. This might
roughly be £100 nowadays, but this would hardly re-erect
even a small timber-framed house. Other types of expenditure are typified by 16s. paid for clasps, hasps, and nails
of silver for the King's great book of Romances in 1237,
and 32s. paid in 1239 to Edward FitzOdo, the well-known
royal clerk and administrator, for cuttings of plants, and
also for planting cherry-trees in the garden at Westminster.
When we come to consider Henry's building works we
shall see other details of the special interest he took in the
upkeep of his homes.

Meanwhile, something must be said of his vast charity
to the poor and to the victims of accident or disease.
Among the payments recorded as "established alms" was
one of 30s. 5d. per quarter to Ellen, who had been Henry's
nurse in childhood; that it was paid by the Sheriff of Surrey
suggests that she lived in that county. In 1229 Master
Robert de Shardelowe, one of the King's clerks, was given
£10 for his sister's use, perhaps in some emergency; for
Christmas of that year 300 robes of russet, consisting of
a tunic and cloak at 10d. a yard, and 300 pairs of shoes,
were delivered for distribution by the treasurer to 300
poor folk. In 1237 another 300 pairs of shoes and 900 ells
of cloth were bought for Brother John, the King's almoner,
to give to 300 poor at Easter. In the same year Emma,
one of the Queen's damsels, was lying sick at Worcester,
and the King gave orders for two horses to be found for

her to ride to London if she were able to do so, or if not, then a good cart with two horses was to bring her to the King. A few months later the poor girl, Emma Biset, had gone blind, and Henry gave her a present of 20 marks. In 1239 he sent 40s. for the benefit of Roger le Panetier, one of his household servants lying ill at Woodstock. When Edward, the King's son, was born, Sibyl, the wife of Hugh Giffard, was so diligent in her attendance on Queen Eleanor that the grateful King made her a grant of £10 a year.

At Christmas 1239 this same Hugh Giffard, constable and keeper of the works at the Tower of London, was ordered to see that the bailiffs of Windsor caused the great hall of Windsor Castle to be filled with poor folk on Christmas Day, and the smaller hall likewise on St. Stephen's Day and at Epiphany, and on St. Thomas's Day with poor chaplains and clerks, and on Innocents' Day with poor children, and to feed them on the said days " in honour of the Lord and of the Saints aforesaid." In 1241 the Sheriff of Norfolk and Suffolk was to make 3,000 tapers and offer them on the King's behalf in the chapel of St. Mary of Walsingham on the Feast of the Assumption, " and to feed as many poor people on the King's behalf as he can find." In 1245 the sheriffs of London were to buy 300 pairs of shoes to be given to the poor at Christmas at 4½d., 5d., or 5½d. the pair. In 1248 Edward of Westminster, the Edward FitzOdo we have met before, was given 3s. 4d. to feed all the prisoners of Newgate on the Monday after Ash Wednesday; £14 11s. 8d. to feed the poor for the soul of King Richard, the King's uncle, on two successive days; £10 to feed the poor in the King's great hall at Westminster, " as many as can get in "; £16 and 1 mark to feed the poor on the two days of St. Peter and St. Paul; £30 12s. 3d. to feed the poor in the great hall at Westminster " for the love of Him who made the King's son safe and sound "; and £10 to feed the friars minors who are to assemble for their general chapter.

Among the most interesting of the King's charities are those at Oxford; in 1240 Henry gave 25 marks to the keeper of St. John's Hospital without the east gate at Oxford "to make a chamber for the use of women labouring in childbirth in the said hospital", an early instance of a lying-in ward. In 1244 the Sheriff of Oxford was to feed 1,000 poor scholars of Oxford on the Friday after the octave of St. Matthias the Apostle, the anniversary of the King's sister, formerly Queen of Scotland. This throws light upon the numbers of Oxford students at this period: Dr. Coulton puts the total number at Oxford's highest point about 1300, as "probably not more than 1,500", and in 1450 as 1,000 or less. How many students were *not* poor may be a question impossible to answer, but they must surely have been fairly numerous. In 1246 "all the poor clerks of the university of Oxford" were to be fed in the King's hall there, and all the friars preachers and minors of Oxford in their houses on the day when obsequies are performed for the soul of Isabella, formerly Queen of England, the King's mother. The Sheriff of Cambridge was ordered to perform a similar duty at the sister university.

The entries relating to building works have long been available in print, and the reader is referred to the first volume of Hudson Turner's *Domestic Architecture* for a detailed picture of Henry III's methods of ordering work. The orders are full of human touches: so anxious was the King for completion that he would add "as they value themselves and their goods", or "though it cost £100". He would give precise instructions as to the patterns and pictures to be painted, or state, as he did of the chapel in Windsor Castle in 1240, that it was to be painted "as the King enjoined by word of mouth". Of the vast number of named artists and craftsmen it is not possible to speak, though we must not forget the famous Master Henry, the chief mason at the building of the new Westminster Abbey, begun in 1245. Apart from Westminster and extensive work at Westminster Palace, Windsor and other palaces and manors, Henry made lavish gifts to the many friaries which were being built in all the important towns of England.

Some thirty friaries in all benefited from the King's generosity within a few years of 1240, besides gifts to abbeys, priories, and hospitals.

We may admit that Henry was extravagant; yet his expenditure was by no means solely or even mainly devoted to selfish ends; his great artistic works provided employment of a kind truly productive in its lasting artistic value, and his charity was on a scale to give substantial relief. Like his descendant, Richard II, he robbed the rich to give to the poor, and in the same manner fell foul of his wealthy barons, determined to pay into the royal exchequer as little as they might and to exact from their peasantry as much as they could. Too single-minded and too lofty in outlook to combat such men on their own ground, Henry had to resort to the support of the Papacy and the singularly forgiving generosity of his brother-in-law, Louis IX, to maintain his position; seemed to have lost everything to De Montfort at Lewes in 1264, but by the brilliant strategy of his son Edward was reinstated in the following year after the compensating battle of Evesham. Supported by his noble son, happy in the continuing love of his dear wife, and in the daily superintendence of the works of his glorious Abbey Church, the old King spent the sunny autumn of his declining years and died at the age of sixty-five on 16 November 1272.

HENRY III AND HIS MASONS

This remarkable view of a King with his mastermason, giving
instructions to be passed on to the workmen engaged on the
building seen to the right, is from Cotton MS. Nero D.i, f. 23v. The
manuscript consists of the *Lives of the two Offas*, by Matthew
Paris (died 1259), but this particular illustration may be an
addition of rather later date. It is, however, an important view
of building processes in the later thirteenth century, showing
the gulf fixed between the master (with his mantle, long tunic,
square and giant setting-out compasses) and the artisans with
their simple, short tunics. The mason-hewers both use double-
headed axes, though the man on the right is dressing a plain
ashlar, and the carver on the left works at a foliated capital.
Two labourers operate the windlass to draw up hewn stones in
a basket, while two setters are engaged on the wall-top, one
using the plumb to test the course for true level. Note that
the ladder consists of a single pole with battens nailed across it.
Only the King and the hewers wear gloves, though one would
expect the setters also to do so, to save their hands from the
sharp edges.

PART TWO: SUMMER

CHAPTER V

EDWARD I

The life of Plantagenet England falls conveniently into three sections or seasons: spring, ushered in by Henry II and brought to full bud by Henry III; the blossom time initiated under Edward I and completed by the blazing glory of Richard II; and the chilly autumn, lasting from Henry IV to Richard III and broken by the little Indian summer of revived culture at the Court of Henry VI and his polished uncles. The great turning-points are the reigns of Edward I and of Richard II. While the culmination of English art took place in the reign of Richard of Bordeaux it was through the achievements of Richard's great-great-grandfather, Edward I, that that wonderful culmination was made possible. Whether or no we consider Edward as the greatest of his race, his was certainly the most formative individual achievement. Famous as a warrior, it was in peaceful administration and in European peacemaking that he scored his most notable successes.

The picture of a granite-faced old man struggling from a sick-bed to keep on hammering the Scots has been too widely spread to be easily replaced by any more balanced portrayal of Edward's character. Like most men in advance of their age, he faced an immensely strong and well-intrenched opposition; and his efforts to overcome this senseless antagonism brought upon him the evils which he had foreseen and attempted to avert. Thus his actual settlement of the problem of Wales, and attempted settlement of the Scottish question, far from showing him as greedy and ambitious, prove his true statesmanship—though in the

King	Year	Principal Events	Year	Art and Literature
EDWARD I	1272	Treaty of Commerce with Flanders	1274	London: Tower of London outworks begun
	1274	First Welsh War	1277	Aberystwyth, Flint and Rhuddlan Castles
	1276		1278	Vale Royal Abbey begun
	1282	Second Welsh War	1283	Conway and Denbigh Castles
			1284	Harlech Castle begun
	1287	Edward's Mediation at Bordeaux	1285	Carnarvon Castle begun
	1290	Treaty with Scotland; Jews expelled	1288	Exeter Cathedral: Choir begun
	1291	Fall of Acre; English embassy to Persia	1291	Eleanor Crosses; York Minster: Nave begun
	1292	Scotland awarded to Balliol	1292	Westminster: St. Stephen's Chapel begun
	1293	Christian missionaries reach China	1293	Southwell Minster: Chapter House
			c. 1293	Lichfield Cathedral: West Front begun
	1296	Balliol's revolt; Edward occupies Scotland	c. 1300	York Minster: Chapter House; Winchelsea Church
			1303	Robert Mannyng's "Handlyng Synne"
EDWARD II	1304	Campaign in Scotland	1306	London: Greyfriars Church begun
	1307	Murder of Gaveston	1307	Lincoln Cathedral: Central Tower
	1313	Invention of Gunpowder	1308	Winchester Cathedral: Stalls
	1314	Great European famine	1309	Exeter Cathedral: Stalls
			1314	Dante begins Divina Commedia
			c. 1320	Lichfield Cathedral: Lady Chapel
			1321	Dante's Divina Commedia; Ely Cathedral: Lady Chapel
			1322	Ely Cathedral: Octagon begun
EDWARD III	1326	Mortimer's rebellion	c. 1329	Wells Cathedral: Retrochoir begun
	1327		1331	Gloucester Abbey: South Transept
	1330	Edward overthrows Mortimer	1332	London: St. Paul's Chapter House begun
	1336	Conquest of Scotland	1334	Salisbury Cathedral: Tower begun
	1337	Edward claims French Crown	1337	Gloucester Abbey: new Choir begun
	1338	Edward visits Rhineland		
	1345	Crops lost through wet weather	1344	Prague Cathedral begun
	1346	Battle of Crecy		
	1347	Taking of Calais	1347	Chester Bridge built
	1348	Founding of Order of the Garter		
	1349	The Black Death or First Pestilence	1349	Richard Rolle, poet, and William Ramsey, mason, died
	c. 1350	English the language of instruction in school		

King	Year	Principal Events	Year	Art and Literature
	1356	Battle of Poitiers	1353	Windsor Castle; Cloisters built; Boccaccio's "Decamerone"
	1357	Turks take Adrianople	1359	Vienna Cathedral: Nave begun
	1360	Peace of Bretigny	1361	Queenborough Castle begun; York Minster: Lady Chapel
	1361	The Second Pestilence		
	1362	Legal Pleadings to be in English	1363	Guy de Chauliac's "Chirurgie"
	1363	Timur begins his conquests	1366	Durham Cathedral: Kitchen
	1368	Mongol Dynasty of China overthrown	1369	Chaucer's "Boke of the Duchesse"
	1369	The Third Pestilence; War: France	1371	London Charterhouse begun
	1370	Sack of Limoges	1374	Petrarch died; London: John of Gaunt's tomb in St. Paul's
	1373	Tunnage and Poundage imposed	1375	Boccaccio died; Westminster Abbey: Nave begun
RICHARD II	1377	The Great Schism in the Church	1376	William Langland's "Piers Plowman"
	1378		1377	Canterbury Cathedral: Nave begun and Black Prince's tomb; Ulm Cathedral begun
	1381	The Peasants' Revolt	1380	Oxford: New College begun; York Minster: Choir begun
	1382	Turks take Sofia	1382	Wycliffe Bible in English
	1384	War: Scotland	1385	Chaucer's "Troilus and Criseyde" Bodiam Castle begun
	1385	War: France	1387	Chaucer's "Canterbury Tales"; Trevisa's "Polychronicon"; Milan Cathedral begun
	1388	Rule of the Appellants	1390	Winchester College begun
	1390	Navigation Act	1391	John Gower's "Confessio Amantis"; Richard II attends London plays
	1392	Statute of Praemunire; and Aliens not to sell by retail	1394	Westminster Hall rebuilding begun; Winchester Cathedral: Nave begun
	1394	Truce with France	1395	Westminster Abbey: Richard II's tomb
	1395	Amnesty in Ireland	1396	Richard II attends York Pageant
	1396	Turks defeat Christians at Nicopolis	c. 1396	Wilton Diptych painted
HENRY IV	1398	Parliament of Shrewsbury; Timur takes Delhi	1397	Canterbury Cathedral: Cloisters begun
	1399			

latter case his reliance on force of arms was the undoing of his cause. Throughout human history, and more than ever at the present day, one of the most vital of problems has been that of the relation between the great state, with its advantages of uniformity in law, language, administration, commerce, and lack of artificial barriers; and the small independent community with its love of independence, its own customs, its own language, its own forms of art, certainly its own provinciality and exclusiveness. Federation is the solution propounded by idealist democracy; beneficent personal union the ideal of monarchy.

Edward I realized that the future lay with the united national state, and sought to build up a union of such states within the geographical frontiers of the British Isles. A feudal subordinate in respect of his overseas possessions, he fulfilled his duties with punctilio, and saw in the due performance by Welsh and Scottish princes of their duties to him as overlord, the traditional and appropriate solution of the unity of Britain. He was no innovator in this, but simply bringing up to date the pre-Conquest theory of the Bretwalda or paramount sovereign of Britain. It was an essential part of his plan that the whole of the British Isles should be governed upon one basic principle of justice, while allowing traditional law and custom full rein wherever it was not in conflict with the central teaching of the Christian-Western concept of natural moral law. Like William the Conqueror, he had no intention of imposing a foreign rule upon subjected peoples; but like him also, he allowed himself to be forced by opposition into this forlorn attempt. So his career is a great half-failure, one of the most poignant might-have-beens of history. His reign, which spelt success and prosperity and the reawakening of a real national life for England and the English, also consolidated into opposition the national consciousness of the smaller groups within his realm.

Born at Westminster on 17 June 1239, Edward was named after the Confessor, his father's favourite and English royal saint. Thus he was from the cradle dedicated to

England to an extent not attempted since the Conquest. It was in 1258, when Edward was nineteen, that Henry III's famous proclamation made the first official use of the English language since the time of the Conqueror. This returning tide of the national language is immensely significant, the more so in that Edward himself was at home in English as well as French and Latin, and could speak it eloquently. Thus as protagonist of a national language and a national culture, Edward comes nearest to Alfred the Great in our history. Alfred and Edward were both nobly and brilliantly national, while at the same time international in their religion, their devotion to a united Christendom and to European peace. Alike also as good men, whose lives set a fine example to rich and poor, both genuinely royal, both simple and at home with all classes of their subjects. Four centuries separate the two men, and thirteen generations; even making all allowances for the inbreeding of mediæval royalty, the ties of blood cannot have been very close; yet, partly perhaps as result of a conscious attempt upon Edward's part, it is to the age of Alfred that we have to return to find a parallel to the great task and the corresponding outlook of Edward. In assessing the relative success of the two Kings it must never be forgotten that Edward's empire was of far greater extent than the English kingdom ruled by Alfred, and that the problems of the thirteenth century were more complex than those of the ninth.

Because of the importance of his public career we tend to paint Edward I as a figure with no private life; an unfortunate impression, for it was precisely from his happy childhood and from his devoted family circle that Edward drew so much of his strength. As a boy his health was poor, and it was perhaps due to this fact that he long remained on terms of exceptional intimacy with his father. When he was fourteen, Henry sailed to Gascony, leaving Edward behind; the boy stood on the shore in tears watching his father's ship until it dipped below the horizon. A year later he himself sailed to join Henry, and in 1254 visited Spain, received knighthood at the hands of King

Alfonso X of Castile at Burgos, and in October was married to Alfonso's half-sister Eleanor at the monastery church of Las Huelgas. The young couple spent the first year of their married life at Bordeaux, then proceeded to England for a short stay, for by this time Edward had been granted the administration of Gascony. Ireland, the Channel Islands, Wales, and the County Palatine of Chester, the whole of the outlying fiefs of Henry's kingdom, were also part of the area directly ruled by the young prince.

This early training in statesmanship was of lasting advantage, but it entailed heavy responsibility. In the autumn of 1256 the North Welsh, under their prince, Llewelyn ab Gruffydd, invaded the coastal plain which had been ceded to the English, and took everything but the fortresses of Dyserth and Deganwy. Edward found himself in difficulties and appealed to his father, but at first was told that he must recoup his losses on his own. Next year, however, Henry relented and accompanied Edward on a campaign into the lost territory, and set up his Court for some time at Deganwy. After this campaign affairs in England became involved; in 1258 the Parliament of Barons put forward its selfish proposals and at Oxford forced upon the King a committee of fifteen of their number. Edward, not yet twenty, they forced to join in the siege of Winchester Castle and expel from it his uncles, the Lusignans, children of Isabella of Angoulême by her second marriage. Such humiliations were not likely to predispose Edward in favour of the baronial opposition. But the fact of his apparent acquiescence made his father suspect his loyalty, and when Henry returned to England after negotiations carried on with Louis IX, slanderers got his ear and made him believe for a fortnight that his son was leagued against him. The King at first refused to see Edward, saying that if they met, "I shall not be able to refrain from kissing him." By means of the King's brother, Richard of Cornwall, father and son were soon reconciled.

By 1263 open civil war had broken out, and Queen Eleanor, attempting to leave the Tower and row upstream in her barge, was abused and pelted with filth by a mob who had taken possession of the bridge, and forced to put back. This insult to his mother was never forgiven by Edward, who in after years often had difficulties with the City of London. All parties in England soon tired of warfare, wherein neither side seemed likely to gain a decision, and in 1263 the leaders took oaths to abide by the arbitration of King Louis. His decision going in Henry's favour, Simon de Montfort broke his oath and started a fresh rebellion, which led first to victory at Lewes, and a year later to defeat and death at Evesham. During the campaign of 1264 Edward captured the town of Northampton, and with his usual chivalry endangered his own life to save that of his cousin and opponent, the young Simon, son of De Montfort. This generosity was ill repaid six years later, when De Montfort's sons murdered Edward's favourite cousin and closest friend, Henry of Almaine, while at prayer in a church at Viterbo.

During the last years of his father's reign Edward was in effective charge of the country, and by 1270 was able to go on crusade; he was absent for four years, and in the middle of his absence his father died, soon after the death of one of Edward's own infant sons. When he received the sad news Edward was in Italy, and it was observed that his grief for his father was far greater than for his son. His reply to inquirers, that this was because, though he might have other sons, he could never replace his father, shows the depth of his family affection. As a crusader, Edward emulated Richard Cœur-de Lion and equalled his bravery, but without any useful result. The one valuable outcome of the journey lay in his contacts with important personages in other lands and in the reputation which his courage and endurance won for him. On his return his progress through Italy was one long triumph; in Lombardy he was met with cries of " Long live the Emperor Edward "; at Padua the doctors made him a member of their university's faculty of law; the citizens of Milan presented him with splendid chargers caparisoned in scarlet trappings. While in France, Edward did homage to King Philip the Bold, son of St. Louis, but betrayed both legal caution and a sense of humour in the wording he chose: "Lord King, I do you homage for all the lands which I ought to hold of you."

For the next thirty years the King's task was heavy, but its outcome was the creation of England as a leading state. The basis of Edward's success lay in the knowledge and experience he had already gained; in his faith in the principle of unswerving personal justice; and in the wisdom with which he tempered justice with mercy. No reign so occupied with rebellions and wars has ever been so unstained by unnecessary executions or personal vengeance. Once when someone ventured to remark in his presence that in a certain instance he *might* show mercy, he flared out: "*May show* mercy; why, I would do that to a dog if he asked my grace." After his crushing of Llywelyn's rebellion in Wales in 1277, the Welsh prince was adjudged to pay a fine, a yearly rent for Anglesey and to give hostages; but once the terms had been complied with, Edward remitted the rent and the fine, and sent the hostages home. Years later he banished his own son Edward from Court for insulting a judge, and on one occasion fined himself twenty marks on finding that he had been in the wrong, the money being paid from his wardrobe account to the offended party.

He was not the serious lay figure that is often presented in his name.* He played at forfeits with his Queen's ladies, persuaded the royal laundress to ride in a horse-race; when he took Anglesey in the second Welsh war he remarked that Llewelyn had "lost the finest feather from his tail". His sense of humour, unlike that of many in high position, did not stop short at himself, for one day he approached some of his barons' sons and asked what they talked about while he was in council with their fathers. At first they were afraid

*His affection for his family is brought out by many entries in the accounts for the purchase of toys and furniture for his children. In 1284 he paid 10s. 4d. for a little boat, made and painted for his son Alfonso, so soon to die.

that he would be angry if they told him, but he encouraged
them to speak out, which they did in rhyme:

> The King wants to take our tanners
> And the Queen our lovely manors,
> And the Quo Warranto
> Will give us plenty to do.*

Edward was not only forbearing himself. In 1279 a French
knight, Jean de Prýé, coming to England, took part in a
tournament, which he feared might get him into trouble
with King Philip on his return. King Edward kindly wrote
the French King a letter on the subject, explaining the
circumstances and continuing "because the same Jean fear-
eth that he hath offended your highness, we affectionately
request and beseech your serenity that you pardon him, and
that (if it please you), you be in no wise angered against
him on this account, but that you may be willing to excuse
him; so far, at least, that he may feel that this, our urgent
request, hath been to him of effectual service."

Edward was fond of the dangerous sport of jousting,
and loved falconry, but was not purely an outdoor sportsman.
He was also fond of chess, and once when in play got up
suddenly from his chair and walked to the other end of the
room; at that moment a great stone fell from the vault above
the place where he had been sitting and crushed his chair
to matchwood. He regarded such incidents (on another
occasion he had a miraculous escape from being crushed to
death when his horse slipped at Winchelsea) as marks of
divine protection, and exposed himself to danger with absolute confidence. Though not noted as a lover of literature,
he carried with him on his crusade an important book of
Romances, which he lent to Rusticiano of Pisa, who drew
from it the raw material from which sprang most of the
European cycle of Arthuriana. He does seem to have been
fond of music, for he maintained many minstrels at his

---

* Le Roy cuvayte nos deneres
  E le Rayne nos beaus maners
  E le Quo Waranto
  Sal mak us all to do.

Court and rewarded those who visited it with the utmost liberality. Though his interest in architecture was largely military, he founded Vale Royal Abbey in Cheshire, supervised the planning of the new towns of Winchelsea and Hull, and showed fine taste in the beautiful monuments which he had erected after the death of his Queen in 1290.

It was almost certainly Edward I who caused the original surveys of England to be made, which resulted in the production of a map, of which a later copy, known as the Gough Map, survives in the Bodleian Library. Apart from rough copies of classical maps, and some generalized sketches, influenced by the maps of Moslem scholars and the charts of Mediterranean seamen, Western Europe was then almost devoid of real geographical knowledge. Although rough-and-ready methods were employed, the Gough Map marks the first appearance in post-classical times of scientific, experimental land-surveying, as opposed to the mere acceptance of tradition. In history Edward was certainly interested; he recognized its importance in connexion with the practice of statecraft, and was always careful to have historical records searched and precedents sought in dealing with important problems. When the bodies of King Arthur and Queen Guinevere were discovered at Glastonbury, Edward himself carried Arthur's coffin to its place of reburial; and in 1284 he accepted the supposed Crown of Arthur which was found, conveniently enough for his great Round Table feast at Nevin, along with the bones of Constantius, father of Constantine the Great.

In the field of learning, the thirteenth century marked a falling-off in experimental science, a hardening of tradition, the consolidation of the gains of the previous century. The scholastic philosophy perfected by Thomas Aquinas and typical of the Dominican outlook was hostile to change and to the free inquiry liable to bring change. It was an age of encyclopædias, summarizing the knowledge already available, rather than of specialized research. In spite of this, some experimental work was carried out in continuation of the earlier spirit, notably by Albertus Magnus (Albert of Cologne), who died in 1280, aged about seventy-five, but Albert was a Dominican and took care not to give offence to the dominant hierarchy. Roger Bacon, on the contrary, set down all his thoughts, and rapidly came into conflict with his Franciscan superiors. Born about 1214, he had a brilliant career at Oxford and at Paris, returned to Oxford about 1250, and was soon famous. Seven years later his lectures were forbidden; he was ordered to Paris, and spent ten years under a cloud. Fortunately, the papal legate in England, Guy de Foulques, interested himself in Bacon's work, and on becoming Pope in 1265 wrote to Bacon and ordered him to send him a treatise on the sciences, taking no notice of the prohibitions of his order. To this enlightened step the world owes the surviving portions of an enormous body of research. Unhappily, after the death of Pope Clement IV (Guy de Foulques), Bacon was again subjected to persecution, and imprisoned from 1278 to 1291. For a little longer he lived at liberty, and then died at the age of eighty.

Bacon preserved the adventurous spirit of the twelfth century and passed it on to a later age; but meanwhile a new world of geographical discoveries was being opened up. From the middle of the century Western Europe had begun to penetrate the enormous Mongol Empire which covered Asia. The rich arts of China, Turkestan, and Persia, were for the first time directly accessible to Europeans, among them Englishmen. The Mongol Tartar rulers were tolerant pagans, not yet converted to Islam, and welcomed Venetian, Genoese, and English traders and ambassadors. The Ilkhan Arghun, ruler of Persia, sent several missions to the West, and in 1289 one of these visited London. Edward I returned the compliment by sending to Persia Sir Geoffrey Langley, an old companion from the crusade of 1270-4. Langley and his suite, by way of Genoa, Constantinople, Trebizond, and Erzerum, reached Tabriz, and presented Edward's gifts to Argun's successor, Kaikhatu. Bringing a live leopard, a present from the Tartar prince to swell Edward's menagerie at the Tower, the ambassadors returned to Genoa at the beginning of 1293. There can be little doubt that the sudden appearance of ogee curves and of geometric diapers based on the equilateral triangle was a direct outcome of these contacts with the East; paintings and woven fabrics brought by the Mongols in 1289 and eye-witness reports of the great buildings of Persia by the companions of Langley must soon have spread these new motives and launched them on the stream of English art.

The buildings, the illuminated manuscripts, the sculpture, the paintings, the literature of the end of Edward's reign were very different from those of his boyhood. This was largely due to the steady progress made by internal development of the arts and crafts, but we must not underrate the part played by the King's insistence on security and justice. Private warfare such as had gone on between the earls of Gloucester and Hereford was stopped; woodlands were cleared away from the main roads to leave no lurking place for highwaymen; even before his own reign began Edward had sought out the outlawed knight, Adam Gurdon, vanquished him in single combat, and opened up a safe road from London to Winchester. In all matters it was by personal example that Edward showed the way; like his great-uncle, Richard, he worked with his own hands at the siege of Berwick; cut off by flooded torrents during the Welsh wars, he refused to take more than his share of the short commons available, and divided up his one cask of wine with his following of private soldiers. Though he could assume great splendour for affairs of state and did not grudge expenditure on ceremonial, he was wont to dress in plain homespun like an artisan. He had the accessibility of Henry II, though to the rebellious and insolent he could be as terrible as Richard, the rumour of whose coming had caused traitors to die of fright.

There seems no reason for believing the stories of his faithlessness and cruelty during the Barons' War; his opponents were themselves without scruple, ready to commit murder and sacrilege and to repay forbearance with cold-

blooded treachery. Their scurrilous toadies among the
monasteries are not worthy of implicit belief; though deprived of the swift circulation of the modern journalist, their
pens were as capable of putting in motion the lie direct, the
cunning prevarication and the tendentious anecdote. But
several articles of accusation levelled at Edward do deserve
to be mentioned, in order that they may be put into truer
perspective. These vexed questions are those of his treatment of the Jews; his adjudication on the Scottish succession;
the trial of Wallace; and the dispute over the Forest Charters.
Before Edward's day the Jews had held a special position
in England: they alone were permitted to lend money at
usury; and in return for the King's protection they were
obliged to lend him money and to pay over to him a heavy
proportion of their gains.

Edward was not satisfied with this state of affairs, for the
exorbitant interest charged for money had become notorious,
and the Jewish community formed an exotic mass segre-
gated from that united national body which it was his purpose to form. In 1275, the year after his return and coronation, he enacted laws forbidding usury and encouraging
the Jews to live by normal trade and labour. Unfortunately
the Jews did not respond, and succeeded in charging even
higher rates than before, and also formed a ring for clipping
the coinage. It must be remembered, in speaking of "the
Jews" of thirteenth-century England, that their numbers
were small and that within their own ranks they were a
highly organized community. Added to economic difficulties
caused by the presence of this alien body was a series of
most sinister crimes committed against Christian children,
including murder (allegedly ritual) and forcible circumcision.
Whatever we may think of the evidence in favour of "ritual
murder" (its existence in modern times among the Indian
thugs is fully substantiated) a number of instances of mysterious child-murder undoubtedly did occur in twelfth- and
thirteenth-century England, at least ten being well authen-
ticated between 1144 and 1290.

The evidence against individual Jews was considered conclusive in the case of Hugh of Lincoln (Little Saint Hugh), murdered in 1255, when, after exhaustive trials before the justices, later adjourned before Henry III in person, certain Jews were convicted and hanged, others being pardoned, apparently as "second-degree" offenders rather than as innocent parties. In vindication of English justice in the thirteenth century it must be pointed out that there was no question of mob-violence or lynch-law; no mass-condemnations, and a scrupulous adherence to form. In law, the evidence of the public records on this case is unassailable; but a stronger argument is perhaps to be found in the poignancy and pathos of the considerable literature of the subject. Best known is the reference in Chaucer's Prioress's Tale, but the memory survived longer and went further in a series of exquisite folk-songs, of which "Little Sir William" and "Oh down, oh down in merry Lincoln" are still well known. Whatever the merits of the case it is difficult to doubt the statesmanship of Edward's decision to remove the whole Jewish community, while one must admire the scrupulous justice with which he executed Englishmen who murdered some of the departing outcasts.

The case of the Scottish succession is much clearer: on the death of Alexander III in 1286, his grand-daughter, Margaret of Norway, was the only direct heir; it was intended that a personal union between England and Scotland should be brought about by her marriage to Edward's only surviving son, Edward of Carnarvon, afterwards King Edward II. But Margaret died, and the next heirs to Scotland were descendants of the three daughters of David, great-uncle of Alexander. By primogeniture the heritage lay with the line of the eldest daughter, whose grandson John Balliol was the first of three claimants. Robert Bruce, son of the second daughter, based his claim on the fact that he was one generation nearer the parent tree than his rival; the third claimant, John Hastings Lord Abergavenny, claimed that the kingdom should be divided by the law of land inheritance between the lines of the three co-heiresses, he himself being grandson of the youngest. No party seriously accepted Hastings's claim; it was held that a kingdom was an impartible inheritance. All three claimants were persuaded by the Scottish regents to submit their claims to Edward's arbitration; after assembly of learned lawyers and clerks, and collection of histories and chronicles to decide precedent, Edward at Norham demanded that all parties should acknowledge his historic claim to be suzerain over-lord of Scotland; after a month's delay spent in scrutiniz-ing the chronicles this was agreed to, and all the Scottish barons swore fealty to Edward. A special court consisting of eighty Scots, forty appointed by Balliol and forty by Bruce, and twenty-four Englishmen chosen by Edward, sat for nearly eighteen months and scrutinized every point. The final decision, on point of law, was in favour of Balliol, who was immediately put in possession of his kingdom. The whole of the subsequent misery and bloodshed in the wars between England and Scotland lies at the door of those rebellious Scots who neither adhered to their King, nor to their oaths of fealty to their supreme overlord, Edward.

The case of Wallace is different; he was not a baron, but an outlawed guerrilla leader, skilful and daring, but ruthless in his conduct. He adhered to no rules of chivalry, but waged total war against man, woman, and child. It was as a leader of sedition that he was formidable, but it was cold-blooded murder and incendiarism which led him to the scaffold after his capture. Had his offences been merely political he would have found the same mercy that Edward's other opponents never sought in vain; but Wallace was not the romantic hero of later legend, but a leader of well-organized criminals in an assault upon society. For 300 years the Borders suffered cruelly for this one man's misdeeds, and it is strange that the Scots, who were the greater sufferers, should have so long idolized their destroyer.

It is unfortunate that Tout's great authority should have countenanced the view that the "Confirmation of the Charters" of 1297 was a concession wrung from the King in favour of the people, and that the late Professor Jenks should have remarked in a footnote that "Edward did not make use of the absolution (granted by Pope Clement V, from his oath to observe the Charters); but he should never have sought it." The only study of the moral problem, that of Seeley in 1872, showed conclusively from citation of the original documents that the outcry for the confirmation of the charters was not in the people's interest, but a baronial conspiracy; and more important as affecting the King's good faith, that Edward's only use of the Papal absolution was to give back to the poor commoners of the forests the rights of common which were being robbed from them by the new owners of the lands disafforested. What Seeley justly called "that remarkable statute" of 28 May 1306, wherein the King, on receipt of the Bull of Absolution resumed his power, contains the highly personal phrase: "we are inwardly tormented with divers compunctions, tossed about by the waves of divers thoughts, and are frequently troubled, passing sleepless nights, hesitating in our inmost soul upon what ought to be done." So far from breaking faith to oppress his subjects, the only outcome of the absolution was the vindication of the rights and livelihood of his poorer subjects who depended on him, and on him alone, for help. "And moreover we will, that they which had common of pasture in the forest before the perambulation was made, and who were restrained of common by the late perambulation, shall have their common of pasture hereafter in the forest, as freely and largely as they were wont to have before the perambulation was made."

Little more than a year later, on 7 July 1307, aged sixty-eight, and worn out with his ceaseless campaigning against the rebellious Scottish freebooters, the great King died. It is impossible not to regret that the peace-lover, the arbitrator, the fountain-head of his country's prosperity and justice, should have exhausted himself in constant war. But it is better to remember his virtues, and standing beside his simple and unadorned tomb in the Abbey to dwell upon the words of the contemporary elegist:

Nou is Edward of Carnarvan
  King of Engelond al aplyht,
God lete him ner be worse man
  Then is fader, ne lasse of myht
  To holden is pore-men to ryht, . . .
Thah mi tonge were made of stel,
  Ant min herte y-zote of bras,
The godnesse myht y never telle
  That with Kyng Edward was.

CHAPTER VI

EDWARD II

The death of Edward I marked the close of an epoch; that of his successor the beginning of a new one. The intervening reign of Edward II formed one of those periods of flux when time stands still. The thirteenth century had seen the complete triumph of Gothic over Romanesque art, the emergence of England as one of the leading states of the known world, important out of all proportion to its size, and the rapid replacement of semi-barbarism by the refinements of a high material civilization. The Dark Ages were put aside, and in thinking of the reign of Edward II as a set-back, an interlude of retrogression in the path of progress, we must beware of likening it to the utter chaos of the reign of Stephen. The late Professor Tout summed up this distinction: " Neither the state nor society ceased to function because the king's weakness made the state a little more ineffective, and the barons' turbulence made social conditions a little more disorderly than were the normal ineffectiveness and disorder of the slack, easy-going times which we call the middle ages."

But the times were out of joint; the forces of rebellion and disorder, only battened down with some difficulty by the genius and indomitable courage of an Edward I, were not to be met by the pleasant, cultured young squire who was his son. Edward II, Edward of Carnarvon, was in almost all respects a country squire of the best type; a good friend and master, fond of his family, pathetically naïve, devoted to sport and open-air exercise, and built for a life of healthy amusement and the gentle routine of estate management. He was physically strong and of fine appearance, with bright curly hair; fond of conversation and quick in rejoinder; by the end of his reign he had become possessor of at least seven magnificent copies of books in French, romances and legends, and the famous poem on his imprisonment, probably from his own pen, eloquently tells of long practice in the art of poetry. By 1300 there was nothing surprising in a prince, or even a layman of much lesser station, being highly literate. Literacy, and even higher education, were no longer clerical monopolies by the end of the thirteenth century. Tout pointed out that this broke down the old hard and fast distinction in the exchequer between the treasurer's clerical officers and the lay "serjeants" of the chamberlains, but the extent of a layman's interests quite away from the Court can be seen in the surviving Estate Book of Henry de Bray, doubtless representative of a much larger body of lay literature, now lost.

Edward II was the first of our Kings to take a personal interest in the theatre, but the plays which he witnessed have not survived: our one surviving fragment of early comedy, the *Clerk and Damsel*, probably belongs to the period of Edward II's youth. All we know is that Walter Reynolds, whom on his accession he appointed treasurer, was described in a monkish sneer as little learned but pre-eminent in stage plays, through which he obtained his preferment. The bishop was presumably a writer and stage-manager rather than an actor, but Edward II did not stand upon his own dignity, and did not expect dignified behaviour from others. The stories of large sums which he lost in betting and in playing pitch-and-toss and of the huge reward which he gave to his serjeant-painter for dancing on a table sufficiently indicate his bent. The seriousness of his father's character had not found a responsive chord in him, and he preferred the company of his gay, witty, and malicious friend Gaveston to that of any well-intentioned adviser of the older generation. There is no need to see anything vicious in his fondness for Gaveston; it was the natural dependence of an introspective and lonely character upon a brilliant exhibitionist. That Edward II must have been terribly lonely can be gauged from his choice of menial companions and the recreations of manual labour. After Gaveston's murder he spent weeks in digging and is reported to have taken part in the making of a new ditch round Clarendon Park. He continued his work even on Sunday, for Robert, one of the household messengers, was prosecuted for saying that when the King should be hearing Mass he was wasting his time at digging and such-like unsuitable occupations. Robert was "bound over", and it can hardly have been his easy-going master who had him prosecuted, but rather the governmental machine which had the King in its clutches.

Rumours were even put around that the King was no King, but a changeling, the son of an obscure carter, and in 1318 an impostor, perhaps a maniac, but certainly an educated man, passed himself off as the true heir to the throne, forcing himself into Beaumont Manor at Oxford, together with a dog and a cat which he took about with him. Through his reign Edward was surrounded by those less scrupulous than himself, prepared to go to any lengths for their own enrichment. His Queen, still remembered as the She-Wolf of France, married him a few months after his accession; she was then sixteen and described as the rose among the fairest. But she already had a will of her own and did not appreciate the amount of time spent by her husband with Gaveston and with humbler companions. Gaveston may even have gone out of his way to irritate her by appearing at her coronation dressed in royal purple sewn with pearls, but throughout the reign she was perpetually ready to oppose anything and anybody well disposed to Edward himself.

That this was a temperamental dislike is probably true; the Queen does not seem to have been ill-natured in other respects: she once met a Scottish orphan boy whom she fitted out with new clothes and then sent to London to be schooled by the wife of one of her French suite, Jean the Organist, after getting him medical attention for some disease of the scalp. The King seems to have been extra-ordinarily unconscious of his wife's attitude to him; as late as 1321 he was taking trouble to order special dress-lengths for the Queen and her damsels at Christmas, and when she had fled to France with the young Prince Edward, he continued to write to her the puzzled, faintly querulous letters of a kindly husband who cannot imagine what has gone wrong. Towards the end he is said to have exclaimed that if he had no other weapon he would crush the Queen with his teeth, but by that time she had shown herself as the leader of armed rebellion.

As often happens with those who become dependent upon others, the King was not fortunate in his friends. Even Gaveston, who felt real affection for him and came to his death by his determination not to desert his master, was not above feathering his own nest, and used his influence at Court to make his own fortune and to pour funds into the coffers of the moneylenders from Gascony, led by his nephew, Bertrand Calheu. The Gavestons were not upstarts, but belonged to the higher Gascon aristocracy; the practice of international finance was not at that time considered incompatible with gentility. What so enraged the English baronage about Piers was his own personality. He had a capacity for searing wit, and for nicknames that stick like a burr and wound like a dagger. Like Edward, he was an athlete; both the King and Gaveston were fond of tournaments, hunting, and racing, and it is pretty to picture the impotent rage of the earls who were unhorsed by the hated Gascon at the great tourney of Wallingford, held a few months after the beginning of the reign. To be exposed to his scathing tongue and not to be able to defeat him on horseback, lance in hand, set alight that real flame of hatred which destroyed him five years later. The fact that the King was not interested in any other courtier when he had Gaveston by his side must have been a constant reminder of their galling inferiority.

For each of the five great earls, Gaveston had a name ready; and some of those names are not dead yet. Gloucester was " whoreson " or " cuckold's bird "; Lincoln, stout and unwieldy, " broste belly "; Guy Beauchamp of Warwick, " black hound of Arden "; Lancaster, " churl ", or " fiddler " or " the player ", " because he's slim and tall "; Pembroke,

who was lean and pale-complexioned, was "Joseph the
Jew". Pembroke, that Aymer de Valence whose splendid
tomb remains beside the High Altar of Westminster Abbey,
was the skilful moderator whose "middle party" was later
to make the best showing in a bad period; Lincoln had
been the faithful servant of Edward I and was completely
honest and loyal; of Thomas of Lancaster, the King's cousin,
little good can be said, except that his death won him a
martyr's crown in popular estimation, though his life was
filled with brutality, vice, revenge, and double-faced intrigues
with the Scots. The Black Dog of Arden, Guy of Warwick,
murderer of Gaveston, has a reputation for learning; he
had a wide knowledge of literature, unusual among the
higher nobility of his time, and we can see in him a fore-
shadowing of that strange marriage between culture and
sadism that was to lend a special horror to some figures
of the next century: Gilles de Rais in France, in England
the butcher Earl of Worcester, John Tiptoft.

Gaveston was murdered in the June of 1312; when the
King heard of it, all he had to say was : "By God, what
a fool he was; I could have told him never to get into
Warwick's hands," but this apparent callousness must have
covered a depth of misery. To lose a friend in such a
manner, and through his own weakness and incapacity, must
have been exquisite torture, only somewhat relieved by the
birth of a son a few months later.

In every way things tended to go from bad to worse.
Edward has been blamed for failing to continue his father's
Scottish war; it is true that he did not fulfil Edward I's
dying wishes on the subject, but was it to be expected that
a bright young man-about-town, fond of his amusements,
should take seriously the notion of boiling down his father's
bones and carrying them on campaign? He did not lack
personal courage, but he was not a particularly capable
soldier, for all his physical strength and manly accomplishments such as swimming. Two years after Gaveston's death
came the fatal field of Bannockburn, the most outstanding
of many English defeats, which occurred with monotonous

John, *from the effigy at Worcester Cathedral, c.* 1230

Henry III, *from the effigy at Westminster Abbey.*
Cast by William Torel of London, 1291

Edward II, *from the effigy at Gloucester Cathedral, c.* 1330

Edward III, *from the effig
Westminster Abbey, c. 137
probably cast by John Orch*

Edward the Black Prince,
*from the effigy at Canterbu
Cathedral, c.* 1377, *probab
by John Orchard*

Edward I, *from Cotton MS. Vitellius A.xiii, c.* 1285. *English*

Margaret of France, second Queen of Edward I, *from a statue at Lincoln Cathedral*

Edward I and Margaret of France, *from the "Alard"
tomb, Winchelsea Church, c. 1305*

Edward II and Isabella of France, *from the Oxenbridge
tomb, Winchelsea Church, c. 1320*

Henry V, *from the painting in the National Portrait Gallery*

Henry VI, *from the painting in the National Portrait Gallery*

Richard II, *from the effigy at Westminster Abbey,* 1395, *by Nicholas Broker and Godfrey Prest*

Richard II and Anne of Bohemia, *from the effigies at Westminster Abbey,* 1395, *by Nicholas Broker and Godfrey Prest*

Henry IV, *from electrotype copy of the effigy at Canterbury Cathedral, early fifteenth century*

Edward IV, *from a painting belonging to the Society of Antiquaries*

Elizabeth Woodville, *from the original contemporary portrait at Queens' College, Cambridge*

Richard III, *from the painting in the possession of the Society of Antiquaries*

repetition for years. In 1318 Bruce took Berwick, and by 1322 won a battle as far south as Byland in Yorkshire; from Bannockburn to the end of the reign the northern counties were never safe. On top of internal disasters came the Great Famine, which spread across Europe in 1314 and 1315; appalling weather, wars, and the incidence of one of those periodic breakdowns in society of which the troubled reign of Edward II was a symptom, had conspired to bring about this terrible result. Not until 1946 was Europe again faced by the menace of dying of sheer hunger.

One age was in its death-throes, another was soon to open. From the end of Edward I's reign to the year of Bannockburn the trial of the Order of Templars had been proceeding in France, a sinister reminder that the encyclopædism of the thirteenth century had ushered in a new orthodoxy and a series of heresy-hunts, as diligent and more far-reaching in their effects than the abominable crusade against the Albigenses, in which the De Montfort family had played so prominent a part. But outside questions of faith, many remarkable matters were being dealt with, remarkable men were dying and coming into prominence. On the Continent the old era's close was marked by the deaths of Jacopo de Voragine, author of the *Golden Legend*, in 1298; of Raymond Lull, mystic and philosopher, in 1314; and of Heinrich Frauenlob, one of the last and greatest German minnesinger, in 1318. Summing up in immortal verse the philosophized theology of Aquinas, Dante began his Divine Comedy in the year of Lull's death, and completed it just before his own, in 1321. Meanwhile, a university had been founded at Rome in 1303, while the Italian arts were taking shape in such great works as the Cathedral and Church of Santa Croce at Florence, both begun in the last decade of the thirteenth century; Giovanni Pisano's pulpit at Pisa, made in 1301; the paintings of Giotto; and in the North, the completion of the choir of Cologne Cathedral in 1322.

The extinction of the older generation in England was symbolized by the death, about 1316, of Walter Odington, a

P.   E musician of European reputation, and the first of whose output we have some signed examples, beside extensive theoretical treatises. Walter of Hereford, the great architect of Edward I's latter years, designer of Carnarvon Castle and of much else, had died by 1309; his work at the Greyfriars Church in London was one of the first portents of fully developed English Gothic, which in another generation was to crystallize into the Perpendicular style. Another Walter also, the great painter of Durham, who executed the paintings on the Coronation Chair, had died about 1308. The over-naturalistic and then over-mannered and lush decadence of the Decorated period had set in, though magnificent monuments which looked both forward to the unknown future, and back to past triumphs, were being built. Among these were the new building of Exeter Cathedral, begun at the east end in 1288; the Chapter Houses at York and Southwell; the beginning of the Gothic cloister at Norwich Cathedral; the central tower of Lincoln Minster, begun in 1307; and the Lady Chapel at St. Alban's Abbey. The most important work was being done by masters from Canterbury at the King's Palace of Westminster, where the work of St. Stephen's Chapel, discontinued after a fire in 1298, was carried on by Master Thomas of Canterbury in rich Decorated style between 1320 and 1326.

Considering the unsettled state of political affairs a large amount of artistic work was carried out, and much of it is owed to the King's personal instigation and taste. He did not spend all his time digging, as his well-composed letters witness, and a court-painter meant more to him than a companion who was prepared to make a fool of himself. One anecdote shows that he was interested in portraits, and incidentally, that collections of royal likenesses were being made. Dining with Abbot Thokey at Gloucester, where he afterwards came to be buried, he remarked on the portraits of his royal predecessors on the walls of the Abbot's Hall, asking with a smile if the Abbot proposed to add one of himself. Thokey made the courtly reply that he hoped the King's effigy would appear in a more distinguished place than those of his predecessors—and so it did, upon his monument.

Towards the end of the reign, under the rule of the two Despensers, the government was doing a certain amount for the benefit of the country, as may be seen from the second ordinance of the Staple, of 1 May 1326, wherein staple towns for the wool trade were set up in England, Ireland, and Wales, and everyone was to use home-made cloth except the King, nobles, and others worth over £40 yearly. Economists are not agreed upon the ultimate effectiveness of such protectionist measures, but the ordinance was one of the most popular acts of government ever published. It gave for the time an immense fillip to the weaving industry, though it may also have unduly promoted national insularity and pride. The great maxim of Justinian, that what touches all should be approved by all, had been quoted by Edward I when he summoned his " Model " Parliament of 1295, and there are signs that even in the age of baronial squabbling which followed the great King's death, some attempts were being made to improve the position of those masses who never were nor are truly represented by the parliamentary machine. Such attempts have been made throughout English history by the Sovereign himself, or by members of the Court Party: from very early days up to the usurpation of the Throne of the Stuarts in 1688, the claim of " popular " representation was used as a misleading mask by parties of self-seeking nobles, barons, lawyers, or tradesmen, intent upon their own advantage, and knowing that in the overthrow of the real power of the Crown lay their only hope of exploiting those humbler masses they pretended to serve.

So although we need not imagine the Despensers as altruistic, their rule as " King's men " was at least more likely to be just than that of a great territorial nobleman such as Lancaster, or a scheming adventurer like Mortimer, who robbed his King both of wife and life. Unfortunately the Queen's crafty lover found submissive tools ready to his hand; men like Adam Orleton, Bishop of Hereford, who, when the King was in Mortimer's power, bullied him into abdication by saying that only thus could he save his children from destruction. Similar methods were used three centuries later to force Charles I to consent to the death of Strafford; in both cases submission to the blackmailers spelt doom for the wretched King. The blackmail used against Edward II was, of all kinds, the most despicable: the levelled pistol of the kidnapper. Edward was not lacking in physical courage, and his strength and endurance were to cause his tormentors considerable difficulty and annoyance before they finally disposed of him; but the threat that the whole Plantagenet line would be wiped out brought him down. It is a pitiable spectacle, and all the more terrifying when we think that it was the deposition of Edward II that formed the precedent for that of Richard II, while both contributed to the fall of Charles I and the final expulsion of the Stuarts and the Regality together. Not the most adept of American kidnappers has gone to the electric chair with the load of evil on his soul that encumbered those of Roger Mortimer and his Christian brother, Orleton.

It is needless to retell the oft-told narrative of the last months of the wretched King's life. He was moved from place to place, from bad to worse, for every expedient was tried to avoid actual violence, in the hope that semi-starvation, insanitary conditions, lack of light, forced absence of sleep—the tortures of the third degree and the concentration camp—would result in death. But the King, aged only forty-three, possessed of a splendid physique and constitution and toughened by his outdoor pursuits, obstinately refused to oblige his captors. Once, for a short time, in July of 1327, he was actually rescued by the noble exertions of two brothers, Stephen and Thomas Dunheved, from the fatal hold of Berkeley. But the brave endeavour did not succeed; the King was retaken and hurried back to his clammy dungeon, where he was soon afterwards murdered with monstrous torments. The date of his death was given out as 22 September, a day which deserves commemoration for the suffering borne by a pathetic and courageous man, a royal martyr even if he were no saint.

CHAPTER VII

EDWARD III

A boy of fourteen at his father's abdication, Edward III was at first a puppet of his mother and Mortimer. His father had been fond of him, and he was attached to the memory of his father, for as soon as opportunity offered, he overthrew Mortimer and sent his mother into an honourable retirement, where she could do no more harm. It must always have been a painful thought to Edward that he owed his throne to a mother both adultress and traitor to her husband, and to the assiduity of her lover, Mortimer, in spreading slanderous calumny against his King and conspiring with every worst element in the country. These circumstances were enough to unsettle any youth, and that Edward III did not suffer more than he did from lack of balance must be considered as due to his fortunate marriage. Edward and the young Philippa of Hainault were married at York on 24 January 1328; for forty years the Queen was by his side, always an influence for kindliness and restraint, a true good genius. We are told how she saved the lives of the defeated burghers of Calais and how she averted punishment from the carpenters whose stands for the Cheapside tournament in 1331 had broken down, to the injury and embarrassment of knights and ladies of the Court.

It has been suggested that Edward's wrath at Calais was simulated, and his hard-won pardon of the burghers a piece of stage-management; but surely this is to attribute a most improbable psychology to a King who lived by the arbitrary exercise of his own will. That the Plantagenet anger was terrible is a fact vouched for by abundant witnesses; looking at the magnificently regal features of the aged King as portrayed on his tomb at Westminster it is easier to believe in his fits of anger than in any subtle elaboration of diplomacy. Yet it is easy also to credit the reports of his splendour and charm of manner. The accessibility and luxurious tastes of his father mingled with the sternness of his grandfather and the violent passions of his mother; but the sum total made up a great King and an outstanding personality.

His Queen had been marked out at the early age of nine; Bishop Stapeldon was sent overseas to inspect her at that age, and this is the report he brought home to Edward II: "The lady whom we saw has not uncomely hair, betwixt blue-black and brown. Her head is clean-shaped; her forehead high and broad, and standing somewhat forward. Her face narrows between the eyes, and the lower part of her face is still more narrow and slender than the forehead. Her eyes are blackish-brown and deep. Her nose is fairly smooth and even, save that it is somewhat broad at the tip and flattened, yet it is no snub-nose. Her nostrils are also broad, her mouth fairly wide. Her lips somewhat full, and especially the lower lip. Her teeth which have fallen and grown again are white enough, but the rest are not so white. The lower teeth project a little beyond the upper; yet this is but little seen. Her ears and chin are comely enough. Her neck, shoulders, and all her body and lower limbs are reasonably well shapen; all her limbs are well set and unmaimed; and nought is amiss so far as a man may see. Moreover, she is brown of skin all over, and much like her father; and in all things she is pleasant enough, as it seems to us. And the damsel will be of age of nine years on St. John's day next to come, as her mother saith. She is neither too tall nor too short for such an age; she is of fair carriage, and well taught in all that becometh her rank, and highly esteemed and well beloved of her father and mother and of all her meinie, in so far as we could inquire and learn the truth." Most of these characteristics can still be traced in the figure of the dead Queen, carved by her compatriot, Master Hennequin of Liége, half a century later.

The Queen was crowned in March 1330, and her eldest son, known as the Black Prince, was born on 15 June. In October, Mortimer and the Queen-mother were overthrown, and the reign began in earnest. The change of government brought about an immediate spurt in artistic activity; the upper chapel of St. Stephen in the Palace of Westminster was pushed ahead, and showed signs of the coming of the " Perpendicular " style; more clearly marked is the innovating character of the work at the new Chapter House and Cloister of St. Paul's in London, by Master William de Ramsey, shortly to be King's Chief Mason; the retrochoir of Wells, and the reconstruction of the south transept at Gloucester. A new golden age had dawned; public order, gravely disturbed under Mortimer, was stabilized, and the gangs of kidnappers who had been imprisoning and holding to ransom travellers on the King's highways were rounded up by the King in person. The free access of foreign merchants to the ports and great towns, provided by Magna Charta, was confirmed in 1332 and further enacted in 1336.

The first six years of Edward's personal rule were halcyon days indeed; the only cloud was the little war against Scotland, but at the time this seemed only a source of easy glory, for a Balliol was restored, and for a few years the dream of Edward I was realized by the occupation of Scotland by English troops. Of more sinister significance were the new tactics adopted by the English soldiers of fortune who fought for Edward Balliol at Dupplin Moor in 1332, and carried out with success by Edward himself at his victory of Halidon Hill in the next year. In brief, the humble archer proved his military value, and by the adoption of this new arm, Edward, the pattern of chivalry himself, doomed to extinction the chivalrous code of knightly warfare in Europe. It would be fanciful to attribute to Edward, or to the household knights who formed his General Staff, a plan of continental aggression based upon this new method of battle; but by unfortunate coincidence the extinction of the male line of the Capetian House of France gave Edward the opportunity his ambition needed. Instead of concentrating upon the unification of Britain and the fulfilment of his grandfather's dreams of peace and prosperity, he laid claim to the throne of France, and embarked upon a war which with slight intermissions was to last for 115 years, and was to exhaust the two major nations of Western Europe.

Although the new methods of war introduced in Edward III's reign were to spell disaster for Europe, Edward himself belonged to the school of true chivalry, even forsaking a hard-won advantage in favour of scrupulous fair play. At the age of fifteen he had been in command of the English troops on the Scottish border, when the Scots invaded England; seeing that his front lay on the River Wear he offered to retire, that the Scots might have a proper foothold and room to fight. It is now amusing to read in Longman's classic work on the reign, published in 1869, that " the usages of chivalry . . . impart to the incidents of the battles and manners of the age, a picturesque interest, which is apt to blind one to the defects, inseparably mingled with that splendid, but imperfect condition of society."

Defects there will always be in human society, but it is the best qualities of each successive society that we must seek: the fourteenth century had much real chivalry beneath its picturesque veneer, and was one of the periods of most outstanding achievement in the arts. Music on a new plan, freed from the tyranny of second-hand theories, was forging ahead in France, where Philippe de Vitri and Guillaume de Machault laid the foundations of a new and practical harmony, to be brought to completion in the next century by the Englishman, John Dunstable. The life of Richard Rolle, first of the great English mystic poets, fills the half-century from 1300 to 1349; Robert Mannyng, the other great English poet of the early century, began his *Handlyng Synne* in 1303, but was still working on his Chronicle more than ten years after the opening of Edward III's reign. Rolle and Mannyng belonged to an earlier generation, but the great outpouring of English literature came from a small group of men roughly contemporary with Edward III and Richard II: John Gower, William Langland, Geoffrey Chaucer, and the author of *Pearl*, probably Ralph Strode. This constellation was as significant as that of the great Elizabethans, or the group of Latin writers of English origin in the twelfth century. And whereas the twelfth-century authors had used a language other than the vernacular, and the form and methods of the Elizabethans were highly un-English, the poets of the fourteenth century not only used the English language, but did so in an English way, with largely English material.

The encouragement to artists given by Edward III and his sons and grandson was very great; without such court patronage the efforts of most of the authors, and of practically all the architects and painters, would have come to nothing. Richard of Bury, the first great bibliophile, was on terms of close intimacy with the King, and the Court was permeated with the new type of humanism that flowed from such sources. In the breezy irony of De Bury's *Philobiblon* we leave the rather dank atmosphere of scholasticism and reach modernity. The books which he collected were all hand-written, for the art of printing was yet to come; but his reproof of the careless user of books remains seasonable: "His nails are stuffed with filth as black as jet, with which he marks any passage that pleases him. He distributes a multitude of straws, which he inserts to stick out in different places, so that the halm may remind him of what his memory cannot retain. . . . He does not fear to eat fruit or cheese over an open book, or carelessly to carry a cup to and from his mouth; and because he has no wallet at hand he drops into books the fragments that are left. . . . Aye, and then hastily folding his arms he leans forward on the book, and by a brief spell of study invites a prolonged nap; and then, by way of mending the wrinkles, he folds back the margin of the leaves. . . . Now the rain is over and gone, and the flowers have appeared in our land. Then the scholar we are speaking of . . . will stuff his volume with violets and primroses, with roses and quatre-foil. Then he will use his wet and perspiring hands to turn over the volumes; then he will thump the white vellum with gloves covered with all kinds of dust . . . then at the sting of the biting flea the sacred book is flung aside, and is hardly shut for another month, until it is so full of the dust that has found its way within, that it resists the effort to close it."

Early in the reign the wonderful school of East Anglian illumination was at work, producing about 1340 as its final achievement the Luttrell Psalter with graphic scenes from everyday life. A great age of wall- and glass-painting was also opening; the chief painters were men of St. Albans and London, and their greatest work was the adornment of St. Stephen's Chapel which, structurally complete by 1349, was fitted with stalls, carvings, and glass, and brilliantly enriched with paintings in the years after the great pestilence. Chief of this group of painters was Hugh of St. Albans who brought into England advanced notions of perspective just reaching the Papal Court at Avignon from Italy and not yet carried into northern France. This priority of England over France was independent of the war, though the military victories were another symptom of France's state. The great reforms of Edward I were bearing fruit, while across the water the break of dynasty and the backswing of the pendulum after Philip III and Philip the Fair made the fourteenth century in France one of disunity and internal strife.

Edward III felt himself upon the top of the wave; his pride and love of glory and splendour, the qualities which even the modern historian cannot altogether tarnish, led him to tread the perilous path of national aggrandizement. In 1336 the Count of Flanders forbade trade with England; Edward in return prohibited the export of English wool to Flanders. The power of France took the offensive, and an invasion was feared in England; Edward made the proud claim that " our progenitors, Kings of England, were lords of the English sea on every side." This assertion was often repeated, and is the historical origin of Britannia's rule of the waves and the salute owed by the ships of all nations to the English flag of St. George. The cult of St. George as a national patron was personally promoted by the King, who founded the Order of the Garter and began to

rebuild the great chapel in Windsor Castle in the saint's
honour. But the way of national patriotism is not smooth;
on the one hand are the noble activities of chivalry; on
the other are more ominous signs of the meaning of warfare.
In 1336 one of the measures taken to put the country upon
a defensive footing was the order that "no man shall cause
himself to be served at dinner, meal or supper with more
than two courses, and each mess of two sorts of victuals at
the utmost." Two years later, when a more serious threat
of invasion was in the offing, it was proclaimed that if the
French set foot on English soil the church bells should all
be set ringing together; while a year earlier the petition
to Parliament of John Codyngton, clerk and attorney, shows
that the Admiralty's conscription board was no respecter
of persons or estates. Edward III, with greater flexibility than
a modern ministry, heard the case and cancelled the calling-
up papers.

The unwisely provocative attitude of the new Valois
King, Philip VI, goaded Edward into claiming the French
Crown for himself, in right of his mother, sister of the last
three Kings, and daughter of Philip the Fair. As legitimate
right was counted in the earlier middle ages, the claim was
moderately good, but it probably would have remained
unasserted had it not been for Philip's arrogant offensives
against England and the English possessions in France.
Like Richard Cœur-de-Lion, Edward in 1340 challenged his
opponent to single combat for the sake of avoiding warfare.
His admirable letter, which failed to awaken a chivalrous
response in the breast of the wily French King, deserves
quotation: " . . . we purpose to recover the right we have
to that inheritance, which you violently withhold from us,
. . . and forasmuch as we have so great an army assembled,
a like power, it is presumed, being assembled on your part,
which cannot remain long in the field without producing
great destruction to the people of the country, which thing
every good Christian should eschew, especially princes and
others, who have the government of the people; it is very
desirable to settle the matter briefly, to avoid the mortality

of Christians, since the quarrel is between you and us only, that the discussion of our challenge should be decided by our own persons, to which arrangement we offer ourselves, . . . and in case you shall not agree to this way, then let us determine our dispute by a battle of one hundred of the most efficient persons on your part, and as many on ours. . . . And we wishing that our said offers should be known by all—for it is our desire it should be known that not from pride or presumption, but from the causes already stated, and to the intent that the will of our Lord Jesus Christ being declared between us, for the greater repose of all true Christians, and that the enemies of God might be the better resisted for the security of Christianity—desire you to consider which of our offers you will accept, and signify the same to the bearer of these letters, and with all convenient dispatch."

Edward's strength lay in the fact that the people of Flanders had been persuaded, through their dislike for their own Count, to acknowledge the King of England as rightful King of France, and thus their own overlord; he also made a diplomatic journey in 1338 to meet the German Emperor Louis, who appointed Edward his Vicar-General over the parts of the Empire on the left bank of the Rhine, the Imperial Princes of the Low Countries being given orders to follow him in war for seven years. Pauli in 1861 printed details of Edward's journey from Antwerp to Coblenz and back, from an account in the Public Record Office. He left Antwerp on 16 August and returned on 13 September; the Queen accompanied him for the first four days out, and met him for the last four days of the return. The intervening three weeks were occupied by travel through Bree, Sittard, Juliers, Cologne, and Bonn, a week of festivity at Coblenz, and a speedy return by Andernach, Bonn, and Düren. The King was entertained by nobles and great ecclesiastics for most of the nights of his journey, but at Cologne he stayed with a rich burgher, Heinrich Scherfgin and his wife, Blida; a sign of the new relationship that was growing up between the Court and business interests. While at Cologne,

Edward interested himself in the work of the cathedral, and gave £67 10s. sterling, perhaps some £6,000 now, to the fabric fund.

All this had to be paid for, and in 1340 a fifteenth was granted in taxation, but "the poor and those who live of their labour" were exempted, a praiseworthy attempt to keep the burden on the shoulders best fitted to bear it. The centre of English policy tended to swing from London to Flanders, and for some years the royal family spent much of its time in the Low Countries, as we are reminded by the nickname of the King's son, John of Gaunt, born at Ghent. In 1346 the King attempted to float a new international currency, valid both in England and Flanders, a fourteenth-century sterling bloc, but it was not a success. This was the year of his memorable expedition through northern France; taking Caen, he discovered documentary evidence of the French plan of 1339 for the invasion of England. He was so enraged at this that he wished to massacre the inhabitants, but his anger was restrained by the soothing words of Geoffrey de Harcourt: "Dear Sire, restrain your courage a little, and be satisfied with what you have done. You have yet a long journey before you get to Calais, where you intend to go." Anxious to maintain his character as a scrupulously Christian monarch, Edward gave strict instructions that no churches should be injured by his troops on the march, and hanged twenty of his men who set fire to one of the great churches of Beauvais. Against great odds Crécy was won, the vital port of Calais taken after a stubborn defence, and the pinnacle of fame was achieved when, on the death of Louis, the German electors voted for Edward as his successor.

But Edward's financial commitments were already too great, and though the renunciation cost him a good deal in personal humiliation, the offer of Germany was declined with thanks. Now that the stern campaign was over and won he could return to his treasured project of the Garter, to the tournament, and to such pleasing fancies as the " harness of white buckram inlaid with silver, namely a tunic and shield, with the King's motto *Hay, Hay the Wythe Swan, by Godes soule I am thy man.*" The Channel crossing turned stormy, and the King petulantly sought for omens, crying: "Holy Mary, my Lady, why is it, that going to France, the sea is calmed with a favourable wind and all is prosperous to me; while, in returning to England, heavy misfortunes and adverse winds happen to me?"

The gallant exploits of the war must be sought in the pages of Froissart, who gathered up eyewitness accounts from the principal actors; so much so that his book suffers from the inconsistency always coupled with first-hand information. But as a guide to the characters of the sovereigns, princes, knights and squires of the age, no book can equal it, except the prologue and by-play of Chaucer's Tales. Good Canon Froissart, courtier and man of peace, loved a war-story, like the exploits of his famous compatriot, Sir Walter Manny, who in 1342 sallied out of Hennebont with 300 archers and broke up the great siege engine which had been built by the French; and when Manny and his companions returned, "the countess [of Montfort] descended down from the castle with a glad cheer and came and kissed sir Gaultier of Manny and his companions one after another two or three times, like a valiant lady." The most apposite of all these stories is that of King Edward's lying in wait for the Spanish fleet in 1350, when "the King stood at his ship's prow, clad in a jacket of black velvet, and on his head a hat of black beaver that became him right well; and he was then (as I was told by such as were with him that day) as merry as ever he was seen. He made his minstrels sound before him on their trumpets a German dance that had been brought in of late by my lord John Chandos, who was there present; and then for pastime he made the said knight sing with his minstrels, and took great pleasure therein; and at times he would look upwards, for he had set a watch in the topcastle of his ship to give tidings of the Spaniards' coming. While the King thus took his pleasure, and all his knights were glad of heart to see how merry he was, then the watch was aware of the Spaniards' fleet, and cried: 'Ho! I see a ship coming, and methinks it is a ship of Spain!' Then the minstrels held their peace, and it was asked of him again whether he saw aught else; then within a brief space he answered and said: 'Yes, I see two—and then three—and then four.' Then, when he was aware of the great fleet, he cried: 'I see so many, God help me! that I may not tell them.' Then the King and his men knew well that these were the Spanish ships. Then the King let sound his trumpets, and all their ships came together to be in better array, and to lie more surely; for well they knew that the battle was at hand, since the Spaniards came in so great a fleet. By this time the day was far spent, for it was about the hour of vespers. So the King sent for wine and drank thereof, he and all his knights; then he laced on his helm, and the rest did likewise." The result was a resounding English victory, the Spaniards losing at least 14 ships out of 40.

Merry as the King and his knights were, a great disaster had recently befallen their country, in common with the whole of Europe. The years 1348 and 1349 had seen the appalling visitation of the Black Death. Though its effects on the economic situation in England used to be grossly exaggerated it was a very real blow, and in London it seems to have led to almost a clean sweep of the earlier masters of the important crafts, who were replaced by fresh comers from the country. This doubtless contributed to the comparative standardization of the new Perpendicular style of architecture all over England, though the new style was already coming into favour in courtly circles some fifteen years before the plague. Another example of centralization is found in the fixing of the Courts at London in 1345; they no longer followed the King's person on progress, and London and Westminster became more fully than before a permanent capital.

Although Court circles suffered less from the pestilence than did the monasteries, King Edward lost his fifteen-year-old daughter Joanna, who died of plague near Bordeaux on 2 September 1348. She had been betrothed to the Infante

Pedro, son of Pedro the Cruel, King of Castile; Edward's letter to the Infante, informing him of Joanna's death, still survives:

Most Noble Infant:

We believe it is not unknown to your Serenity, how that multifarious negotiations between the magnificent prince, the King of Castile, your father, and our procurators and messengers have been held, at different times, about the contraction of a marriage between you and Joanna, our dearest daughter; and at last, desiring to keep faith in reference to these treaties, we thought fit to transmit our aforesaid daughter to Bordeaux, thence to be led to other parts of Spain, at the time appointed by your father. And subsequently according to the last agreements . . . lately made and accorded, we had decreed to send our daughter, before the approaching feast of All Saints, to Bayonne, with an honourable company, as was fitting; there to be received by your officers, and united to you, in the marriage bond. And we had moreover, not without much difficulty, and great loss of our exchequer, prepared to fulfil each and every condition in reference to the dower which we were to pay with her. But, whilst we with paternal affection thought to have had an adopted son to our mutual comfort, behold—what with sobbing sighs, and a heavy heart, we sorrowfully relate,—Death, terrible to all the Kings of the earth, which takes indifferently the poor and the powerful, the youth and the alluring virgin, with the aged man, without respect to person or power, has now by a subversion of the wonted laws of mortality, removed from your hoped-for embraces, and from ours, our aforesaid daughter, in whom all the gifts of nature met; whom, also, as due to the elegance of her manners, we sincerely loved beyond our other children. Thus the bond of this adoption is broken by a dire mode of emancipation, and a grievous sort of divorce. Whereat none can wonder that we are pierced by the shafts of sorrow. But although our bowels of pity lead us to such groans and complainings, yet we give devout thanks to God, who gave her to us, and has taken her away, that he has designed to snatch her, pure and immaculate, in the years of her innocence, from the miseries of this deceitful world, and to call her to heaven; where, united to her celestial spouse, for ever to reign in the choir of virgins, her constant intercession may avail for us . . .

The second part of the reign, after the Black Death, was a disappointment. After the blaze of glory which surrounded the young King and his splendid designs, the defeats and difficulties of his later years seem disconcerting and surprising. But in truth he had undertaken more than any man could perform, and his every action did but entangle him deeper in the morass of debt and frustration. His son's victory at Poitiers and the subsequent captivity of the French King, though they led to the apparently satisfactory Peace of Brétigny, were illusory benefits. The Dauphin and the influential men of France were determined not to recognize such a peace, and though their decision entailed a century of almost unmitigated misery and desolation it was ultimately vindicated by the verdict of history. We in England are accustomed to think of ourselves as the outstanding example of undaunted pluck; it might do us good to contemplate the picture of fourteenth- and fifteenth-century France, ravaged by the scum of England and the worst mercenaries of Europe, constantly defeated, constantly acknowledging defeat on paper, yet never despairing of ultimate victory. No nation has any monopoly of courage, nor any corner in abstract justice; and the futile waste and abuse of these qualities in war will go on until a victor appears, great enough not only to forgo the fruits of victory, but to apologize to the vanquished and make heartfelt restitution.*

In spite of the gloomy picture given by the political world

* The enormous historical influence of the Indian Emperor Asoka (264-227 B.C.) seems due to his close approach to this ideal.

of the latter part of Edward's reign, in the cultural sphere progress continued. It was this period that saw the great triumphs of renascent English letters: *Pearl*, the first version of *Piers Plowman*, Chaucer's *Boke of the Duchesse*. At Westminster, at Windsor, at other royal palaces and many of the greater churches was immense architectural activity; the master masons Henry Yevele and William Wynford shared with the carpenters William and Hugh Herland the design of the King's works, and in all parts of the country their colleagues were busy. The scientific field also was not barren: Archbishop Thomas Bradwardine, the most learned mediæval geometrician, died in the Black Death, but in John Arderne of Newark the practice of medicine found its first modern surgeon. Arderne, whose *Art of Medicine* appeared in 1370, looked forward, and it is interesting to find that his reputation was not confined to the vaguely heretical and free-thinking Lancastrian circle which first patronized him, for he was a consultant at the Infirmary of Westminster Abbey in 1378, taking a gown and retaining fee. His great contemporary in France, Guy de Chauliac, produced his *Chirurgie* in 1363, and had it not been for the effects of war, pestilence, the closing of the ancient trade routes to Asia by the fall of the Mongol dynasty in 1368, and the concurrent expansion of the Turks, the fifteenth century might have seen a far truer and wiser revival of learning than that actually reserved for the sixteenth.

Experiments were made in internal affairs: in some ways the leaders of fourteenth-century statesmanship were wiser than their twentieth-century descendants. Thus the King made a firm stand against the growing practice of " county " seats in Parliament being represented by lawyers from the towns. On seven occasions from 1330 to 1372 lawyers and " maintainers of quarrels " were excluded from sitting as county members, and the principle was carried even further under Henry IV, when in 1404 no lawyer was permitted to sit in Parliament at all. It was felt that by the nature of his business a lawyer was unfitted for genuine representation of country interests; and his aptitude for special pleading and "maintaining" the quarrels of individuals was against impartiality. In another direction the century was in advance of modern practice: in firm adherence to the principle of the Fair Price. The Black Death, upsetting the balance of population and supply of labour, caused incipient inflation, with the beginning of a "price-spiral". Severe laws were introduced to fix wages and prices and to enforce the customary laws against selling otherwise than in the open market. The blissful Longman, basking in the sunlight of Victorian Free Trade, could criticize a clause fixing the price of herrings in the following sarcastic terms: "Justice to the poor fishermen, who toiled for the herrings and were fairly entitled to as much as the herring consumers were willing to give, seems never to have entered into the minds of the legislators." What did not enter Mr. Longman's mind, nor the minds of his contemporaries who knew neither the mediæval nor the twentieth-century "black market", was the disastrous effect of absolute free trade in a period of financial uncertainty. But, as a matter of fact, Edward III was aware of the difficulties of the fishermen; in 1350 he gave special orders to the keeper of the Channel Islands that in collecting taxation from the fishermen he was not to impoverish them, and to abate the usual levies in view of the poverty caused by the plague.

Edward survived Queen Philippa by eight years, long enough to celebrate the jubilee of his reign in 1377, six months before his death. It is charitable to draw a veil over his dotage, sponged upon by his avaricious mistress, Alice Perrers, and a crowd of unworthy hangers-on. The parliamentary difficulties between his sons, Edward the Black Prince and John of Gaunt, and the former's long illness and premature death, did nothing to relieve the sorry picture of the great King's last years. It is even said that at his death Dame Alice snatched the jewels from his body, and that his corpse lay deserted for some hours. We may hope that this is a picturesque exaggeration, and take consolation that he did in the end come to burial, as he had wished, in the great Abbey of his patron "between our ancestors of famous memory Kings of England, where we have chosen our royal sepulture ", and next to his own dear Queen. The glorious monument, masterpiece of his own craftsmen, reflects his former and not his later state, and the tired old face of bronze distils some of that godlike grace and charm which had enriched the happier days of youth.

CHAPTER VIII

RICHARD II

The reign of Richard II, as a recent historian has said, marks the culminating point in English mediæval history. For a reason quite different from that commonly assigned (that it contained the admission of the supremacy of Parliament), it may be said to be the actual culmination of English history as a whole. Modern research has demolished the theory of a continuity of parliamentary progress, of a steadily growing domination of English affairs by the principles of true representative government. It is nevertheless true that through a long series of actions, lasting for some seven centuries, English administration took on the familiar forms of the nineteenth century, still regarded as " the last word ", though they have already been silently replaced by a new autocracy, government by semi-despotic orders and regulations.

Richard II is important because he was in the highest degree the type of his family, of the whole House of Plantagenet, and because he represented in the most personal manner the supreme case for Divine Kingship. His insistence upon the sacred and indissoluble nature of the regality conferred on him by his consecration, and upon the maintenance in full of the rights of the Crown, was due to his prescience of the nature of all that would follow, once this barrier was swept away. It is neither sentimentality nor romanticism to see in Richard a highly intelligent and supremely cultured man, fully abreast of the high intellectual attainments of his age, and gifted with a greater insight than most men, even most sovereigns, into the essential character of government. He could see that the purpose of statesmanship is not merely, in a material sense, the greatest happiness of the greatest number; it must be founded in the

first place upon quality. Thus it is not sufficient to improve
the standard of living, and to improve it impartially throughout society; this is not even the most important aim; the
first essential is to raise the standard of sensibility, of
artistic perception and capacity, of cultural inspiration,
throughout the masses of the governed, starting at the top.

If we are to credit the notion of a purposive universe, it
is probably true that in historic time at least there has
been some human advance rather than human retrogression.
Yet it is one of the commonest and most widely spread of
errors to suppose that because a period is more remote
in time, it is more barbarous, worse equipped, and less
sophisticated. The flawless poise of the Greece of the sixth
and fifth centuries B.C., and the exquisite line of the sculpture,
painting, and literature of the Pharaoh Akhnaton a thousand
years earlier still, are enough to teach us that. Similarly, the
fourteenth century saw the attainment of a supreme peak
of European existence, and we shall be nearer the mark if
we picture Richard II as a superman, wiser and better equipped than ourselves, than if we suppose him a crude potentate
in an age of splendid savagery. It is probable that Europe
proper has not, since the fourteenth century, seen any individual capable of appreciating Richard at his proper value.

The events of Richard's reign are of such far-reaching
importance, so terrific in their after effects, that it is a
shock to learn that the King himself was only thirty-three
at the time of his death, the same age as Alexander the
Great and perhaps a little older than the Emperor Julian.
It is with men such as Alexander and Julian that he is to
be compared. All alike shared the impossibly high ideals,
the meteoric brilliance, the brittle glory. Not that there
are many points of resemblance between their careers; but
all three were conscious exponents of the highest type of
monarchy: Alexander so nearly restored the world empire
of remote antiquity; Julian in lonely isolation all but preserved the noble flame of paganism in a dying era; Richard
made the most nearly successful attempt to combine the
highest cultural aims with the welfare of the common man.

Alone of the three, to Richard belongs the special credit of perceiving, in the midst of a world gone mad with warfare, the one overruling necessity was peace. He saw the utterly illusory nature of even successful war; the fact that the law of the conservation of energy means that even the war of good aims, the justified war, brings irreparable loss to both parties. Towards the end of his reign attempts were made to interest him in a new Crusade, but there is little reason to suppose that he had any intention of armed conflict with the infidel; he was at home the last King to stand out against the burning of heretics, and his benevolent toleration is the nearest approach in Christian Europe to the exalted calm of Julian or Akbar. It is significant that while in the later years of his grandfather the two main parties in the state had been led by William of Wykeham and John of Gaunt, Richard was able to make friends of both. In all respects we must see in Richard, not a pacifist indeed, but a peacemaker.

Who were Richard's opponents? It would not be thought that a policy so equitable, so ultimately profitable to all, would meet with serious opposition. Yet, like similar policies before and since, it was fiercely opposed, and in the end wrecked by determined troublemakers. As usual, they may be summed up briefly as vested interests, but the interests were not solely material. The most obstinate were the leaders of the war party; those who could see nothing but the crushing of France as a worthy aim; the exponents of a war, intolerable and expensive as it might be, to end war. In short, men who lacked the ability for compromise, or even to understand its nature. Ably seconding these leaders were the ambitious men of big business in the City of London and elsewhere, and that ever-present section of the clergy who exhort to arms. In all essentials this was a party of what is now miscalled the "Right", though it was as the spearhead of the "Left" that it left its mark. It was typically this party, so critical of the King and his absolute rule, that cruelly and treacherously rescinded the pardons he had given to the deluded peasants of 1381. This victimization of the "true commons", who, in spite of their bitter revolt against famine and bureaucracy, responded to the personal courage and leadership of their young King, was the first step that led to the great tragedy of 1399.

Richard was born at Bordeaux on 6 January 1367, and was in his eleventh year when the death of his grandfather brought him the crown. The details of his descent are revealing in connexion with the extent to which he brought together the qualities of the House of England. His father, Edward the Black Prince, was great-grandson of Edward I, of Philip the Fair of France, and of Charles of Valois, Philip's brother. But Richard's mother had Edward I for grandfather, her father, Edmund of Woodstock, being the child of the great King's old age, by his second Queen, the lovely and charitable Margaret of France, half-sister of Philip the Fair. Through the Black Prince's maternal grandmother, only five generations separated Richard II from Elizabeth, princess of the nomad Cumanians and bride of Stephen V, King of Hungary; while he was more distantly descended from Emperors of Byzantium, Viking Kings of Dublin, and the Cid Campeador himself. Three-sixteenths of Richard's blood was that of Edward I, and in other directions he and Edward I shared many common ancestors. Through his mother's grandfather, John Wake of Liddell, he received a strong Welsh strain from the ancient Celtic princes through Llewelyn the Great, who had married King John's daughter, Joan.

To the influence of heredity was added that of environment: the Black Prince chose as his son's tutor an old friend and companion in arms, Sir Simon Burley. It is now impossible to discover details of Burley's teaching, but he was certainly a strong royalist and a well-informed one; he gave Richard a thorough grounding in the historical principles underlying the regality, to such purpose that his young charge was later to send to the Pope a book of the miracles of Edward II, with a request for Edward's canonization. Richard perfectly understood the dangerous precedent, and his whole reign shows him endeavouring to create and develop counter-precedents in favour of the Crown. Burley encouraged the young King to read, for we know that in 1384 he possessed a dozen books of French Romances, including one of King Arthur, one of Percival and Gawyn, and the Romance of the Rose, as well as a book of lays. Richard himself composed lays, ballads, songs, and rondels, " well and fairly " and sang in the services of his chapel; we know of his personal encouragement of Chaucer and of Gower, whose great English poem was begun at Richard's suggestion when King and poet met on the water of Thames. Froissart also was richly rewarded by the King for his gift of one of the chronicler's books, treating of matters of love, beautifully illuminated and bound.

Richard attended performances of plays and loved exquisite costumes and furnishings.* He was referred to after his death in the famous cookery book, *The Forme of Cury*, as " the best and ryallest vyander of alle cristen Kynges "; a tribute to his taste and palate which bears out the universal character of his culture. The architecture, painting, and illumination carried out for him and for members of his Court are of magnificence coupled with restraint; the work done for Richard II was no mere repetition of the lush art of Edward II; it was instinct with a vividness and unity of aim which stamp the masterpieces of the end of the fourteenth century as the high water-mark of English achievement. It is generally admitted that in technical perfection the fourteenth century showed a great advance upon the thirteenth, but it is common to speak of the spiritual values of the thirteenth century as though later work had been conceived upon a lower, more material and commercial plan. The earlier period of Gothic art had the springtime promise of an uncertain future. These are great virtues; but viewed without preconceptions, the unity and grandeur of such works as the new Westminster Hall, the new

* In 1380 he made a present of 10 marks to John Katerine, a Venetian dancing-master; in the previous winter John of Gaunt had had a special floor laid in the Priory Hall at Kenilworth for dancing at Christmas.

nave of Westminster Abbey, and the nave of Canterbury
Cathedral, more than counterbalance any loss of the quality
of surprise. A good deal of the prejudice in favour of early
Gothic has been due to failure to distinguish between the
culminating work of the best period, which died with
Richard II, and the inferior output of the fifteenth century.

In sculpture, the Madonnas of Winchester College, belonging to the last decade of the century, will stand comparison with any English work of earlier or later periods, and
with the best work of France. Even if such carving was
produced as shopwork it is clear that it could not have
been mass-produced, but was the outcome of technical mastery
wedded to personal genius on the part of William Wynford
or some unknown master. Similarly we know that the great
London painters, men such as Gilbert Prince, had their
shops and their many assistants, but few paintings of any
period are of higher quality than that on the tester of the
Black Prince's tomb at Canterbury, and than the Wilton
Diptych, probably none. John Siferwas, the outstanding
miniaturist of the time, is in the highest rank both as a
portraitist and as an observer of nature: his named figures
of English birds in the margin of the Sherborne Missal
have a fidelity and spirit seldom found in this field, except in
China and Japan.

All or almost all the artists and architects of the front
rank, most of the poets and writers, the musicians, the gold-
smiths, broderers, cooks, and others, were in direct dependence upon the taste of the King and on that of his
uncle, John of Gaunt, and a few prominent members of
the Court circle. It is good taste which calls forth good
art; never the contrary. The introduction of artistic masterpieces into another country, for example, will have no
effect unless there is already there a body of real appreciation. The correspondence between periods of great art and
eras of great patrons, especially great kings, is far too close
to admit of any doubt upon this crucial point. Art for
art's sake is a superficially attractive theory, but in reality

the artist has to live by selling his wares, and their nature
will be decided in the main by the nature of demand. In
the history of English art the highest inspiration and the
highest technique only coincide for some two generations,
from about 1330 to 1400, and as we should expect, it is
precisely at that period that the throne was occupied in succession by our two most splendid and most distinguished
kings, Edward III and Richard II.

Richard's personal share in this cultural outburst is em-
phasized by his modern biographer, Mr. Anthony Steel,
who writes: " If for no other reason he should go down
to history as the inventor of the handkerchief, the *chef
d'œuvre* of a dilettante of genius." That Richard was personally responsible for the invention cannot be proved, yet
the clerk who recorded his personal expenses thought it
worth while to specify that the cloths supplied were " little
pieces made for giving to the lord King for carrying in his
hand to wipe and cleanse his nose." The evidence that
Richard was an individual of the highest sensibility is abundant and undoubted, but it is wrong to think of him as
a dilettante, for he was both a thoughtful statesman and
a man of action of great physical and moral courage. All
the hostile attempts to explain away his interview with the
rebels in 1381 have ended in failure; the plain fact remains
that the King, a boy of fourteen, saved the situation single-
handed by force of character and faith in his divine mission,
when his elder relatives were panic-stricken and incapable
even of intelligent co-operation.

Very shortly after the revolt came a second occurrence of
vital interest: the King's marriage to Anne of Bohemia,
daughter of the Emperor Charles IV, in January 1382.
The new Queen, a girl of Richard's own age, brought with
her a retinue of Bohemians but no dowry, and these facts
contributed to the campaign carried on by the great nobles
and their toadies against the King and his intimates. At
this time Bohemia was the leading country of central Europe
and in close touch with artistic circles around the Court of
France. But in Bohemia there was also strong Byzantine

influence, and certain unwestern motives in English illumination of this period have been alleged as marks of the Bohemian contact. However this may be, there can be no doubt of the link between the heresies of Wycliffe in England and of those of the Bohemian "reformer", Huss. In spite of this trend the English King remained strictly orthodox in his own behaviour, but his natural tolerance no doubt was strengthened by contact with the views of his Queen's household. It must be remembered that the policy of Wycliffe was one not merely of reform, but of revolution; had his way been followed, even less of English civilization might have been spared than actually survived the ravages of Thomas and Oliver Cromwell.

Personally, Richard became deeply and passionately attached to Anne, and she in return worshipped him. When the caucus of Appellants had secured the condemnation of the King's friends in 1388, the Queen knelt at the feet of their leader, the King's uncle, Thomas of Woodstock, duke of Gloucester, to beg for Sir Simon Burley's life—in vain; and when Anne herself died at Shene six years later, Richard's grief was so great that he ordered the destruction of a wing of the palace, and never visited it again. The behaviour of Gloucester and the rest of the Appellants was cruel to the point of being sub-human. It is hardly surprising that after Anne's death the King's thoughts turned more and more to revenge, for with his wife gone and his early companion, Robert de Vere, Earl of Oxford, dead in exile, everything conspired to remind him of the happiness of which he had been robbed by this group of selfish men.

The problem of the King's policy and outlook after the death of his Queen is difficult and involved. Richard set himself to undo all that had been done by the Appellants and to make sure that they were deprived of all power for future evil. But it is going too far to suppose that he deliberately undertook to have them judicially or secretly murdered. The one execution, that of Richard, earl of Arundel, was merited not only by the part which Arundel had played in the actions of the Appellants, but by his calculated provocation of the King at Anne's funeral in 1394 and by later conspiracy. Whatever may be the facts of the duke of Gloucester's death at Calais, he deserves no sympathy, for he had throughout been the villain of the piece, acting with cruelty and malice, steadily plotting the downfall of the King and the King's policy. And yet, though it is too much to say that Richard in the last years of his reign was an unbalanced neurotic, it is likely that the bitterness of his personal losses, added to the senseless opposition of which he was the victim, did cloud the King's judgment.

Against the theory of neurosis is the genuine statesmanship of the King's expedition to Ireland in 1394-5, his carefully managed policy of resisting the encroachments of the vested interests, and his steady pursuance of great artistic projects such as the rebuilding of Westminster Hall. The expedition to Ireland was, in fact, one of the greatest acts of intellectual politics ever carried out by an English ruler. Had Richard's second visit in 1399 not been cut short, together with his policy and his life, by Henry Bolingbroke's revolution, the sister island might well have been saved centuries of misery. From the time of John's stupid insult to the Irish princes up to the present day, Richard's was the only English initiative of truly benevolent conciliation. Its importance in the history of international relations can hardly be overestimated and equals the significance of its author's proposals for lasting peace with France. Richard's easy trust in the professions of the Irish leaders on his first expedition has been criticized, but at least proved the real sincerity with which he approached a problem already over two hundred years old and which, after another five centuries, has not been happily settled yet.

Richard realized, as neither his forerunners nor his successors did, that the two problems to be faced in Ireland were those of the Anglo-Irish who opposed English rule; and of the absentee landowners, who spent their time in England. With the latter he dealt summarily by ordering them all back to their Irish estates; his views on the former are expressed in one of his extant letters, sent from Dublin to his uncle, the duke of York, his regent in England, in the early spring of 1395. "Because that in our land of Ireland there are three kinds of people, the Wild Irish, our enemies, the Irish Rebels, and the obedient English, it appeareth to us and our council that, considering that the Irish rebels are, perhaps, so rebellious by reason of the grievances and wrongs done unto them on the one part, and that redress hath not been made to them on the other part; and that likewise if they be not wisely managed, and put into good hope of favour, they will probably join our enemies; wherefore, it shall not be any fault of ours that a general pardon be granted them. . . ." The enemy "Wild Irish" he treated kindly, and might have won over had he been permitted to continue his generous policy.

Probably the greatest single factor leading to Richard's downfall was his constitutional loneliness, added to the natural isolation of his position. As a boy he had the elder companionship of Burley, and until her death in 1385, the affection of his beautiful and popular mother. Then, in the period of his first attempt at personal rule, he came under the influence of his elder contemporary, Robert de Vere. There is no evidence that De Vere was morally vicious; he was of good birth and undoubted culture, but beyond this there is little to be said. He shared the King's artistic tastes, and his extreme unpopularity with the opposition may have been due in part to his possession, like Gaveston, of the gift of stinging repartee and an intellectual brilliance naturally obnoxious to the men of saddle and spur over against him. His flight and death abroad had taken place before the final disaster—the Queen's death—in the summer of 1394. As happened with his grandfather and with Edward I, Richard's temperament deteriorated after the death of a dearly loved wife. Always subject to outbursts of violent rage, he was now deprived of the one consoling factor which moderated both his personal misery and its ill effects. Left with no intimate friends, he placed most reliance on Sir Baldwin Raddington, Burley's nephew and holder of the important confidential position of controller of the wardrobe until the end of 1397.

The King's second marriage, to Isabella of Valois, was the keystone of the new policy of peace. But Richard became fond of his child-bride, only twelve at the time of his death, and made generous provision regarding her dowry in his will. This will, principally concerned with his own funeral arrangements and with the continuance of the new work of Westminster Abbey, was never fulfilled. It was drawn up on 16 April 1399, and seems evidence of a premonition of disaster. Gaunt's death on 3 February and Richard's subsequent confiscation of the vast Lancastrian estates and prolongation of Gaunt's son Henry's exile from ten years to life, had just taken place, and the last phase was at hand. Whether he foresaw the end or merely wished to settle his affairs before undertaking a fresh expedition to Ireland, the will's insistence on the pomp and ceremony of death and the exact fulfilment of posthumous wishes, reads after the event with a sinister irony. Whatever the circumstances, the phrasing of some clauses makes it certain that Richard was taking every step he could to ensure that his successor should be bound to follow out his own line of regal policy.

In taking the opportunity of uniting the inheritance of Lancaster to the Crown of England, Richard acted with wisdom as well as justice; it is now, to all, as it was then to the King, obvious that a great state within the state was an impossible anachronism, and Richard was only continuing the policy of Henry II and of Edward I; besides, the behaviour of Henry in 1388 and again ten years later had shown his disloyalty; the only puzzle is that recognizing Henry as a traitor, Richard still took no precautions against what was about to happen—the armed invasion of England by Henry and the exiled plotter, Thomas Arundel, brother of Earl Richard, and late Archbishop of Canterbury. Faith in his own divine right seems to be the only satisfactory explanation, for Richard's bodyguard of Cheshire men, wearing his livery of the White Hart, stands as proof that he was not oblivious to danger. His trust was misplaced, and his voyage to Ireland (rendered necessary by the murder in ambush of his deputy, the earl of March) was promptly followed by Henry's to Ravenspur.

Throughout the reign we are astonished by the cruelty, ill-faith, and irrational treachery of the great men and of the King's own close relatives. The consistent plotting of Gloucester, the double-dealing of Norfolk, the abominable treachery of Henry Bolingbroke himself; all are in such sorry contrast to cultural and artistic glories, and the long forbearance of the King. The sorriest spectacle of all is that of the King's betrayal by his former Archbishop of Canterbury. Like his predecessors, Becket and Hubert Walter, and like Bishop Orleton, he counted treason as nothing. With the earl of Northumberland, whose complicity in the plot is not certain, he persuaded Richard to leave the security of Conway Castle, only to fall into an ambush and be carried a captive to Flint, whence in due course he was removed with indignity to London, to deposition, Leeds, Pontefract, and death. Henry's responsibility for all this is undoubted, but the part played by Arundel, ostensibly a man of God, is the more revolting and inexcusable.

The failure of Richard's epic attempt to restore the full force of royal government in England spelt not merely the fall of absolutism, but the continuance in the saddle of the vested interests, of the war party, and of the heresy-hunting clerics; it meant in the long run the extinction of the power of the Crown to succour the humble oppressed. We have seen this power exercised by Edward I in the famous instance of the Forest Charter; Edward III remitting taxation upon the poor and the plague-ridden; Richard II refusing to agree to the " Commons " Bill of 1391 to prohibit villein education.* The distant future was to hold

---

* Richard's Statute of Mortmain of 1391 ordered that a proportion of the fruits of a benefice appropriated to a monastery should be distributed to the poor of the parish. The Appellants, on the contrary, had in 1388 passed a draconic act against begging and vagrancy.

the vain attempts of Charles I to restrain the business men
of his day; of Charles II to prevent the formation of the
tyranny of the Whig grandees; and of George III to form
a patriotic administration independent of political jobbery
and financial manipulation. That these attempts were vain
was due in large measure to Richard II's prior failure;
the selfish opportunism of Henry Bolingbroke opened the
flood-gates to a rising tide that was to overwhelm piecemeal
the defences that were left, and in time to bring, not one
nation alone, but the whole world to a state so pitiable
that only the reinstatement of kingly power could lead to its
recovery.

So the tragedy is not of Richard II only; not of one lonely
individual, but of millions upon millions of human beings,
spread over 500 years of time and the whole surface of
the globe. The grand significance of this lone figure, cham-
pion of order against chaos, has not passed unnoticed:
Queen Elizabeth I in a dangerous hour was shown an old
portrait of Richard, and flared out: "I am Richard the
Second; know ye not that?"—recognizing the meaning of
his last ditch stand and martyrdom. But as has been said
in a less serious connexion, nothing succeeds like a failure;
and the tragedy of Richard will outlive many generations.
Within twenty years his murdered body came to rest
beside that of his dear Queen Anne, and though time has
stolen the linked hands of their recumbent figures, they have
lain through wars and revolutions and continue to lie
" among the royals " at Westminster, augury of the resur-
rection of a happier day to come.

PART THREE: AUTUMN

CHAPTER IX

HENRY IV

The usurpation of Henry IV did not go unmarked by signs of divine displeasure: the year 1400 saw the rebellion of King Richard's friends, followed by his murder at Pontefract; an outbreak of plague, which had been quiescent since 1369, and the revolt of Owain Glyndwr. Not daunted, Henry and his Parliament in the next year passed the Statute "De Heretico Comburendo" which Richard had avoided introducing. To political misgovernment was to be added religious persecution in its most cold-blooded form. Fitly enough the greatest men of the stricken era—Chaucer, Langland, the architect Henry Yevele, the painter Gilbert Prince—did not survive into this gloomier age. The last years of the old century saw a great reaping.

This new century, opening with usurpation and rebellion, death and pestilence, was to be the saddest, as it was the last, of the Middle Ages. An atmosphere of lassitude immediately settles over the scene; the grand architecture which had been rising in the last ten years now withered as if struck down by a premature frost. The completion of Westminster Hall was perfunctory; that of the nave of Westminster Abbey indefinitely postponed; that of the extensive new works at Canterbury Cathedral long drawn-out and uninspired in comparison with the works of genius that had gone before. The literary pupils of Chaucer: Hoccleve and Lydgate, much as they revered their master, lacked his spirited genius, his deep irony, his light-handed sense of humour. The new school relied upon sonorous verbosity and upon sheer length and weight; a substitution of quan-

King	Year	Principal Events	Year	Art and Literature
HENRY IV	1399	Rebellion of Barons and Owen Glendower	1400	Geoffrey Chaucer and Henry Yevele, mason, died
	1400			York Minster: East window
	1401	Statute De Heretico Comburendo	1405	John Thornton's glass at York Minster
	1403	Revolt of the Percies	1407	York Minster: Central Tower rebuilt after collapse
	1405	Northumberland Conspiracy		
HENRY V	1409	Treaty with Teutonic Order	1408	John Gower, poet, died
	1413		1411	Thomas Hoccleve's De Regimine Principum
	1414	Lollard Rising: Council of Constance		London: Guildhall begun
	1415	Agincourt Campaign	1415	Thomas à Kempis's "Imitation of Christ"
	1417	Norman Campaign		
	1420	Treaty of Troyes: Henry V enters Paris		
	1422			
HENRY VI	1424	Bedford's victory at Verneuil	1421	Catterick Bridge built
	1428	Siege of Orléans	1423	Canterbury Cathedral: South-West Tower begun
	1430	Disenfranchisement of Small Freeholders	c. 1430	Sherborne Abbey: Choir begun
	1431	Henry VI crowned at Paris: Council of Basle	1432	York Minster: South-West Tower begun
	1435	Death of Duke of Bedford	1433	Tattershall Castle begun
	1436	Loss of Paris	1437	Thomas Damett, composer, died
			1438	Oxford: All Souls College begun
			1441	Eton College begun
	1447	Deaths of Gloucester and Beaufort	1443	Warwick: Beauchamp Chapel begun; Cambridge: King's College Chapel begun
	1448	War: France, Scotland	1448	Eton College Chapel; Cambridge: Queens' College begun
	1450	Jack Cade's Rising: York appointed Protector	1449	York: Guildhall begun
			1450	Gloucester Abbey: Tower
			c. 1450	Thomas Hoccleve, poet, died
			1452	Leonardo da Vinci born
	1453	Turks take Constantinople: Loss of Guienne	c. 1452	John Lydgate, poet, died
	1455	Wars of Roses begun	1453	John Dunstable, composer, died
			1455	Bishop Reginald Pecock's "Repressor"

King	Year	Principal Events	Year	Art and Literature
EDWARD IV	1461	War: France; Turks take Trebizond	1463	Norwich Cathedral: Nave vault
(HENRY VI)	1470	Warwick restores Henry VI	1470	Sir Thomas Malory's "Morte D'Arthur" written
EDWARD IV restored	1471	War: Hanseatic League	1472	Norwich Cathedral: Presbytery vault
			1474	Oxford: Magdalen College begun; Windsor Castle: St. George's Chapel begun
			1475	Eltham Palace Hall
	1475	Treaty of Picquigny		
	1476	Caxton printing at Westminster		
	1480	Bristol ship sails for "Brasile"; Turks take Otranto, besiege Rhodes	1480	Oxford: Divinity School vaulted
				Leonardo da Vinci invents parachute
			1481	Rome: Sistine Chapel frescoes by Botticelli and others
				Venice: Colleoni Statue by Verrochio
EDWARD V	1483	Hastings and Rivers executed; Buckingham's conspiracy	1484	London: College of Arms incorporated
RICHARD III				
HENRY VII	1485	Battle of Bosworth	1485	Malory's "Morte D'Arthur" published
	1486	Marriage of Henry and Elizabeth of York	1486	Thomas Ashwell and Gilbert Banister compose music for Royal Marriage
	1487	Simnel's rebellion; Diaz reaches the Cape		
			1488	Ely: Bishop Alcock's Chapel; Oxford: Duke Humphrey's Library opened; Taunton: St. Mary's Tower begun
			1490	Oxford: Magdalen College Bell Tower begun
			1491	William Caxton, printer, died
	1491	War: France		
	1492	Discovery of America; Spanish conquer Granada		
	1493	Flemings banished from England	1493	Canterbury Cathedral: Bell Harry Tower
	1494	France invades Italy	1495	Leonardo da Vinci begins "The Last Supper"
	1496	War: France and Scotland	1496	Colet begins to lecture at Oxford; Peterborough Abbey: New Building begun
	1497	Warbeck's and Cornish revolts; Discovery of Newfoundland; Vasco da Gama rounds the Cape		
	1499	Earl of Warwick and Warbeck executed	1498	Windsor Castle: Henry VII's Tower

tity for quality in poetry, the art least able to afford such a debasement of the coinage.

Though a good deal of this artistic decline was due to the political revolution it cannot be set down as the crime of Henry personally. He increased Chaucer's pension, and towards the rank and file of the administration and civil service acted with conspicuous fairness. Except for the leading friends of the late King, who were put to death or severely handled, as, for example, Richard's outspoken defender, Thomas Merke, sometime monk of Westminster and Bishop of Carlisle, imprisoned and later translated *in partibus infidelium,* the aftermath of the crisis passed off in an atmosphere of clemency. Henry himself had been brought up in the art-loving circle of his father, Gaunt, and was no unlettered knight, but a man of culture, though not in that higher flight that Richard had adorned. Born on 3 April 1367, only two months later than Richard, Henry had the dubious advantage of being the first King since the Conquest to be born and bred in England of an English father and an English mother. On the day of his birth at Bolingbroke, Lincolnshire, his father in far-off Spain was winning the great victory of Najera over the usurper Henry of Trastamare, a victory crowned by the capture of the French leader, Bertrand du Guesclin.

The stars which presided over the fortunes of the House of Lancaster on that day saw to it that throughout his life Henry's material success and spiritual defeat should go hand in hand. He was indeed intensely ambitious, and his great inheritance and the royal state in which he was brought up (though John of Gaunt's title as King of Castile came only with his second wife, Constance, after the death of Henry's mother, Blanche) were calculated to instil into him dangerously exalted ideas. From the portraits and his effigy at Canterbury we can see that he was not good looking like his cousin Richard; Richard was tall and slender, with magnificent auburn hair like his mother's, piercing blue eyes, and an unusually refined and arresting face. Henry, on the other hand, was short and reddish haired, but instead of good looks he had that stocky strength which was so valuable to the mounted knight of the time and which Richard lacked. This diversity of physique and temperament led to a mutual jealousy.

It would be unnatural for Richard, with his comparatively frail physique and dependence on spiritual courage, not to have during youth some envy of this cousin whose career was one perpetual victory at field sports and the martial arts in which his own father had so excelled. On Henry's side there was the feeling that Richard, to him a strange incomprehensible nervous being, was undeservedly enjoying everything for which he himself was built. In an earlier age Henry could have carved out a kingdom for himself, as the Norman princes had done in Sicily and Constantinople; but there were no such chances in the fourteenth century. Had he but been the son of his father's second wife he might have had the throne of Castile, of which John of Gaunt had for long been King in name and state. At the time of Richard's "first tyranny", when the King and he were just turned twenty, he ruined Richard's hopes by his defeat of De Vere at Radcot Bridge in December 1387. This would have been hard for Richard to forgive, though when it was too late Henry did something to make amends by standing up for Sir Simon Burley. But as soon as the King seized real power in 1389, Henry found it advisable to leave the country.

His first journey was a kind of crusade with the Teutonic knights against their old enemies the Lithuanians, in spite of the fact that Jagiello, Grand-duke of Lithuania, had been converted from paganism to Christianity five years before. Henry, earl of Derby as he was then, reached Danzig on 10 August 1390; in September he took part in the siege of Vilna, went into winter quarters at Königsberg, and in the spring returned to England by way of Braunsberg, Elbing, Marienburg, Dirschau, and Danzig. After a year in England he left for Palestine, but travelled overland by way of Prague, Vienna, and Venice. It may be that he hoped to obtain Lithuania for himself but if so nothing came of it.

He spent Christmas of 1392 at Zara in the Adriatic, then sailed by way of Rhodes to Jaffa, and rode up to Jerusalem as a pilgrim. In February 1393 he returned by Cyprus and Venice, and in July was again in England.

After the famous quarrel with the duke of Norfolk, the abortive trial by combat, and his banishment by Richard, Henry lived at Paris, until occasion offered for his fatal temptation, the invasion of England in 1399. His claim to the Crown was made on 30 September; he was crowned on 13 October, and by the middle of February had the guilt of the true King's death upon his soul. The guilt weighed him down for the remaining thirteen years of his life, and the throne proved little more than a sorry responsibility. Success could not be won, even by the wide extent of his diplomatic negotiations; for he maintained correspondence with his contemporaries all over Europe and even farther afield: the Emperors of Constantinople and Abyssinia, the King of Cyprus, and the dreaded Timur, who was greeted by Henry as an ally against the Ottoman Turks. Timur's victory over Sultan Bayazid gave Christian Europe a much-needed breathing space, and Henry, with the other western monarchs, hoped to renew the prosperous interchanges with the Mongol realms which had formed such a feature of the preceding century, under Kublai Khan and his successors and their Persian viceroys. The visit of the Byzantine Emperor Manuel II to England in 1400 was the last flicker of the crusading spirit which preceded the final downfall of Christianity in the Near East.

There was hardly any direction in which progress was made during Henry's reign; the state of uncertainty, renewed piracy around the coasts, invasions by the Welsh, the Scots, and the French, combined to depress the country to a level of mediocrity horrifying after its recent brilliance. Henry was not recognized by Charles VI of France, who referred to him, in speaking to the English ambassadors, as " the lord who sent you ". Henry's other foreign contacts did not achieve anything permanent, and the stream of England's trade dried up, until by the middle of the century it flowed only through Calais. So soon as 1402 "much people desyred to have Richard Kynge again", and Henry's waning popularity was further depressed by his second marriage in that year to Joan, widow of John, duke of Brittany, and widely reputed to be a witch. Next year the revolt of the Percys and Henry's victory at Shrewsbury led to a temporary respite, but a new conspiracy in 1405 caused Henry to have Richard Scrope, Archbishop of York, beheaded. This sacrilege was visited upon him, as contemporaries said, with a leprosy, from which he never recovered. From the time of Scrope's death the King was seldom well, and in the end became almost bedridden. His former energy was gone, his plans for a new crusade postponed indefinitely.

Henry himself felt that vengeance was upon him, for in his serious illness in the winter of 1408-9 he made his will, which breathes the spirit of guilt and fear. But in spite of the reiterated phrases of abasement: "I Henry, sinful wretch . . . my sinful soul . . . whiche (my) lyffe I have mispendyd . . . y ask (my lordis and trew peple) forgivenes if I have missentreted hem in any wyse . . .", it never seems to have occurred to him to make restitution to Richard's true heirs. Henry's only important action in connexion with art was the sending in 1407 of Master William Colchester, chief mason of Westminster Abbey, to York Minster, to take charge of the building of the central tower, which had just collapsed. Even this initiative was not altogether fortunate, for Colchester and his assistant were grievously wounded by the York masons, whose indignation at this outside interference must have been aggravated by the recent martyrdom of their Archbishop. The minor arts of London were quite expensively patronized by Henry, but there was a marked falling off in all departments of the royal works establishment.

Of all the Kings of his House, Henry IV had the least to recommend him; he possessed the family energy, the family courage, the love of adventure, but fell short in true vitality and fire. He had not even the excuse of a constitutional scepticism, like John's; he was, on the contrary,

slavishly orthodox, to the point of abetting virulent persecution. In spite of the romantic interest of his travels
he himself remains more a lay figure than any of his race.
His father and his sons are real personages; his mother,
described for us by Froissart, "gay and glad she was,
fresh and sportive; sweet, simple and of humble semblance,
the fair lady whom men called Blanche"; his sister, the
shadowy English princess who went to Portugal, lives as
the mother of that extraordinary family which included
Henry the Navigator and the heroic Ferdinand, the Constant
Prince. The only picturesque tradition of Henry's career
is that which concerns his death; it had been foretold
that he would die in Jerusalem; he comforted himself that
until he undertook his long-promised crusade his life was
safe. Visiting the shrine of St. Edward in Westminster
Abbey in the spring of 1413, he was attacked by a sudden
seizure, and carried to the Abbot's chamber, where he even-
tually regained consciousness. Learning that the room was
called "Jerusalem" he realized that his end had come.
It is difficult to find pity for so unsympathetic a figure, but
remembering Henry's early vigour and talent for success,
one cannot but wish they had been expended in a better
cause.

CHAPTER X

HENRY V

At a first glimpse the character of Henry V seems to transport us from the gloom and mediocrity of the early fifteenth century to the eager faith and chivalric vitality of the twelfth or thirteenth. It is only when we make a deeper study of the keen hatchet face, and ponder upon the strange inconsistencies of this complex character that we see Henry as a true child of his age, partaking in a full measure of the grotesque qualities that cast a wan and flickering light upon the scene. For though Henry only reigned for nine years he sets the key for the whole period through which he might have lived. Let us imagine that this prince, born at Monmouth on 9 August 1387, had lived out the scriptural span of seventy years, dying in 1457. What did those years contain? The year of his birth was to close with his own father's guerrilla victory over the royalist forces of Robert de Vere, earl of Oxford; this petty skirmish at Radcot Bridge on the Upper Thames was the cast of the die, the opening move of a tragic game, a game which would sweep all the pieces off the board before it was played out.

Radcot Bridge made possible the criminal career of the Lords Appellant; their murder of the King's friends and of old Simon Burley; Queen Anne's vain pleading for Burley's life; Richard II's bitter humiliation and decision to be avenged upon the men who had so humbled him; his overhasty shutting of the Lancastrian jack-in-the-box, so that the rebound knocked him off his throne. On another part of the stage the Church was waiting its turn to rob, to torture, and to massacre all dissidents. Restraints of morality and honour once shaken off by the leaders of Church and state, a large following was soon assured. All was fair in love and war; men's and women's minds began to turn to witchcraft and sorcery, any means by which they might work

their will. Twelve years from Radcot Bridge saw a throne
usurped, a King murdered; fifteen, Englishmen burning at
the stake; twenty-three, the young Prince Henry of Monmouth attending the flames, giving a half-roasted wretch
the offer of a pension for recanting, and on the bribe's
refusal, cold-bloodedly supervising his return to the fire.
The victim, a blacksmith, was guilty of saying and maintaining
that the Sacrament received in Church was not the Body of
Christ, but inanimate matter.

The lapse of twenty-eight years saw France once more
ravaged, her knighthood overthrown, her countryside raped
and plundered; thirty-one years after Radcot Bridge the
city of Rouen was being besieged, and drove out from its
gates 12,000 *bouches inutiles*, women, old men, and children
who devoured rations but could not fight—between the city
walls and the English lines, in the appalling weather of a
Norman midwinter, they perished, for Henry refused to
let them pass through to such safety as they might find.
This was the man whom his very opponents called "the
most virtuous and wise of all the Christian princes who
reigned in his time." Here indeed was the spirit of the
age with a vengeance. By the standards of the time Henry
actually was magnanimous, comparatively mild in his methods
of warfare, generous to the poor, accessible, a good man of
business. Lord Mersey has described him as "a general,
a statesman, . . . the restorer of the English navy; . . . a fine
type of the mediæval hero, a leader worthy of England and
without doubt her most popular King." It is permissible
to wonder just how well Henry V does compare with other
English heroes of the whole mediæval period: Alfred certainly, and William the Conqueror probably, never caused by
their personal act the death of 12,000 non-combatants.
Richard Cœur-de-Lion bears the reproach of having, under
considerable provocation, been a party to the death of some
2,000 Saracen prisoners-of-war, taken in arms; Edward III
wished to hang six burgesses in cold-blooded revenge, but
his Queen stayed his hand.

I must repeat, it was the spirit of the age that had so

declined. From the murders committed by the Appellants onwards, mercy was a word unknown, except to the gentle and pious Henry VI. State trials and executions, mass murder of the defeated leaders after the battles of the civil war, scenes of bloodshed and inhumanity by the score, were to be witnessed by those seventy years beginning in 1387. We have seen Henry's attitude to a heretic and to a body of 12,000 non-combatants whom he claimed as his own subjects; let us consider his response to the appeal for mercy of Richard, earl of Cambridge, his first cousin once removed, involved, though not as a prime mover, in a conspiracy against Henry early in 1415. After condemnation Cambridge wrote: " Myn most dredfull and sovereyne lege Lord, i Richard York yowre humble subgyt and very lege man, beseke yow of Grace of al maner offenses wych y have done or assentyd to in heny kinde, by steryng of odyr folke eggyng me ther to, where yn y wote wel i have hyll offendyd to yowre Hynesse; besechyng yow at the reverence of God that yow lyke to take me in to the handys of yowre mercyfulle and pytouse grace, thenkyng yee wel of yowre gret goodnesse. My lege Lord, my fulle trust is that yee wylle have consyderacyoun, thauth that myn persone be of none valwe, yowre hye goodnesse wher God hath sette yow in so hye estat to every lege man that to yow longyth plenteousely to geve grace, that yow lyke to accept chys myn symple reqwest for the love of oure Lady and of the blysfulle Holy Gost, to whom I pray that they mot yowre hert enduce to al pyte and grace for theyre hye goodnesse." Neither Cambridge's trust nor love of Our Lady and the Holy Ghost melted the King's heart of stone, true ancestor of Tudor ruthlessness.

Through all the apparent injustice of history we sometimes seem to catch a glimpse of God's mills grinding slowly, and to what a terribly fine grist did they reduce the proud House of England for its fratricidal bitterness and hardness of heart. Before the seventy years were up, all English France was lost, save Calais, and the poor King had become a scarecrow figure being torn to pieces between rival relatives.

The trial and burning of Joan of Arc, the imprisonment for witchcraft of a queen and a royal duchess, were minor incidents in these generations of wretchedness and the fear of death. Not in England only, but all over Europe men's minds were turning to the pain-racked figure on the Crucifix and to the grisly reiterated figure of Death Himself leading the dance of Macabree. Yet outside England there was already some sign of returning daylight; the arts were not cut short. But in England and in Scotland the poets who were left were punctuating their verses with the terror-struck refrain: *Timor mortis conturbat me.*

I have dwelt upon the miseries of the fifteenth century and the crimes of Henry V because they point the moral that even the best of men and of kings can be corrupted by the spirit of their age. Compared with the nineteenth century exploiters of child labour, or the twentieth-century exponents of total war, Henry V was not a wicked man, but it is evident that he suffered from a serious decline in the standards of his age. The apophthegm that " power corrupts, and absolute power corrupts absolutely " does not cover the facts, for Henry IV and Henry V were ostensibly far more " constitutional " and less absolute than their predecessors. Not power in itself, nor absolutism was to blame for this return of barbarism; but the lust for power, and the greedy maintenance of power unlawfully obtained. Without order, society returns to chaos, and the usurpation of power from its rightful holders was the denial of basic order.

It would be unfair to Henry to look only on the dark and horrifying aspect of his character; he revived many of the cultural virtues of Richard II, and in his personal life a pleasing characteristic is his gratitude. Of this the most striking example is his prompt translation of Richard's body from Langley to Westminster, in accordance with Richard's will. Henry as a boy had been a hostage in Richard's power in 1399, and accompanied the King to Ireland, but Richard's generosity did not permit him to use the weapon placed in his hand, and Henry clearly felt some compunction about the part played by his family. Though he did not bring himself to the renunciation of the throne it is possible to see a conscious attempt at continuity with the policy of his father's victim. Unfortunately, though he did something to revive the arts in general and a great deal for music, his renewal of the French war was disastrous. Even here he went to considerable lengths to avert hostilities, and made to the Dauphin the same offer of personal combat that Richard Cœur-de-Lion had made to Philip Augustus, and Edward III to Philip VI. In July 1414 he had written to King Charles VI " our Cousin and Adversary ", reminding him of former peace between England and France, and requesting him to avoid a deluge of blood by restoring Henry's minimum demands, with the Princess Katherine, for whose hand negotiations had already been proceeding. On 16 September 1415, shortly before Agincourt, he wrote to the Dauphin: " considering it hath pleased God to visit with infirmity our cousin your father . . . we offer you to decide this our quarrel, with God's grace, by combat between our person and yours." He further offered that Charles VI should retain the throne of France for life " from reverence to God, and because he is a sacred personage." It is remarkable, even admitting the force of chivalric traditions, that three Kings of England, in the twelfth, the fourteenth, and the fifteenth centuries should have made the same offer, and that in each case the rulers of France should have been too crafty or too pusillanimous to accept.

Looking at Henry's portraits, one can see in the prominent nose, lantern jaw, and compressed lips, the lineaments of the determined fanatic. Henry was dominated by a piety as earnest as that of his son, but it was a piety closely linked to the advancement of Lancaster; what might have been commendable firmness in a better cause was degraded by his father's usurpation and his own failure to do justice to the real heirs of the Crown. The execution of his cousin, Cambridge, for promoting the true heir's interests, was the crime of a man with a guilty conscience. But apart from this besetting sin, his obstinate continuance of a bad cause, he had much to recommend him. His face is not alone fanatical; it has also intellectual power and artistic appreciation. When he was a boy of ten he already had a harp and a number of books, and his learning and love of music kept pace with his athletic and military career. He could run as fast as a deer, and was a brave soldier as well as a brilliant general. His piety and his love of music were seen together when he ordered his household clerks to sing a hymn of praise to God on the field of Agincourt. Whether a first draft of the famous hymn can have been composed on the spur of the moment or no, the existing music undoubtedly belongs to the royal school of composition, and the fact that it has come down in several versions shows how popular it was.

The picture of Harry of Monmouth's riotous youth, so familiar from Shakespeare, cannot have much foundation, for while still youthful he had command of troops on the Welsh Marches and was already showing himself a responsible and careful strategist. But there is a pleasant tradition that he was a foppish scholar at Queen's College, Oxford, going about dressed in " a gown of blue satin full of oilet holes, at every hole the needle hanging by a silk thread." The Falstaff of drama is, of course, a mythological figure, and bears no relation at all to the historical Sir John Fastolf, one of the important generals of the French war. Perhaps there is some foundation for the prince's supposed love of low company, for he did, during his reign, do a great deal for humble individuals, and would note on petitions in his own hand: " See that the poor partye have right." No matter connected with the war was beneath his notice, and he corresponded personally with master masons and ships' carpenters. The following example is a letter from the chief mason at Calais, John Pynkhill, in 1421:

Souveraine Lorde, in as humbly wise as any true liege-man can think or deme, I recommend me unto youre noble grace; having in myne hert continuelly emprinted, amonges youre other high comaundments, yeven to me at youre departyng from Caleys, that speciall

commandment, by the whiche ye charged me, that I
shulde algates write unto youre highnesse, from tyme
to tyme, of all matiers that me semed necessarie or
expedient to signiffie unto youre highnesse. In par-
formyng of the which youre commaundement, like it
youre highnesse to conceive, that the fundament of youre
chappell, withinne youre castell of Caleys, and the
walles over (height above the grounde, in the lowest
place, viij. fete) whereof I send yow the patrone by John
Makyn, servant to Thomas De la Crosse, bringer of
this. . . . And as touching the stone of this cuntre, that
shuld be for the jambes of your doores and windowes
of your seid chapell, I dare not take upon me to sett
no more therof upon your werkes, hit freteth and fareth
so foule with himself, that, had I not ordained lynnessde
oyle to bed hit with, hit wolde not have endured, ne
plesed youre Highnesse. Wherefore I have purveyed
xiij. tons tight of Cane (Caen) stone, for to spede
youre werkes withall. And more I shall purveye, in all
the haste possible, for I cannot see that none other stone
wolle be so proffitable for your seide werkes; and, for
God's love, souveraine lorde, like yow, of youre benign
grace, to have me excused now and at all tymes, of my
rude and uncunnyng writyng to youre highnesse; the wich
anbassheth me ful mochel, to write unto youre high
estate of any matter, savinge youre wille and com-
mandement aforesaid; the which I shall ever obeye and
perfourme, to the uttermoste that is possible unto me,
whiles my lyf endureth. Souveraine lorde, I beseche
Almightie gode kepe yow in continuel prosperitee,
to his plesaunce, and your herts desire, and send yow
victorye of all your enemys for his muche mercye.

Henry promoted more than military architecture; he endowed monasteries at Sheen in Surrey and near Brentford,
and enabled the rebuilding of the nave of Westminster Abbey
to go forward, besides beginning an extensive chantry for
himself. His craftsmen made his father's tomb at Canterbury, a splendid work, almost recapturing the fine finish

and freshness of the late fourteenth century; in addition to the monument there is a tester of carved wood of excellent design and workmanship, and a series of interesting paintings. But it is in connexion with the growing school of English music that Henry's services were of particular importance: three of the most significant composers of the century, a number of whose works survive, Thomas Damet, Nicholas Sturgeon, and John Pyamour, received pensions or grants at his hand, and the more famous John Dunstable, who served Henry's brother, John, duke of Bedford, in after years, probably began his career in connexion with the Chapel Royal. Expert opinion now regards the King Henry whose own musical works appear in the " Old Hall Manuscript " as Henry V, for the evidence of Henry V's keen interest in the members of his chapel and in musical services is extensive. His reign saw the founding of a song school at Durham in 1414 and a reawakening of art in general.

A conscious imitator of the champions of an earlier heroic age, Henry V was an unusual figure; his aims were great (his last words were a wish that he might live to rebuild the walls of Jerusalem), and if his earnest purpose blinded him to the defects of his own cause, his blindness was less than that of most of his contemporaries, and a large proportion of humanity before and since. When he died at Vincennes on 31 August 1422, there perished the last of the paladins.

CHAPTER XI

HENRY VI

If the Character of Henry V showed how a great man could be degraded by the faults of his age, that of his son was an even more eloquent witness to the capacity of exceptional spirits to rise superior to environment. Within two months of his father's death Henry VI's grandfather, Charles VI of France, also died, and at the age of one year he was sovereign of two great kingdoms. He had been born, fittingly enough, at Windsor Castle, on 6 December 1421; at three he was brought to open Parliament and "schriked and cryed and sprang; and he was then led upon his feet to the choir of St. Paul's by the Lord Protector and the duke of Exeter, and afterwards set upon a fair courser and conveyed through Chepe." The King's tutor was Richard Beauchamp, earl of Warwick, to whose fine character and strict up-bringing the young Henry was so deeply indebted. Warwick, who had made pilgrimage to Jerusalem and travelled in most parts of Europe, was given by the Emperor Sigismund the honorific title of "Father of Courtesy", and seldom can such a title have been better deserved.

The child King was made to give, by way of an official enrolment, permission for his own corporal chastisement, and this permission was used by the great earl with so deft an admixture of severity and tact that his charge was soon brought "for awe thereof . . . (to) forbear the more to do amiss and intend the more busily to virtue and learning."* The lessons of courtesy, kindliness, and true religion that Henry learnt from Warwick were never forgotten, and were to enable him to sustain with fortitude many years of trouble and humiliation. A foretaste came when he was

* When Henry was sixteen he was using a wooden stamp of his signature, one of the earliest examples known. It has been suggested that it was made for him as a toy.

thirteen and received a letter from the duke of Burgundy announcing that the alliance with England was broken off; seeing that he was not addressed as King of France, as well as of England, Henry burst into tears. After his gorgeous coronation at Paris three years before, this must have been a rude awakening. A year later his uncle, the duke of Bedford, died, and the collapse of the English rule over northern France speedily followed. Bedford had been a statesman as well as a competent soldier, and for a dozen years fought a losing battle against the national consciousness of resurgent France. The loss of Bedford to the English cause completed the harm begun by Joan of Arc, and from that moment the final expulsion was foredoomed.

Although Bedford was Regent of France he had been able to exercise some check upon the rivalry of the different persons, his brother Humfrey of Gloucester among them, who aspired to control the King. After his death rivalry broke out into open conspiracies, and also took some stranger forms. In 1441 Gloucester's reputation was seriously damaged by revelations concerning the activities of his wife, Eleanor Cobham. She was tried and convicted of treason, as also were several of her abettors, " master Thomas Southwell a canon of St. Stephen's chapel at Westminster, master John Hum a chaplain of the said duchess, and master Roger Bolyngbroke a man expert in necromancy, and a woman called Margery Jourdemayne surnamed the witch of Eye beside Winchester, to whose charge it was laid that (they) should, at the request of the said duchess, devise an image of wax like unto the King, the which image they dealt so with, that by their devilish incantations and sorcery they intended to bring out of life, little and little, the King's person, as they little and little consumed that image." Eleanor was henceforward imprisoned in a succession of fortresses—Chester, Kenilworth, and perhaps also the Isle of Man.

During the early part of the reign, under the patronage of the King's uncles, Bedford and Gloucester, much important artistic work was done. Both the dukes gave special en-

couragement to musicians, Gloucester being the early patron
of Henry Abingdon, for many years to be Master of the
Chapel Royal, while Bedford had in his service the even
greater musician, John Dunstable. Two royal captives—
King James I of Scotland and Charles, duke of Orleans—
were whiling away their time by composing poems in English
much nearer to Chaucer in spirit than the work of their
English contemporaries. A wave of church building was
in progress, and to this was added a new era of collegiate
foundations at the universities. Archbishop Chichele's All
Souls College at Oxford was begun in 1438, and the educational fervour of the period took hold of the impressionable
young King. By the time he was twenty he was planning
a new scheme for a school and a university college, which
rapidly took shape at Eton and at King's College in Cambridge, where the chapel gives a clue to the scale of the
mighty establishment he designed. In France under English
rule new universities had been founded in 1431 at Caen
and Poitiers, and the strength of the new movement in
Europe can also be judged from the founding of the University
of Louvain in 1426, of the Platonic Academy in Florence in
1440, and of the universities of Glasgow, Freiburg, and
Basle, in 1451, 1457, and 1459. In spite of the depression,
the seed sown in the fourteenth century was beginning to
spring up.

Henry's will, which gives minute directions for the building
of both colleges, shows how intensely personal was the
King's interest. The care taken over his education by Warwick had borne fruit; probably no single person has ever
been responsible for so great and successful an educational
establishment as Henry, and behind Henry we sense the
figure of that great gentleman, his boyhood's governor.
Nor did the King's interest end with planning, but extended
to the individuals who were the first pupils. John Blacman,
chaplain and later Carthusian monk, Henry's first biographer,
tells us: "whenever he met any of [the boys who were
brought to be put to school] at times in the castle of
Windsor . . . he would advise them concerning the following

of the path of virtue, and with his words he would also give them money to attract them, saying: 'Be you good boys, gentle and teachable, and servants of the Lord.' And if he discovered that any of them visited his court, he sometimes restrained them with a rebuke, bidding them not to do so again, lest his young lambs should come to relish the corrupt deeds and habits of his courtiers." When the King's great-uncle, Cardinal Beaufort, died in 1447 he left Henry a legacy of £2,000, which Henry refused. He told the astonished executors: "He was a very dear uncle to me and most liberal in his lifetime. The Lord reward him. Do ye with his goods as ye are bound: we will receive none of them." But in the end he was persuaded to take the gift for the benefit of his colleges.

Like all his family, Henry was extremely liberal to the poor, doing all that he could to relieve destitution. His devotional life and notorious holiness were such that when he was only twenty-five Pope Eugenius IV sent him the Golden Rose, the most precious honour he could bestow. Blacman gives many details of his life: "He was a simple man, without any crook of craft or untruth . . . with none did he deal craftily, nor ever would say an untrue word to any." When the King was going about his business he was constantly engaged in meditation and prayer, "so that many times he would let his royal cap drop to the ground even from his horse's back, unless it were quickly caught by his servants." Even his turbulent nobles respected him and took heed of his warnings not to bring hawks, swords, or daggers into church, or to conduct business discussions there. Instead, he enjoined upon them frequent prayer, "according to the word of the Saviour, 'My house is a house of prayer': and they obeyed him devoutly." He wore round-toed shoes and boots like a farmer's, a long gown with a rolled hood like a townsman and a full coat, reaching below his knees, with shoes, boots, and footgear all of black, "rejecting expressly all curious fashion of clothing."

Of his modesty two stories are told: once "at Christmas time a certain great lord brought before him a dance or show of young ladies with bared bosoms who were to dance in that guise before the King, . . . who very angrily averted his eyes, turned his back upon them, and went out to his chamber, saying: 'Fy, fy, for shame, forsothe ye be to blame.'" On another occasion he visited Bath, "where are warm baths in which they say the men of that country customarily refresh and wash themselves. The King, looking into the baths, saw in them men wholly naked with every garment cast off. At which he was displeased, and went away quickly, abhorring such nudity as a great offence and not unmindful of that sentence of Francis Petrarch 'the nakedness of a beast is in men unpleasing, but the decency of raiment makes for modesty.'" If in some respects his views seem unduly strict his kindly wisdom still has much to teach us. When he heard that one of his servants had been robbed he sent him a present of twenty nobles, advising him to take better care of his goods in future, but not to prosecute the thief.

In an age of cruelty and barbarity almost equal to our own, he maintained an absolute and not merely a relative standard. "Once when he was coming down from St. Albans to London through Cripplegate, he saw over the gate there the quarter of a man on a tall stake, and asked what it was. And when his lords made answer that it was the quarter of a traitor of his, who had been false to the King's majesty, he said: 'Take it away. I will not have any Christian man so cruelly handled for my sake.' And the quarter was removed immediately. He that saw it bears witness." When four of the greater nobility had been condemned to death for treason he had them immediately released, and on another occasion he pardoned three other lords who had conspired against his life, and also all their followers. Even when, during his imprisonment, a man severely wounded him in the neck, all his reproof was: "Forsothe and forsothe, ye do fouly to smyte a kynge enoynted so." When riots broke out in 1450 the King put on armour and rode through the streets demonstrating great physical courage, but he would never fight against his fellow-

Christians in battle, but simply stood his ground until either the fight was over, or he were captured.

Henry was not alone in condemning the fratricidal wars of his age; the brilliant and thoughtful Reginald Pecock, Bishop of Chichester, remarked in his *Repressor of over-much Blaming of the Clergy*, that the clerical order, with all its faults, was at any rate free of the guilt of war. " Take me all the religiose men of Englond, whiche ben now and han ben in religioun in Englond this thritti yeeris and mo now eendid, in which xxxti yeeris hath be contynuel greet werre bitwixe Englond and Fraunce; and lete see what schulde have worthe of the men in these yeeris, if thei hadden not be mad religiose . . . whether not thei schulden have be . . . gileful artificers, or unpiteful questmongers and for-sworn jurers, or sowdiers wagid into Fraunce forto make miche morther of blood, yhe, and of soulis, bothe in her owne side and in the Frensch side?" and Pecock elsewhere shows that truth was the first casualty in war, for " al the tyme of werre during these xl yeer bitwixe Ynglond and Fraunce, wist I not scant iii or iiii men, whiche wolden accorde thorough out, in telling how a town or a castel was wonne in Fraunce, or hou a batel was doon there." King Henry was murdered, and Pecock deprived and imprisoned by the barbarity of the age they criticized.

Henry is reproached for having been too weak to govern, and even for having acquired some taint of mental instability from his grandfather, Charles VI. But the strong and ruthless kings were not more successful than he in maintaining order and justice. It was not the brute force of an Edward I that commanded respect, but his passion for justice; while the combination of exceptional courage with a reasoned policy of peace has always aroused sympathy for Richard II. Even during Cade's rebellion of 1450, Henry VI was well loved, just as Tyler's peasants had held by " King Richard and the true commons ". With England and Europe in their stricken state the King may have been wise to concentrate upon devotion and personal kindliness. Blacman gives an amusing picture of the difficulties of his way of life: " the lord King himself complained heavily to me in his chamber at Eltham, when I was alone there with him employed together with him upon his holy books and giving ear to his wholesome advice and the sighs of his most deep devotion. There came all at once a knock at the King's door from a certain mighty duke of the realm, and the King said: ' They do so interrupt me that by day or night I can hardly snatch a moment to be refreshed by reading of any holy teaching without disturbance.' "

Henry's views on his right to the throne have been preserved and show the doctrine of royal consecration as held by a conspicuously fair man. When imprisoned under Edward IV, Henry was reproached with his usurpation, and replied: " My father had been King of England, possessing his crown in peace all through his reign; and his father, my grandfather, had been King of the same realm. And I, when a boy in the cradle, had been without any interval crowned in peace and approved as King by the whole realm, and wore the crown for wellnigh forty years, every lord doing royal homage to me, and swearing fealty as they had done to my forefathers; so I may say with the psalmist, ' The lines are fallen unto me in a pleasant place, yea I have a goodly heritage.' ' My help cometh of God, who preserveth them that are true at heart.' " That Richard II left no direct heirs greatly furthered this doctrine so favourable to the Lancastrian cause; the legitimate claim was too roundabout to make good propaganda.

One particularly interesting source of first-hand information regarding Henry VI consists of depositions taken down years afterwards from monks and other inhabitants of Westminster regarding his visits to the Abbey to choose his tomb. These are given as an appendix to the first three editions of Dean Stanley's *Memorials of Westminster Abbey*, so I here give simply a few extracts. On different occasions between about 1448 and 1460 the King visited the tombs of his predecessors around St. Edward's Shrine, attempting to find a suitable place for his own sepulchre. At one visit, members of his entourage suggested that Queen Eleanor's monument should be moved, but the King "shewed his mynde and saide, that it myghte not well be in that place but if it shuld prejudice the body of the Quene that there then lay as it yit dothe. Whiche, as he said he wold in no wyse doo." Philip Ilstowe, aged ninety, and lavender or laundryman of the Abbey forty years, remembered being present when Abbot Kirton suggested "that it was metely for (the King) to lie in the chappell by his fadre Kyng Henry the vth. Whereunto he answered and said: 'Nay let hym alone he lieth lyke a nobyll prince I wolle not troble hym.' And therupon the seid Kyng Henry callyd unto hym . . . Syr Richard Tunstall, and after hys commyng to hym the said Kyng Henry lened upon his sholdre and askyed of the forsaide Abbat if the Relyques which then stode upon the northsyde of Seint Edwardys Shryne myghte not be removed in to some other place. The which answerd and saide that for his pleasure the saide Reliques shuld shortly be removed in to somme other place. And then incontynently the foresaide Kyng Henry the vith with his owne feete mett out the length of vij. foote befoore and nyghe the place wher the Reliques than stoode. And commawndyd a mason than beyng present callyd Thurske . . . to marke oute there the place where he shulde lie, which Thurske at the saide commawndement markyd out there the foresaid place withe an iron pykkes. Which done the said Kyng Henry seid to such as then there were present these wordes—'Forsoth and forsoth here is a good place for us.'" Another witness, Thomas Humfray, who had been Abbot Kirton's barber, mentioned that the mason "Thurske" was at the time "master-mason in the makyng of the Chapelle of King Henry the vth", a post which John Thirsk held from 1421 until his death in 1452. He was appointed also master-mason of the King's works in Windsor Castle on 28 June 1449, and perhaps owed this promotion to his meeting with the King.

Notwithstanding the disasters of Henry's reign in the world of politics, it was able to show compensating factors in art. I have already spoken of the great composers, under whom

England was for a generation the leading musical centre of
Europe. In sculpture there was the lofty figure of John
Massingham, who seems to have learnt anatomy from the
warden of the London Barber-Surgeons' Company, Roger
Webb. Humfrey, duke of Gloucester, was busily collecting
manuscripts of the classics from Italy. By a strange irony
he obtained from overseas a copy of Vitruvius on Architecture, a work which, unknown to duke Humfrey, existed in
several English monastic libraries and whose earliest extant
manuscript was written in England in the eighth century A.D.
From England copies of the manuscript were sent to the
Court of Charlemagne and to Germany and Italy, and so,
after a lapse of six or seven centuries, back to the eager
hands of duke Humfrey. Meanwhile the drama, as exemplified by the moralities of *Perseverance* and *Wisdom* and
the cycles of Coventry and York plays, was emerging, and
Bishop Pecock was laying the foundations of an English
prose style.

Within a few years of 1450 the older generation of states-
men, poets, musicians and architects, was passing away.
Gloucester and his rival, Cardinal Beaufort, both died in
1447, Occleve and Lydgate soon after 1450, Dunstable in
1453. Their place was taken by the Queen, Margaret of
Anjou, whom Henry married in April 1445. The King
was twenty-three, his bride just sixteen years old. She
was the daughter of René, titular King of Sicily, one of the
most cultured men of his age. Unfortunately Margaret did
not resemble her father, but was fiery and tempestuous, unlike her husband, and unsuited to his meek and forgiving
temperament. Through the rest of the reign and beyond, the
great struggle was between the Duke of York, now beginning
to assert his legitimate claims to the throne, and Margaret,
who, on behalf of her husband and later of her young son,
upheld the cause of Lancaster. While Henry's presence at
a battle almost invariably spelt defeat, his wife was usually
successful, until her fatal overthrow at Tewkesbury. Had
it not been for his marriage to Margaret, Henry would have
come to some satisfactory arrangement with York, and the

disaster of the Wars of the Roses have been averted. But where Henry would go to meet his adversary, Margaret sprang to arms and never admitted compromise. To her fierce determination to dominate she sacrificed the lives of her husband and her beloved son and her own chances of success. Seldom has a woman shown such undaunted courage under repeated misfortunes, seldom has there been a clearer demonstration that courage can be so misplaced as to be a dreadful liability.

Poor Margaret, though a good general, was no woman of affairs. In 1461, after Edward IV's successful seizure of power, she retreated to the North, and in her obstinate pursuit of an obsession sold Berwick to the Scots for present assistance; Berwick once surrendered, the Scots took no further interest in the Lancastrian cause, except to give the royal exiles rather precarious asylum. Various strongholds, especially in Wales, long held out for Lancaster, and in 1464 there were hopes of a successful rising against Edward. Henry was lured southwards into Lancashire by these hopes of restoration, and there in the following year he was captured. The next five years he spent a prisoner in the Tower, until Richard Neville, the great King-maker earl of Warwick and son-in-law of Henry's old tutor, turned against his master, and set up Henry as King once more. For a few months Henry remained a puppet King, but the period of his " readeption " was short, and early in 1471 Edward re-entered London and again sent him to the Tower. There, apparently on 24 May, he was murdered, though not by Richard of Gloucester, who was away at the time. His body was at first buried at Chertsey Abbey, then in 1484 removed to Windsor by Richard III. When the tomb was opened in 1910 the skeleton was found to be that of a fairly strong man about 5 feet 9 inches tall, with a rather small skull, to which brown hair still adhered.

Henry's life and death and the thwarting of his noble designs are one of the sorriest tragedies of English history. He was the victim of forces outside his control, for whose existence he was not responsible, but set in motion by his

grandfather's crime and his father's one-sided ambition.
Inheriting, with the love of justice and the accessibility of
his Plantagenet forefathers, the artistic culture and the melan-
cholia of Charles VI of France, his character was in sharp
contrast with that common to his age, possessed in a marked
degree by his wife. In his charity, his love of art, and his
spirit, he was a true Plantagenet, though a paradoxical one.
His facets of temperament were needed to round off the
many-sided aspects of his House, and brought the wheel
round full circle, emulating his distant ancestor Fulk the
Good. Like Fulk, he saw the world as a place of brief
sojourn in which to do good, to learn courtesy, and to seek
God. There was nothing political in his martyrdom; except
as the shadow of a name and as the crowned and anointed
husband of Margaret he represented no threat to anybody in
the world. Yet the callous and sacrilegious hand that struck
him down, though it ended a gentle and devotional life
on earth, ensured that Henry's virtues and lasting benefits
should be perpetually brought to the minds of oblivious
posterity.

CHAPTER XII

EDWARD IV

When the House of York at last reached the throne over two generations had passed since the tragic end of Richard II. There is a cruel necessity which takes little account of abstract right and wrong. From the standpoint of legitimacy, Edward IV was Richard's true heir; but the England to which he succeeded was not the England of Richard. Those two generations had witnessed the unfolding of the great crisis of European and of English history: the victory of the Church over toleration; the victory of selfish interests over the disinterested leadership of the Crown; the victory of war over conciliation. Those sixty years had seen the final, though as yet unbelievable, severance of England from the last remnants of the continental empire of Henry II —England, cut adrift from the direct contacts with the wine, the women, and the song of the warm South, contacts which had held a prime importance from Eleanor of Aquitaine to Margaret of Anjou, was henceforth to carve out a new empire, new spheres of interest across wider seas. But the new links, though in the end they were to encompass the globe and reach from the Equator to the Poles, were to be forged from the hard, cold iron of the North. Henceforth the Englishman was to stand with his face towards the Pole and his back to Europe.

The restlessness, the energy, the constant ebullition of the English temperament were to seek new outlets, and during that short quarter-century separating the victory of York from the final destruction of Plantagenet, English expeditions were to begin the search for the riches of the Indies and the fabled islands of the western sea. All the initial, critical stages of development, the origins of that new Renaissance world for which the House of Tudor in England has received credit, had taken place before the end of the reign

of Edward IV. In common with the whole western world,
England had in the Dark Ages lost higher civilization and
higher culture together; the story of the Middle Ages is
the tale of how those classic qualities came to be recaptured;
how they were, for brief periods, and in one part or another
of Europe, re-established. So far as England is concerned,
there was no reason why there should not have been a continuous development from the spark of returning life fanned
by Alfred the Great, up to a new flowering of the arts
in the sixteenth and later centuries. No reason, that is,
apart from the failure of continuity in the royal House itself.

It is one of the puzzles of history that the new humanism
of the Renaissance world should have taken a wrong turning
and riveted on fresh shackles of an imitative formalism, in
place of the elastic bonds of old tradition. The traditions
which had been in process of growth for some six centuries
and of perfected Gothic life for four were to be jettisoned,
in order that a cargo of half-baked antiquated notions might
be put in their place. The spurious imitations of classical
Rome would never have won acclaim from the royal houses
of Europe unless the traditional Gothic standards, at their
best so vivid and alive, had first been debased. In France the
debasement was due to the physical ravages of war; but
in England the cause can be identified with much greater
accuracy: it was the replacement of the high cultural inspiration of Richard II by the mediocre outlook of Henry IV,
followed by the breakdown in spiritual values consequent
upon this flagrant contamination of the fountain-head of
justice, of administration, and of art. The tragedy of great
wrongs is that they cannot be undone; even if further wrongs
are not added the initial obliquity is enough to turn the
stream out of its proper channel. It was to a country
whose stream of life had been thus twisted out of line that
Edward IV succeeded.

When the elder generation of royal kinsmen and ad-
ministrators had disappeared, the generation of Bedford,
Cardinal Beaufort, and Gloucester, men's disappointed hopes
came to centre more and more upon the person of Richard,

duke of York, Edward's father, and in right of his mother, Anne Mortimer, heir general of Edward III. Of Edward III's sons who lived to have children, the second was Lionel, duke of Clarence, whose daughter, Philippa, had married Edmund Mortimer, third earl of March; their son Roger was succeeded by his son Edmund, fifth earl of March, on whose death without issue the line passed to his sister Anne. Anne married Richard, that earl of Cambridge who was executed by Henry V in 1415 and who was heir to his brother Edward, duke of York (author of the hunting treatise *The Master of Game* and who died at Agincourt). Edward and Richard were the two sons of Edmund, duke of York, the fourth of Edward III's surviving sons, coming after John of Gaunt. Thus the Yorkist claims in the male line were subsequent to those of Lancaster, and their right of succession depended on the validity of two descents through females: Philippa, daughter of Lionel of Clarence, and Anne, daughter of Roger and sister of Edmund Mortimer. It was because such rights were not definitely recognized in the fifteenth century that Richard of York's claim went so long unasserted. Even when the rule of Henry VI's queen and her advisers had continued for some years and the affairs of England had reached their lowest ebb, York did not put forward claims to the throne, but merely demanded a share in the government.

A few months after the final loss of Bordeaux, York was made Protector of the kingdom, on 5 April 1454. He made oath of allegiance to Henry VI, appending seal and signature to the formal deed, which declared that in the event of breaking his oath he, York, was to be "unabled and held and taken as an untrue and openly foresworn man." York did not retain the Protectorship, and in his efforts to regain it, broke, reaffirmed, and again broke his oath. In the midst of an age when evil-doers for the most part flourished like the bay-tree, there is poetic justice in the fact that York's final recourse to arms in 1460 ended in his death at Wakefield, after he had actually tasted the triumphs of claimant and heir-designate. His head, adorned with a paper crown, was stuck above the walls of York by Queen Margaret's orders, and so it was his eldest son Edward who a few months later became King in his stead.

Edward was born at Rouen on 28 April 1442, seven years after the fall of English rule in Paris, but while Normandy was still held. When he was twelve his father became Protector, and Edward and his brother Edmund were left at Ludlow Castle in the March of Wales. From thence the two boys wrote to their father letters of congratulation on his victories, and inserted in them matters of personal moment. In one, " we thank your noblesse and good fatherhood of our green gowns now late sent unto us to our great comfort ", and ask " that we might have some fine bonnets sent unto us by the next sure messenger, for necessity so requireth." At the same time the two boys complained to their father of " the odious rule and demeaning of Richard Crofte and of his brother "; Crofte was their tutor. Edward's youthful interest in fine clothes was to continue through his life and to be matched by magnificent and luxurious tastes in other directions. All descriptions agree as to his extraordinary personal beauty, which he inherited from his mother, Cecily Neville, youngest daughter of Ralph, first earl of Westmorland by his second wife, Joan Beaufort, daughter of John of Gaunt. Edward was six feet tall when he came to the throne, with exquisite polished manners, as well as considerable military skill and experience. All gentlemanly accomplishments were his: he excelled in dancing as well as in outdoor pursuits; he was the first of our kings to cultivate his own handwriting. He brought the management of different classes of his subjects to a fine art, and was said to know the names and fortunes of everyone of any standing all over the country. This knowledge he employed to obtain large loans and gifts which freed him from dependence on the subsidies granted by Parliament.

There was in this a good deal of subtle policy, but he achieved the extraordinary task of freeing the Crown from its burden of debt. In the Middle Ages there was no distinction between the public and private revenue of the

P.   G

King; it was, in fact, constantly suggested that the King should "live of his own", that is, pay the cost of the whole administration out of the profits of the Crown Lands administered as a private estate. The grant of subsidies was as far as possible restricted to occasions of national defence and the conduct of foreign wars when they were proving successful and popular. So Edward's financial acumen and the amorous relations with citizens' wives, from which he reaped a second golden harvest, are more in his favour as King than against his personal character. Though he had, toward the end of his life, a reputation for avarice as the result of his fight against debt, he was no niggard, and provided daily food for 2,000 persons, besides undertaking the architectural schemes which flourished through his last years. There is a good deal of spite in Commynes' verdict that the King of England "thought of nothing but upon women, and that more than reason would, and on hunting, and on the comfort of his person."

Edward's relations with women were not altogether ill-advised; he said himself that he had "three concubines which in diverse properties diversely excelled, one the merriest, the other the wiliest, the third the holiest harlot in the realm." The merry bedfellow was the famous Jane Shore, wife of a London mercer. Years afterwards Sir Thomas More was to write of her: "This woman was born in London, worshipfully friended, honestly brought up, and very well married, saving somewhat too soon, her husband an honest citizen, young and goodly and of good substance. Proper she was and fair; nothing in her body that you would have changed but if you would have wished her somewhat higher. Thus say they that knew her in her youth, albeit some that now see her (for yet she liveth) deem her never to have been well visaged." Men took special delight "in her pleasant behaviour. For a proper wit had she, and could both read well and write, merry in company, ready and quick of answer, neither mute nor full of babble, . . ." Beyond this she had a warm heart, and "where the king took displeasure, she would mitigate and appease his

aind; where men were out of favour, she would bring them
a his grace. For many that had highly offended she obtained
ardon; of great forfeitures she got men remission. . . ."

Edward was not so lucky over his marriage. The most
nportant problem was the inheritance of the Crown, and
was precisely this that Edward failed to solve. Even before
is father became Protector, a son had been born to Margaret
f Anjou, on 13 October 1453. There were grave doubts
s to whether Henry VI was the father, for the royal saint
imself in a moment of lucidity declared that the young
rince "must be the son of the Holy Spirit". But the
hild was accepted by the Lancastrians as heir, and Margaret's
nergies were henceforth to be centred on obtaining universal
ecognition for her son. When Edward of York gained the
irone this Lancastrian Prince Edward, though "on the run",
'as still a prospective rival, and the best counter-move would
ave been an approved diplomatic marriage and the pro-
uction of a recognized male heir. Here Edward's hot-
looded temperament led him into difficulties. It is now
npossible to prove the story that he entered into a con-
act of marriage with Lady Eleanor Butler to seduce her,
ut that the tale had some *prima facie* probability is shown
y the success with which Richard III used it as evidence
f his nephews' illegitimacy. According to Canon Law,
revious contract of marriage invalidated a subsequent mar-
age ceremony; and the offspring of the later union would
e bastards. This was the case on which Richard III's
laim was to rest; but even if this episode was a political
abrication, Edward's actual marriage to Elizabeth Woodville
as unquestionably an affair of impulse.

Elizabeth, five years older than Edward and widow of
ord Ferrers of Groby, was no match, by the social stan-
ards of the day, for the King of England, though she was,
a fact, very well born. Her mother was the Dowager Duchess
f Bedford, who, after the great Regent's death, had re-
aarried to Sir Richard Woodville, or Wydeville, later created
ord Rivers. Jacquetta, duchess of Bedford, was the daughter
f Pierre de Luxembourg, Count of St. Pol, by his wife,

Marguerite des Baux; on both sides she came of the best blood in Europe, and through her second marriage this blood came to the nobility of England and to the Royal House. It was an irony of fate that the match between her daughter and Edward, so suitable in fact, should have been so unequal in seeming as to have led to disaster. The marriage took place on May Day, 1464, when Edward was twenty-two; it was conducted in the greatest secrecy at the bride's home at Grafton Regis, the King having slipped away from his household on pretext of hunting. For several months the marriage was kept unannounced, but in the autumn the King admitted the facts when the great ear of Warwick's negotiations for a foreign princess left him no alternative. Finally, Elizabeth was crowned Queen on Whit-Sunday, 1465, and the ceremony was carried out with magnificence and solemnity.

The City of London made quite extraordinary preparations for welcoming the Queen: the bridge was decorated with gold and coloured papers, tinfoil, buckram, sundry images, and other decorations, and six ballads were specially illuminated for presentation. Forty-five loads of sand were sprinkled on the roadway, and the musical celebrations were entrusted to singing boys and twenty-five members of the Company of Parish Clerks. At the state banquet at Westminster the great nobles served the new Queen in the customary manner, and between the courses "the kings mynstrallys & the mynstrallys of other Lordys" played and piped "in theyre instrymentys grete & small before the Queene full melodyously & in the moste solempne wise." Although his hasty marriage was to cost Edward IV a great deal of opposition from Warwick and others, and his sons their lives, the Queen herself was popular. In her generous refounding of her rival's college at Cambridge, still known as that of the two Queens, Margaret of Anjou and Elizabeth Woodville, she showed herself worthy of her ancestry.

When Edward first became King, a youth of nineteen, he seems to have had two main preoccupations: the first, to restore justice; the second, to stabilize the finances of the Court and government. In pursuance of the first he revived the ancient custom of sitting in person on the bench, while to save money he revoked Lancastrian grants, from the munificent foundations of Henry VI at Eton and Cambridge, down to the fees of office of the royal workmen. Financially, these measures may have had justification, but they must have caused much personal hardship to unoffending men whose whole livelihood was bound up with the civil service. The discharge of the Lancastrian office-holders, including those of humble station, was not a mere formality; many of them seem to have been thrown permanently out of the King's service. This was a new departure: no previous political revolution had entailed loss of office upon the household rank and file. The Acts of Resumption of Henry VI's later years made very considerable exceptions in favour of servants and officers with years of good service to their credit; Henry IV's usurpation in 1399 had been followed by reinstatement of practically the whole of Richard II's staff. Edward IV's behaviour was undoubtedly that of an impulsive young man, who saw the disease more clearly than the means to a cure. His obstinate determination to root out even the memory of Henry VI's acts led him, only a few months after his accession, to obtain from Pius II a bull for the abolition of Eton College, and for some six years it was only the determination of Bishop Waynflete that stood between Henry's two colleges and complete extinction. In the end, by the exercise of much tact, Edward was won round, from 1467 Eton was given some slight encouragement to revive, and in 1471, when Edward returned from his temporary exile, he visited the college three times with his Queen. Finally, in 1482, the year before his death, the King dined at King's College, Cambridge.

In the first years of his reign, largely spent in London on reorganization, Edward is said to have led a licentious life and permanently undermined his splendid constitution. His death at forty-one makes this supposition only too probable. But he was not solely concerned with personal pleasures;

from 1463, and perhaps earlier, he was engaged in the wool trade on his own account and on a large scale. It was largely owing to this private trading that the King was able to rebuild the family fortunes, and thus the financial equilibrium of the state. Such personal attention to business simply carried a stage further the close relations which had existed between Edward III and the merchants of the realm, and that in its turn had reflected the attention with which Edward I fostered trade and the commercial prosperity of England and Guienne. But while Edward I and Edward III had been unwise enough in the end to abandon the interests of commerce in favour of the questionable glories of war, Edward IV preserved throughout his cool capacity and forethought.

For the first time the craft and subtlety of the Valois were well matched by subtlety across the Channel. Louis XI, Edward's exact contemporary in reign, was the fine flower of his race as regards statecraft and the ability to get his ends by devious ways; but by means of a shrewd display of force and then a corresponding display of personal splendour and tact combined, at the famous meeting with Louis on the Bridge of Picquigny in 1475, Edward contrived not to be outdone by his great rival, and to extort from him considerable payments. Edward was more far-seeing than his subjects, or indeed anyone of his time except Louis; he knew, as Louis knew, that for the future England would live apart, and that the dreams of a reconquest of France by the English were phantoms. But an English invasion could have wrecked Louis's plans, and it was well worth his while to pay: he paid. And if Edward shares with Charles II the obloquy of the knaves and fools who would have had them plunge into glorious war, he shares with his great descendant in the truer glory of maintaining an unpopular peace. His determination may have been strengthened by a fortunate accident of family policy. In 1459, when Margaret of Anjou's ministry was tottering to its final downfall, the unpopular measure of universal conscription had been introduced. Commissions of array were

sent all over the country, ordering men to be taken to fill
quotas from every town, village, and hamlet, both within and
without liberties. One of the last acts of Richard, duke of
York, had been to issue a manifesto against, among other
abuses, this new imposition, never before seen, namely,
the conscription of men after the French manner.

Edward, pursuing his father's declared policy, would
in any case have been anxious to avoid such measures; and
he saw many of the inevitable ill results which would arise
from such a policy, so insidiously departing from the old
principles of the national levies, strictly for home defence,
and for the limited period of forty days only. Attempts
have been made, notably by Dr. Coulton, to maintain that
the principle of conscription is typically English, as against
the mercenary army maintained by the absolute monarchs of
France from the fifteenth century onwards. But York's manifesto makes it clear that conscription *for a standing army* was
a complete innovation in 1459, and regarded as "upon the
French model". The Anglo-Saxon fyrd and its later counterpart in feudal times had been not an army but a police-force
and, in the case of actual invasion, defence body. It was
only in emergency that the fyrd could be taken outside its
own county. In the time of Edward III it is clear that
attempts were made to extend the scope of national training,
in view of the war with France, but even then the chances of
booty were the chief means of attracting recruits. Besides,
the older system of impressment left open the loophole of
paying for a substitute, which was still operative until our own
days. Under Edward I, who was a great and popular general,
there had been plenty of evasion of the draft, and the Hales-
owen Court Rolls of 1295 contain the amusing case of one,
Thomas Hill, who had gone in turn to each of the men
chosen to fill the local quota for Edward's army in Wales;
each had paid Hill to act as substitute, but after collecting
the cash Hill disappeared.

It is a pity that Edward IV's record in some other respects
is more open to criticism. In 1468 two Lancastrian agents,
Cornelius and Hawkins, were examined under torture; the

first proved use of torture in English law. In connexion with the same conspiracy Chief Justice Markham lost his office at the instance of Lord Rivers, but with Edward's connivance, solely for his scrupulous fairness; in 1477 the King interfered personally against the accused in the trials of Thomas Burdett, John Stacy, and Thomas Blake, for witchcraft and the unlawful casting of horoscopes; in 1481 accounts passed in the Exchequer show the bribes paid to juries to convict. These are symptoms of the disease of the spirit from which the fifteenth century was suffering; another was the introduction by John Tiptoft, Earl of Worcester, in 1470 of the punishment of impalement for traitors. Tiptoft had the special approval of the King for this horrible innovation and earned for himself the just title of " the butcher of England ". But Tiptoft was undoubtedly an extreme and morbid instance of the fifteenth-century link between sensibility and sadism; he was the greatest English humanist of his time, had travelled to Rome, Jerusalem, Venice, and Padua, and spent much time in Italy collecting rare books.

In religious questions, too, Edward carried out the bigoted policy brought in by the House of Lancaster. He was noted for the extent to which he leaned on ecclesiastics, and in return his severity to heretics was all that the Church could desire. When, in 1474, Edward was making a personal tour of England to gather money for his great show-expedition into France, he combined pleasure with business by detecting heresy; not so much the old heresy of the Lollards, now mostly burnt away, but the new followers of wise Bishop Pecock. In all this may be seen the inwardness of the fall of the House of York, as of Lancaster: men as courageous and noble as Henry V, as wise and justice-loving as Edward IV, became corrupted by an all-pervading miasma of the age. This insidious temptation to do evil that good might ensue, to meet violence with violence, treachery with treachery, crime with crime, proved too much. The very qualities in the Plantagenets which had made them great—their bravery, their fiery temper, their justice, their forethought—all were in process of transformation.

The great climax of Edward's reign was Warwick's successful rebellion of 1470 and the short restoration or readeption of Henry VI. Edward was in bed at Doncaster when the serjeant of his minstrels burst into his room with the news that his enemies were only six or seven miles away and hoped to capture him. The King made no attempt to join his Queen in London, but fled the country by way of Lynn, crossing the Wash with such precipitancy that several of his faithful supporters were drowned. Queen Elizabeth, finding herself deserted, took sanctuary at Westminster with her three daughters and her mother. Henry VI, released from his captivity in the Tower, learned that Queen Elizabeth expected shortly to be confined, and with his usual generosity appointed Elizabeth Lady Scrope to wait upon her, paying Lady Scrope's expenses. He also saw that Queen Elizabeth was permitted to have food sent in to her from London tradesmen. Whether it was the outcome of Warwick's policy, or of Henry's merciful nature, the only victim of the new government was the infamous Tiptoft, and even he was given a fair trial. Edward was at Bruges, preparing a new invasion of England; in February he proceeded by land to Damme, instead of taking boat, so that the Flemings might have the pleasure of witnessing his procession; following the precedent of Henry Bolingbroke he landed at Ravenspur in Holderness, and said that he had come to claim, not the throne, but only his Duchy of York.

Marching on York and using King Henry's name, he persuaded the citizens to admit him; then proceeding southwards he waited only until his company had grown to formidable dimensions to throw off the mask and reclaim the Crown. The whole proceeding echoes the broken faith of Bolingbroke, the treachery that trapped Richard II, the broken oaths of Richard duke of York, Edward's father. And these actions were echoes; echoes of the original treason against Edward II, and echoes of the fratricidal warfare of the sons of William the Conqueror and of Henry II. A house divided against itself must perish. Edward made straight for London, and in London, direct to the Bishop's Palace by St. Paul's, where King Henry was staying. There is a pathetic nobility and resignation about Henry's greeting of his cousin; offering to embrace him he said: "My cousin of York, you are very welcome; I know that in your hands my life will not be in danger." As soon as he had ordered Henry back to captivity Edward adjourned to Westminster Abbey, where the crown was again set on his head in token of his restoration, and then to his Queen's lodgings in the sanctuary. During his ill-omened absence his first son, afterwards for so short a time Edward V, had been born.

At the last battle with Warwick, fought at Barnet, Edward displayed much bravery and tried to save the great rebel's life, but the Kingmaker's captors had slain him on the spot. About 1,500 were killed altogether; a high total for a mediæval battle, but for the first time Edward had refrained from giving his customary order to spare the common folk; his exile had exasperated him with his subjects. No sooner was Warwick disposed of than Queen Margaret landed in the west and gathered another Lancastrian army. It was her last hope, and she put into it everything she had. The star of Lancaster had set and the field of Tewkesbury at last annihilated Margaret's all, for not only was her army defeated, but after the battle her only son, Edward, for whom she had risked so much, was murdered by the victors. There does not appear to be any foundation for the tradition that it was the hand of Richard of Gloucester that struck the young prince down, but three weeks later another murderer removed King Henry from the Tower. Soon it was to be the turn of the survivors of the House of York; Lord Mersey calculated that between 1400 and 1485, 4 Kings, 12 princes of the blood, and 12 near relatives fell by battle, murder, or sudden death.

The age was not altogether bad; Edward himself was more nearly just than his contemporaries, and his attempt to save the rebel Warwick's life compares strangely with modern doctrines of war-guilt. Even in regard to treason, Edward was more lenient than recent case-law, for in writing to James III, King of Scots, early in his reign to demand the surrender of King Henry, Queen Margaret, and their supporters, he made exception in their favour if the King of Scots should grant them naturalization: "We exhort and require you, . . . to deliver unto us without delay our said traitors and rebels, if they become not your lieges and subjects; and if it so be, to certify us the same under seal . . ."

The second half of Edward's reign, from his restoration in 1471 to his death in 1483, was a brilliant period. He patronized the new invention of printing, brought in by Caxton, whose work in Flanders he probably saw during his exile; he spent large sums on the transcription of books in manuscript; he was especially interested in history, the Life of Caesar, a Summary of the Roman Emperors after Caesar, Valerius Maximus in French, the up-to-date chronicles of Jean de Waurin; in theology he read St. Augustine, for recreation the Decameron and Raoul le Fevre's *Recueil des Histoires de Troie*. John Hardyng dedicated his chronicle, and John Capgrave his Annals to Edward; in his reign appeared the great political treatise of Sir John Fortescue on *The Governance of England*, and the legal handbook on *Tenures* of Sir Thomas Lyttelton, described by Coke as "the most perfect and absolute work that ever was written in any human science." Apart from the encouragement of printing and the royal support accorded to early expeditions to the western ocean, Edward is noteworthy for his establishment of a postal system in 1482, whereby relays of horsemen at every twenty miles were enabled to carry dispatches from London to the Scottish Border at the rate of 100 miles a day, or about three times the rate of fast ordinary travel.

The musical and architectural harvest of the reign was a glorious one; from the restoration of 1471 onwards, there was a breath of new life and energy sweeping through the arts, and though some of the initiative undoubtedly came from the Netherlands, a great deal was due to the sturdy

English traditions which were still able to swell into a glorious renaissance, to culminate in Tudor times with the building of Henry VII's Chapel by Robert and William Vertue, and the great school of Church and keyboard composers led by such men as William Newark, Hugh Aston, and Robert Fayrfax. When Edward died on 9 April 1483 he left a country that he had brought from dereliction to great prosperity, from the valley of the shadow of death to the threshold of a new land of promise. For, with all the faults of his time and of his own personality, Edward combined an extraordinary quality of success; his achievement, so subtly and quietly carried out that it has often been unperceived, was a great one—less obvious than the work in France of Louis XI, Edward's in England was no less enduring. The last unquestioned King of England saved his country from disintegration, and in setting the keystone of Plantagenet achievement, laid the foundation of a new world.

CHAPTER XIII

RICHARD III

The character of the last Plantagenet King, Richard III, is the most enigmatic of all, for the careful propaganda of the Tudor dynasty makes it impossible to reach absolute certainty as to any of the crucial transactions of his career. Controversy over Richard has been waged furiously for nearly two centuries, and there seems little hope of further vital evidence ever being discovered. The traditional story is that which was told by Archbishop Morton to Sir Thomas More and by other contemporaries at the Tudor Court to Polydore Vergil; this monstrous legend of a hunchback of superhuman subtlety and cruelty passed into Holinshed and was thus the foundation for Shakespeare's plays, which, one after another, build up an overpowering sense of horrifying wickedness, redeemed only by physical courage. The patient research called forth by controversy has at any rate disproved much of this legend.

Several portraits, contemporary or based upon contemporary originals, have survived, and neither these nor the descriptions lend much support to the allegation of deformity. It may be that Richard had a withered arm, possibly from birth, though the story of his outburst in the Council, soon after Edward IV's death, seems highly improbable. He is said to have accused Lord Hastings, Jane Shore, and Queen Elizabeth Woodville of causing his arm to shrivel by incantations and witchcraft; there is something incredible about his linking of the Queen with her rival and with the chief opponent of her family. But Richard's behaviour after his brother's death does appear strange: within a few months he had disposed of two of his old friends and allies, Hastings and Buckingham, and was publicly reported both in England and France to have had his two young nephews murdered. The cumulative evidence in favour of his guilt of this crime is hard to overcome. But of a large proportion of the minor crimes, which in Shakespeare's hands build up the atmosphere of consistent plotting, he can be acquitted. Ten years younger than Edward IV, he played no part in public events until the period of Warwick's rebellion in 1470, when he loyally supported the King his brother. Eight years later he again supported Edward at the time of their brother George's rebellion, but there is no evidence to show that he was active in securing Clarence's death. The tale that Clarence was drowned in a butt of malmsey wine may be true, but if so, Richard was not the agent.

It is likely that he was always suspicious and critical of the Woodville faction at Court, and the underhand character of Edward's marriage must have caused resentment on Richard's part; after Clarence's death and the attainder of his line, only Edward's offspring by Elizabeth stood between Richard and the throne, and the temptation to find reasons for seizing it must have been great. What Richard seems to have done is not more cold-blooded than John's murder of Arthur. But there does seem to have been a good case against the legitimacy of Edward V and his brother and sisters, and it was in accordance with contemporary custom for Richard to make the most of it. Let us set aside the allegations that he murdered the young Lancastrian Prince Edward after Tewkesbury, and Henry VI in the Tower—the evidence in both cases is strongly against his guilt; let us rule out as a mere atrocity story the suggestion that he wished to divorce his wife, Anne (to whom he was deeply attached), in order to marry his own niece, Elizabeth of York. These secondary charges, so useful as Tudor propaganda, are too bad to be true when it comes to serious history, and have really formed the basis of the modern defence.

It has been argued that if Richard was innocent of nine-tenths of the abominable charges made against him by opponents with an axe to grind, it is unreasonable to convict him upon the main charge: causing the murder of his nephews for his own advancement. Taken with the evidence of Richard's courage, loyalty to his brother Edward, and popularity with his own tenants and retainers, this makes a specious case. But it has the fatal flaw of making out Richard a far better character than he could reasonably be; a better and truer man than his unscrupulous brother Edward and fickle brother George, and a shining light amid the gloom of an exceptionally dark period. The execution of Hastings without trial, of Lord Rivers, and Richard Grey, Edward IV's half-brother, the bloody repression of Buckingham's rebellion, tell a different tale. We cannot really doubt that Richard was as representative of the ruthless spirit of the Renaissance as his brother Edward had been, as his great-nephew Henry VIII was to be. By perjury, treason, and bloodshed, Lancaster had usurped the throne of Richard II; by the same means it had itself been overthrown by York; by the same means York was to be brought low by the hand of Richard III, and he, last of all, was to perish.

Born on 2 October 1452 in that Castle of Fotheringhay where Mary Queen of Scots was to die 135 years later, Richard was the eighth and youngest son and eleventh child of his parents. To judge from his portraits he was by no means ill-looking,* and there is a tradition that Katherine "the Old Countess of Desmond", who was known to Sir Walter Raleigh and died early in James I's reign at the extraordinary age of 140, used to say that as a girl she had danced at the English Court with Richard, when he was duke of Gloucester, and that "he was the handsomest man in the room except his brother Edward, and was very well made." One of Richard's surviving letters, dated in 1483-4, contains instructions that the then earl of Desmond should "renounce the wering and usage of the Irisshe Arraye; and from thensforth to geve and applie him self to use the maner of th'apparel for his persone after the Englisshe guyse, and after the fasshon that the Kinges Grace sendeth

---

* He was tall and lean, with delicate arms and legs, according to the German, Nicolas von Poppelau, who met him in 1484.

unto him . . . aswele of gownes, doublettes, hosen, and bon-
ettes, and soo folowingly in tyme comyng, as the caas or
chaunge of the said fasshion shall require."

Richard continued the policy of the latter part of Edward
IV's reign, and in his management of affairs showed great
ability. His short reign of two years is notable for the
first laws written entirely in English, and for the publication of Sir Thomas Malory's *Morte d'Arthur*. Richard
patronized the same musicians and artists who had served
his brother, and displayed consideration towards Lancastrians
who under Edward had been deprived of their offices. A
larger gesture of the same kind was his translation of Henry
VI's body from Chertsey Abbey to Windsor. He was undoubtedly eager to ingratiate himself, but in many directions
gave proofs of a genuine desire for conciliation. In the
sphere of foreign politics he concluded a truce with Scotland,
thus assuring his northern frontier against invasion and
limiting his commitments. As a private individual he had
much of the address and charm of Edward, but was more
energetic and active and less licentious, though he had
bastards, one of whom hid himself in the obscurity of a
bricklayer's apprentice after Bosworth, and ended his days
as master of the building of Sir Thomas Moyle's mansion
at Eastwell in Kent, where he was buried in 1550 aged
over eighty, under the name of Richard Plantagenet.

Richard's only legitimate son Edward, Prince of Wales,
predeceased him in 1484; Edward IV's legitimate sons
perished in the Tower; the only legitimate son of George,
duke of Clarence, was Edward, earl of Warwick, executed
under Henry VII in 1499. Warwick was the last legitimate
male of the House of Plantagenet; his sister Margaret,
countess of Salisbury, married Sir Richard Pole and was
beheaded under Henry VIII in 1541; Cardinal Reginald
Pole, the faithful friend of Queen Mary I, was one of her
sons. Confusingly, another family of Plantagenet heirs
bore the surname of De la Pole, being the children of
Elizabeth, sister of Edward IV, by her marriage to John de
la Pole, duke of Suffolk, who died in 1491. Of these

children John, earl of Lincoln was killed at the battle of
Stoke in 1487, and left no issue; Edmund, last earl of
Suffolk, died in 1513, leaving an only daughter, who became
a nun; and Richard, known as " The White Rose ", was
killed at the battle of Pavia in 1525. Two other sons entered
the Church. Richard de la Pole, who called himself duke
of Suffolk and declared himself heir to the English throne,
was the last serious Plantagenet claimant; the reason for
the De la Pole claim being advanced and taken more
seriously than that of their senior rivals, the Poles, was
the fact that John de la Pole had been declared heir by
Richard III after the death of his own son. Plantagenet
descents through females are innumerable, and the Marquis
de Ruvigny's patient attempt to record them fills several
enormous volumes. Of greater general interest is the direct
male descent of His Grace the Duke of Beaufort, with only
one illegitimacy, from John of Gaunt.

The man who was to win the Crown had one of the
thinnest and poorest personal claims of all: Henry Tudor
was descended from John of Gaunt through his mother,
Margaret Beaufort, though apart from ancient Welsh blood
on his father's side he had also the benefit of descent from
the House of Valois through the marriage of his grandfather, Owen Tudor, to Katherine, widow of Henry V.
Henry Tudor, earl of Richmond, was an astute and competent man of business; while others risked all, and lost,
he bided his time. When at last the time seemed ripe he
sailed from Harfleur in Normandy and landed at Milford
Haven, on 7 August 1485. In the course of a fortnight
he had traversed his paternal land of Wales, gathering strength
as he went, and by way of Shrewsbury came to Lichfield,
following that section of the old Roman Watling Street
which runs eastwards into the Midland Plain. King Richard,
who had been in the North, assembled a much larger force
than Henry's at Nottingham, and marched to Leicester.
Between Leicester and the Watling Street there ran a Roman
branch road, joining the Street at Mancetter by Atherstone.
Along this ancient way came Henry from the west, Richard

from the east; their armies were in sight of one another at nightfall on 21 August, and they encamped on each side of the little river Tweed, a couple of miles south of Market Bosworth.

Though Richard's army was more than double the size of Henry's, it was half-hearted, and the King was betrayed by Lord Stanley, who raised a private army of 7,000 men and so posted himself that he could join the winning side. The battle, fought on 22 August, lasted two hours and cost only some hundred men on each side. But among the slain was Richard, who performed prodigies of valour, and when urged to flee replied: " I will not budge a foot; I will die King of England." In the heat of battle the golden coronet from his helm was hacked off, and fell into a hawthorn bush, whence it was later retrieved and placed on Henry's head by Lord Stanley. Thus Henry enlisted on his side the magic of symbolism; but his cautious mind did not rest content with that. His victory was won, but it had to be assured: in a short time he would bring to his aid Dynastic Continuity by marrying Elizabeth, heiress of Edward IV, but now he had to take more immediate steps to avoid any suggestion of an interregnum.

The battle over, Henry was dictating letters to an army of clerks, to publish the news of his victory far and wide and show that he was King in deed:

Henry by the grace of God, king of England and of France, Prince of Wales, and Lord of Ireland, strictly chargeth and commandeth, upon pain of death, that no manner of man rob or spoil no manner of commons coming from the field; but suffer them to pass home to their countries and dwelling-places, with their horses and harness. And moreover that no manner of man take upon him to go to no gentleman's place, neither in the country, nor within cities nor boroughs, nor pick no quarrels for old or for new matters, but keep the King's peace. . . .

And as soon as written, the fair copies were put into the hands of messengers, to ride with all speed throughout the kingdom, to Scotland, to Cornwall, to London, to Dover, whence the news would pass to parts beyond sea, to Ireland and the Isles, to Henry's own land of Wales. But even as they set out, another, slower messenger was hoisting King Richard's body, wounded and despoiled, upon a packhorse, to be taken for burial to the charitable Greyfriars of Leicester. Along the ancient highway, across the great rolling open fields, the loaded horse plodded on, while the long summer gloaming deepened into dusk. Night fell.

APPENDIX I

Song of Richard Cœur-de-Lion made in captivity, 1194.

Ja nus hons pris ne dirat sa raison
Adroitemant s'ansi com dolans hons,
Mais par confort peut-il faire chanson.
Moult ai d'amins, mais povre sont li don;
Honte en auront se por ma réançon
   Suix ces .ii. yvers pris.

Ceu sevent bien mi home et mi baron,
Englois, Normant, Poitevin et Gascon,
Ke je n'avois si povre compaingnon
Cue je laissasse por avoir an prixon.
Je no di pas por nulle retraison,
   Mais ancor suix je pris.

Or sai-ge bien de voir certainement,
Ke mors ne priset ne amins ne parent
Cant on me lait por or ne por argent.
Moult m'est de moi, mais plus m'est de ma gent,
C'apres ma mort auront reprochier grant
   Se longement suis pris.

N'est pas mervelle se j'ai lo cuer dolant
Cant mes sires tient ma terre en tormant.
S'or li manbroit de nostre sairement
Ke nos féimes andui communament.
Bien sai de voir ke séans longemant
   Ne seroie pas pris.

Mes compaingnons cui j'amoie et cui j'aim
Ces dou Cahiul et ces dou Porcherain,
Me di chanson, qui ne sont pas certain,
C'onques vers aus n'an oi cuer faus ne vain.
Cil me guerroient, il font moult que vilain
   Tant com je serai pris.

Or sevent bien Angevin et Torain,
Cil bacheler ki or sont fort et sain,
C'ancombreis suix, lons d'aus, en autrui mains.
Forment m'adaissent mais il n'i vient grain;
De belles armes sont ores veut cil plain,
   Por tant ke je suis pris.

Comtesse, suer, vostre pris soverain
Vos sat et gart cil a cui je me claim
    Et par cui je suis pris.
Je nou di pas de celi de Chartain
    La meire Loweiis.

Leroux de Lincy: *Chants Historiques Français*, 1841, I, pp.
56-9.
    A Provençal version of the 1st, 2nd, 3rd, 4th, and part of the
7th verses of the above poem, probably by Richard himself, will
be found in Raynouard: *Choix des Poésies des Troubadours*, 1819,
IV, pp. 183-4.

English translation from the French version.

    If captive wight attempt the tuneful strain,
        His voice, belike, full dolefully will sound;
    Yet, to the sad, 'tis comfort to complain.
        Friends have I store, and promises abound:
    Shame on the niggards! Since, these winters twain
    Unransom'd, still I bear a tyrant's chain.

    Full well they know, my lords and nobles all,
        Of England, Normandy, Guienne, Poictou,
    N'er did I slight my poorest vassal's call,
        But all, whom wealth would buy, from chains withdrew.
    Not in reproach I speak, nor idly vain,
    But I alone unpitied bear the chain.

    My fate will show, " the dungeon and the grave
        Alike repel our kindred and our friends."
    Here am I left their paltry gold to save!
        Sad fate is mine; but worse their crime attends,
    Their lord will die; their conscience shall remain,
    And tell how long I wore this galling chain.

    No wonder though my heart with grief boil o'er,
        When he, my perjur'd lord, invades my lands;
    Forgets he then the oaths he lately swore,
        When both, in treaty, joined our plighted hands?
    Else, sure I ween, I should not long remain,
    Unpitied here to wear a tyrant's chain.

    To those my friends, long lov'd, and ever dear,
        To gentle Chaill, and kind Persarain,
    Go forth my song, and say, whate'er they hear,
        To them my heart was never false or vain.

Should they rebel—but no; their souls disdain
With added weight to load a captive's chain.

Know then the youths of Anjou and Touraine,
    Those lusty bachelors, those airy lords,
That these vile walls their captive king restrain?
    Sure they in aid will draw their loyal swords!
Alas! nor faith, nor valour, now remain;
Sighs are but wind, and I must bear my chain.

Sister, countess, your prisoned sovereign
Prays, may He keep you, to Whom I complain,
And by Whose awful hands I now am ta'en.

Translation by G. Ellis in Walpole: *Catalogue of the Royal and
Noble Authors of England, etc.*, ed. T. Park, 1806.

Sirvente by Richard Cœur-de-Lion, addressed to the Dauphin of
Auvergne *c.* 1198. In the Poitevin dialect.

Dalfin, jeus voill déresnier,
Vos e le comte Guion,
Que an ceste seison
Vos féistes bon guerrier
E vos jurastes ou moi;
E m'en portastes tiel foi
Com n'Aengris a Rainart:
Et semblés dou poil liart.

Vos me laïstes aidier
Por treive de guierdon,
E car saviés qu'a Chinon
Non a argent ni denier;
Et vos voletz riche roi,
Bon d'armes, qui vos port foi.
Et je suis chiche, coart,
Si vos viretz de l'autre part.

Encor vos voill demandier
D'Ussoire s'il vos siet bon;
Ni s'in prendretz venjeison,
Ni logaretz soudadier.
Mas une rien vos outroi,
Si beus faussastes la loi,
Bon guerrier a l'estendart
Trovaretz le roi Richart.

Je vos vi au comensier
Large de grant messïon;
Mais puis trovetz ochoison
Que por fortz castels levier
Laissastes don e donoi,
E cortz e segre tornoi:
Mais nos cal avoir regart
Que Franssois son Longobart.

Vai, Sirventes, je t'envoi
En Auvergne, e di moi
As deus comtes de ma part
S'ui més font pes, Dieu les gart.
Que chaut si garz ment sa foi?
Q'escuiers n'a point de loi:
Mas des or avant se gart
Que n'ait en peior sa part.

Leroux de Lincy: *Chants Historique Français*, 1841, vol. I,
pp. 65-7.

English translation.

Dauphin, let me ask the reason
Both from Count Guy and you,
What like good warriors you do
In this year's season?
The oaths you swore to me
Are true, as all may see,
As to Reynard, Isengrin:
You've the hare's skin.

Your aid vanished hence
When my pay ceased to flow;
At Chinon, well you know,
We've no silver nor pence.
A rich King would suit,
Brave, and faithful to boot;
But I'm miser, poltroon,
Now you've changed your tune.

Let me ask you to say
If Issoire you've in mind?
Would you now vengeance find,
And make warlike array?
But a word let me say:
If your oath you betray,

A good man by the standard
You'll discover King Richard.

In the long distant days
You were generous and kind;
But you then took in mind
Strong castles to raise.
Gifts and largess cut short,
You left tourney and court:
To remember's not hard
That the French are Lombard.

To Auvergne, then, Sirvente,
Tell the two Counts I sent
To pray: God give increase!
If they mean to keep peace.
What avails a boor's troth,
Or a lout's broken oath?
But he'd better take care
If he would not worse fare.

APPENDIX II

Edward III's challenge to Philip VI, 26 July 1340.

Edward by the grace of God King of England and of France, and lord of Ireland, to the right noble and puissant lord Philip earl of Valois.

We have for a long time besought you by messages and all other ways, in the most reasonable manner, that you would restore unto us our heritage of France, which you have this long time detained and forcibly withheld from us; and whereas, fully perceiving that you intend to persevere in your injurious intention, without offering an honest reply to our demand, we have entered the land of Flanders as its sovereign lord, and are passing through the country. And we signify unto you that, aided by our lord Jesus Christ and our right, with the power of the said country, our people, and allies, we purpose to recover the right we have to that inheritance, which you violently withhold from us, and will at once decide our rightful challenge, if you will approach. And forasmuch as we have so great an army assembled, a like power, it is presumed, being assembled on your part, which cannot remain long in the field without producing great destruction to the people of the country, which thing every good Christian should eschew, especially princes and others, who have the government of the people; it is very desirable to settle the matter briefly, to avoid the mortality of Christians, since the quarrel is between you and us only, that the discussion of our challenge should be decided by our own persons, to which arrangement we offer ourselves, for the causes already stated, and in consideration of the great nobleness of your person and superior intelligence. And, in case you shall not agree to this way, then let us determine our dispute by a battle of one hundred of the most efficient persons on your part, and as many on ours. And if you will not allow one way or the other, then assign a certain day to be before the city of Tournay for a combat of all your power, which day to be within ten days after the date of this letter. And we wishing that our said offers should be known by all—for it is our desire it should be known that not from pride or presumption, but from the causes already stated, and to the intent that the will of our Lord Jesus Christ being declared between us, for the greater repose of all true Christians, and that the enemies of God might be the better resisted for the security of Christianity—desire you to consider which of our offers you will accept, and signify the same to the bearer of these letters, and with all convenient despatch.

Given under our privy seal at Chyn, in the fields opposite Tournay, the 26th day of the month of July, in the year of our reign in France the first and in England the fourteenth.

Translation in J. O. Halliwell (– Phillipps): *Letters of the Kings of England*, 1846, vol. I, p. 47 (from the Norman-French).

APPENDIX III

Last Will of Richard II, 16 April 1399.

In the name of the whole and undivided Trinity, Father and Son and Holy Spirit, of the most Blessed Mother of God and Virgin Mary, of Saints John the Baptist and Edward the most glorious Confessor and of the whole celestial Court, Amen. Since Death's inevitable sentence defers to none at the last, but with an equally poised lance puts an end to nobility, power, energy, race, age and sex, it would be too bitter to a reasonable being unless after the course of this life of wavering continuance a more blessed life were to be hoped for in an abiding place: and accordingly since it was determined by the law of nature that nothing is more certain than death, nor more uncertain than the hour of death, the wisdom of human foresight has grown accustomed to provide for the hour of dissolution not only by virtuous and meritorious works but by a careful bestowal of worldly goods; that thus the unexpected hour, anticipated by a wise ordering, may be awaited the more free from care.

Wherefore we Richard, who by the grace of God have already for some time since our tender age submitted our neck by the mercy of the supreme King to the burden of the government of the English, considering in the weighing of our royal discretion the making of our testament and the declaring in royal wise of our last will while to this present time we enjoy a whole memory, have determined to proceed in this manner.

First inasmuch as we live in the purity and sincerity of the catholic faith we bequeath to almighty God our creator our soul which He has redeemed with His precious blood, and commend it to Him in the most intense devotion that we can with the whole desire of our mind.

And for our body in whatever place it shall happen that we should depart from this light, we have chosen a royal burial in the church of Saint Peter at Westminster among our ancestors Kings of England of famous memory; and in the monument which we have caused to be erected as a memorial for us and for Anne of glorious remembrance once Queen of England our consort, we wish it to be buried, of which our burial or funeral we wish the exequies to be celebrated in royal wise namely that for the said exequies four convenient herses of royal excellence should be fittingly prepared in the places underwritten by our executors for the more honourable fulfilment of the same funeral.

Two of these herses, each of five excellent and beautiful lights, fitting for royal exequies, shall be honourably set in the two principal churches through which it shall happen that our body be carried; and the third with as many lights of like form shall be in the church of Saint Paul of London; the fourth, which is to be greater, more principal and honourable, copiously supplied with splendid lights and befitting the royal eminence, and magnificently adorned shall be duly placed at Westminster at the disposition and discretion of our same executors. Also we will and ordain that when our body must be taken from the place where it shall happen that we leave this light to Westminster, it shall be borne fourteen, fifteen or sixteen miles a day according to what suitable hostelry can be found. And throughout the whole journey twenty-four torches shall be borne continually burning about our body to the place where it shall happen that our body shall rest for the night according to the discretion of our executors, where at each evening immediately after the body is borne in we will that the exequies of the dead be solemnly sung, with a mass on the morrow before the body is borne away from that place, twenty-four torches always and continually burning about the body both during the exequies and the mass; and to these twenty-four torches shall be added one hundred burning torches, when our said body has to be carried through the city of London. But if it shall happen that we should not decease within sixteen, fifteen, ten or five miles at the least outside our palace of Westminster, we will that in the four more important places intermediate (and if there should be no such intermediate places, in other suitable places) according to the direction of our executors, herses of this manner shall be appointed for four successive days with the foresaid solemnities. But if it shall happen that we decease within our palace of Westminster, we will that for four days solemnities be made, with one most solemn herse, but that more honourable exequies be made upon the last day. [We will also that if by adverse fortune (which may God of His mercy avert) our body should be snatched from the sight of men by hurricanes or tempests of the sea or in any other manner, and cannot be found, or that we should pay the debt of nature in such parts and regions that our body cannot be carried to our realm of England by reason of manifest obstacles, that all the aforesaid solemnities which are disposed in the present testament to be done about our body, and especially on the monument images and all other provision for us and for Anne of good remembrance aforetime Queen of England and France our consort thus ordained, and also the remaining funeral obsequies and everything else to be fully observed, be in no wise altered.] Also we will and ordain that our body shall be clothed and also interred in white velvet or satin in a royal manner, with royal crown and sceptre gilded but without any stones, and that upon our finger in kingly wise a ring shall be placed with a precious stone of the value of twenty marks of our money of England. Also we will and ordain that each catholic King shall have one cup or bowl of gold of the price or value of forty-five pounds of our English money. And that all gold crowns, cups, bowls, ewers and vases and other jewels of gold whatsoever and also the vestments with all apparel belonging to the chapel of our household, as well as all beds and all altar-clothing shall remain to our successor so long as the same our successor shall fully confirm our last will and shall permit our executors wholly and freely to execute this our will in its every part. And that he shall ratify and confirm all annuities and fees granted by us to familiars who have laboured about us and our person continually who by our licence for necessary causes as sickness or age have withdrawn from our presence, and to those who afterwards have served and serve us and especially about our person but according to the free discretion of our said successor and our executors. Also we will and ordain that from all our jewels remaining, namely circlets nowches and other jewels whatsoever, the new work of the nave of the church of Saint Peter at Westminster, by us begun, shall be completed and the residue (if any be) shall remain to our executors to dispose according to this our last will. Moreover we will and ordain that six thousand marks of gold shall be specially reserved for the expenses of our burial and of the bringing of our body from the place where it shall happen that we should depart from this light to Westminster. Also we will that lands rents and tenements as many as shall suffice for the proper sustenance of fifteen lepers and of a chaplain to celebrate for us in the church of Saint Peter at Westminster shall be procured; for doing which we ordain and bequeath the sum of a thousand marks. We will also that our servants who so far shall not have been rewarded or promoted by us (if such there shall be) shall be particularly rewarded from our goods up to a total of ten thousand marks to be distributed between them according to the discretion of our executors.

Also we bequeath to our beloved nephew Thomas duke of Surrey ten thousand marks and to our beloved brother Edward duke of Albemarle two thousand marks and to our beloved brother John duke of Exeter three thousand marks and to our faithful and beloved William Scrope earl of Wiltshire two thousand marks. [And reserved to our executors five or six thousand marks which we will shall be expended by our said executors for the freer sustenance of the lepers and chaplains ordained in their presence to celebrate for us at Westminster and Bermondsey.] Also we will and ordain that the residue of our gold (the true debts of our household chamber and wardrobe being paid, for which payment we bequeath twenty thousand pounds) shall remain to our successor so long as he shall approve ratify and confirm, keep and cause to be kept and to be firmly observed all and every of the statutes ordinances appointments and judgments made done and returned in our parliament of the seventeenth day of the month September begun at Westminster in the twenty-first year of our reign and in the same parliament prorogued to Shrewsbury and there held as well as all ordinances judgments and appointments of the sixteenth day of the month September in the twenty-second year of our reign at Coventry and afterwards at Westminster on the eighteenth day of March of the aforesaid year made had and returned by authority of the same parliament; but that if our foresaid successor shall be unwilling or refuse to perform the premisses (which we do not believe) we will that Thomas Edward John and William the dukes and earl abovesaid shall have and hold the residue mentioned (the debts of our household chamber and wardrobe first paid [and five or six thousand marks reserved] as above) for the sustaining and defence of these statutes appointments ordinances and judgments according to their ability even to the death if need be, whom and each of whose consciences we charge therewith as they shall wish to answer on the day of judgment; we ordain and set aside for the fulfilment of all and singular the premisses the sum of ninety-one thousand marks, of which sixty-five thousand marks are in the keeping of sir John Ikelyngton and twenty-four thousand marks in the hands and keeping of our dear nephew Thomas duke of Surrey of which sum we will that our same nephew be paid the ten thousand marks above bequeathed to him by us. And two thousand marks of advance for the expenses of our household are at present owed to us for the time when the reverend father Roger our Archbishop of Canterbury was made treasurer by us. Also we will that all the jewels which came to us with our most dear consort Isabella Queen of England and of France shall wholly remain to her if she should survive us; but that if we should survive her then we will that the said jewels should wholly remain to us and to our executors for the execution of this our last will. Also we will that all garments and robes of our body (pearls and precious stones excepted) should remain to the clerks yeomen and grooms who have laboured and labour continually about our person, to be distributed among them according to the discretion of our executors. Of this our royal testament we nominate make and depute executors the venerable fathers in Christ Richard bishop of Salisbury Edmund bishop of Exeter Tideman bishop of Worcester Thomas bishop of Carlisle and Guy bishop of Saint Davids; our beloved brother Edward duke of Albemarle our nephew Thomas duke of Surrey our brother John duke of Exeter and William earl of Wiltshire to each of whom we bequeath a gold cup of the value of twenty pounds and our beloved and faithful clerks [master Richard Clifford keeper of our Privy Seal] master Richard Maudeleyn master William Fereby and Master John Ikelyngton clerks and John Lufwyk and William Serle laymen, to each of whom we will shall be paid their expenses and necessary costs while it shall happen that they or any of them are employed about the execution of our present last will, but according to the discretion of their said co-executors.

Whom all and singular we have charged and charge that they shall do as much as in them is for the due execution and fulfilment of this our last will as they shall wish to answer before God. We create ordain depute and make overseers of this our will the reverend fathers in Christ archbishops Roger of Canterbury and Richard of York William bishop of Winchester and William abbot of the monastery of Westminster Edmund duke of York our uncle and Henry earl of Northumberland our cousin. Whom all and singular as far as regards us we require and request in the Lord that they should duly and carefully supervise as far as need shall be what is in this our last will and disposition and should cause its execution to be duly demanded; that they should strike with the censure of the church those resisting or gain-saying the premisses and should duly control and restrain them as far as their office requires as they shall wish to give reason to God; and to each of these our overseers we bequeath and assign a gold cup and ewer of the value of forty marks.

In witness and present security of all and singular the above matters we have caused the page or present testament containing our last will above-written to be reduced to writing and to be signed with our privy seal and signet and to be confirmed by the affixing of our great seal and the subscription of our own hand. The present testament was given written and ordained in our palace of Westminster in the year of the Lord one thousand three hundred and ninety-nine in the seventh indiction on the sixteenth day of the month of April in the twenty-second year of our reign; present the reverend father Robert bishop of London and the noble and vigorous men John marquis of Dorset Thomas earl of Worcester and others.

Translation from the Latin original printed in J. Nichols's *Wills of the Kings and Queens of England, &c.*, 1780, pp. 191-200. A somewhat different version is printed in *Foedera*, VIII, 75.

(Signed):   +le Roy. (Sealed with the Great Seal; the Signet with the Confessor's Arms impaling France Ancient quartering England; and, now missing, the Privy Seal.)

The text has been collated with the original sealed copy in the Public Record Office (E.23/1) and marginal additions and interlineations marked by the insertion of square brackets [ ]. It should be noted that the first of the marginal additions suggests a date immediately before Richard's journey to Ireland (29 May 1399).

APPENDIX IV

Henry V to Charles VI of France, 28 July 1414.

Most serene Prince, our Cousin and Adversary:

The two great and noble kingdoms of England and France, formerly brothers, but now divided, had usually been eminent throughout all the world by their triumphs. They combined but for the generous object of enriching and adorning the House of God, to place peace in all her boundaries, to make it flourish within its whole extent, and to join her arms against her adversaries, as against public enemies. They never encountered them, that they did not happily subdue them. But alas! this faithful union is vanished; we are fallen into the unhappy condition of Lot and Abraham. The honour of this fraternal friendship is buried; her death and her sepulture have revived dissension, that old enemy of human nature, which may justly be called the mother of Hatred and of War.

The Sovereign Judge of sovereigns will be our witness one day, of the sincere inclination with which we have sought peace, and how we have employed prayers and promises to persuade you to it, even by giving up the possession of a State which belongs to us by hereditary right, and which nature would oblige us to preserve for our posterity. We are not so wanting in sense and courage, but that we are resolved at last to fight with all our strength, *even to death*. But as the law of Deuteronomy commands that whoever appears in arms before a town should offer it peace before it is besieged, we have, even up to the present time, done all which our rank allows peacefully to recover the possession of that which belongs to us by legitimate succession, and to reunite to our crown that which you wrongfully and by violence possess; so much so, that, from your refusing justice, we may rightfully have recourse to the force of arms.

Our honour, however, and the testimony of our conscience, oblige us once more, in going against you, to demand the reason of your refusal, and to exhort you, in the name of the merciful bowels of Jesus Christ, to do us justice, and to say to you that which He teaches, " Friend, give me that which thou owest me." —*Amice, redde quod debes, et fiat nobis ipsius Dei Summi nutu.*

To avoid a deluge of human blood, restore to us our inheritance, which you unjustly detain, or render us, at least, that which we have so many times demanded by our ambassadors. Only the love and fear of God, and the advantage of peace, have made us contented with so little; and we are willing, on that account,

P.   H

to remit fifty thousand crowns of that which we have been offer
in marriage, to show that we are more inclined to peace than
avarice; that we prefer the title which our father has left us
those to which we have legitimate pretensions by representati
from our forefathers, and that we are disposed to lead an innoce
life with your fair and noble daughter Katharine, our very de
cousin, than to enrich ourselves with the treasure of iniquity,
adore the idol of riches, and to extend and increase our crow
(which God forbid!) to the prejudice of our conscience.

Given under our hand and seal, in our town of Southampto
upon the sea-side, the 28th of July.

Translation in J. O. Halliwell (—Phillipps): *Letters of the Kin
of England*, 1846, vol. I, p. 78.

Henry V's challenge to the Dauphin of France, 16 Septemb
1415.

Henry by the grace of God King of France and England, Lord
Ireland, to the high and mighty prince, the Dauphin of Vienn
our cousin, eldest son of the very powerful prince, our cousin an
adversary of France.

Whereas, from reverence to God, and to avoid the shedding
human blood, we have many times and in many ways, sued an
sought for peace, and have not been able to obtain it; and no
withstanding this, our desire of having it increaseth more an
more. And well considering that our wars occasion the death
men, the desolation of countries, the lamentations of women an
children, and so many evils in the general, as every good Christia
ought to mourn and have pity on them, and especially oursel
whom this matter chiefly affects; and that we ought to use a
diligence to find every means that one can, to avoid the ills an
distresses above-mentioned, in order to acquire the grace of Go
and the praise of mankind. And as having taken all thought an
advice herein, it seemeth to us, (considering it hath pleased Go
to visit with infirmity our said cousin your father) that th
remedy rests upon ourself and you. And to the end that ever
one may know that we on our part will not withdraw from it, w
offer you to decide this our quarrel, with God's grace, by comba
between our person and yours.

And if it seemeth to you that you cannot accede thereto, b
reason of the great concern which you suppose our said cousi
your father hath in it; we declare unto you that, if you are willin
to listen to it and to carry it into effect, we are well pleased t
suffer our said cousin, from reverence to God, and because he
a sacred personage, to have and enjoy what he hath at presen
for the term of his life; whatever happen between ourself an

u, as it shall be appointed by his council, ours, and yours.
hus, if God giveth us the victory, that the crown of France, with
appurtenances, as our right, shall instantly be surrendered unto
without demur, after his decease. And hereto all the lords,
d estates of the realm of France to bind themselves in form, as
all be accorded between us.

For it is better, cousin, to determine this war thus between
r two persons for ever, than to suffer the infidels, by occasion
our wars, to destroy Christianity, our holy mother church to
ide in divisions, and the people of the living God to slaughter
e another. And we will pray heartily, as you have so great a
sire to avoid this, and to attain to the blessing of peace, that
u will not refuse to pursue every means that can be found for
taining this peace. And we hope that no means so good and
ort as this will be found. And, to this disburthening of our
ul and to the burthening of yours, if great evils ensue hence-
rward, we make you the aforesaid offer; protesting always, that
is our offer, which we make to the honour and in fear of God
d for the above causes, is of our own mere motion, without our
yal kinsfolk, councillors, and subjects at present around us,
ving presumed in so high a matter to advise us. Nor can it at
y future time be alleged to our prejudice or to the prejudice of
r right and title which we now have to the crown aforesaid with
appurtenances, nor to the good right and title which we
w have to other our lands and heritages on this side of the
a, nor to our heirs and successors, if this our offer does not take
ll effect between ourself and you in the manner aforesaid.

Given under our privy seal, at our town of Harfleur, the 16th
y of September 1415.

ranslation in *Letters of the Kings of England*, vol. I, p. 80.

APPENDIX V

Poem by Henry VI.

> Kingdoms are but cares,
>   State is devoid of stay,
> Riches are ready snares,
>   And hasten to decay.
>
> Pleasure is a privy prick
>   Which vice doth still provoke;
> Pomp, imprompt; and fame, a flame;
>   Power, a smouldering smoke.
>
> Who meaneth to remove the rock
>   Owt of the slimy mud,
> Shall mire himself, and hardly scape
>   The swelling of the flood.

Printed in *Nugae Antiquae*, by Sir John Harington, ed. T. Park
1804.

BIBLIOGRAPHICAL NOTE

This is not intended to be a bibliography of the whole subject, but simply a list of some of the more important works, with emphasis on those mainly consulted. There are extensive detailed bibliographies to the relevant chapters of the *Cambridge Mediæval History*, 8 vols., 1924-36, and the standard, though somewhat outdated, book of reference is C. Gross's *The Sources and Literature of English History, to about 1485*, 1915. The County Libraries Section of the Library Association publishes a good general list of books, *Reader's Guide*, New Series No. 44, *Mediæval Britain*, 1958.

GENERAL

BIGHAM, THE HON. C. (LORD MERSEY): *The Kings of England, 1066-1910*, 1929.

CLARKE, M. V.: *Fourteenth Century Studies*, 1937.

ELLIS, SIR H.: *Original Letters* (1st series, 3 vols., 1824; 2nd series, 4 vols., 1827; 3rd series, 4 vols., 1846). Series 2, vol. 1; Series 3, vol. 1

(GRANT, E.): *The Muse of Monarchy, Poems by Kings and Queens of England*, 1937.

GREEN, V. H. H.: *The Later Plantagenets, 1307-1485*, 1955.

HALLIWELL (– PHILLIPPS), J. O.: *Letters of the Kings of England*, 2 vols., 1846.

HARDY, W. J.: *The Handwriting of the Kings and Queens of England*, 1893.

HAYES, G.: *King's Music*, 1937.

JOLLIFFE, J. E. A.: *Angevin Kingship*, 1955.

LANCASTER, O.: *Our Sovereigns, 871-1937*, 1937.

LINDSAY, P.: *Kings of Merry England, Eadward the Confessor to Richard the Third*, 1936.

MUNRO, C.: *Letters of Queen Margaret of Anjou, &c.* (Camden Soc., LXXXVI), 1863.

NICHOLS, J.: *A Collection of all the Wills . . . of the Kings and Queens of England, &c.*, 1780.

RAE, J.: *The Deaths of the Kings of England*, 1913.

STRICKLAND, A.: *Lives of the Queens of England*, 12 vols., 1840-9.

TURTON, W. H.: *The Plantagenet Ancestry . . . of Elizabeth (of York)*, 1928.

VAN THAL, H.: *The Royal Letter Book*, 1937.

HENRY II

BOUSSARD, J.: *Le Gouvernement d'Henri II Plantagenet*, Paris 1956.

GREEN, A. S.: *Henry the Second*, 1919.

KELLY, A.: *Eleanor of Aquitaine and the Four Kings*, 1952.

LLOYD, R.: *The Golden Middle Age*, 1939.

NORGATE, K.: *England under the Angevin Kings*, 2 vols., 1887.

SALZMAN, L. F.: *Henry II*, 1914.

RICHARD I

HAMPDEN, J.: *Crusader King*, 1956.

HENDERSON, P.: *Richard Cœur-de-Lion*, 1958

NORGATE, K.: *Richard the Lion Heart*, 1924.

WILKINSON, C. A.: *Cœur de Lion*, 1933.

JOHN

D'AUVERGNE, E. B. F.: *John King of England*, 1934.

NORGATE, K.: *John Lackland*, 1902.

PAINTER, S.: *The Reign of King John*, 1950.

WARREN, W. L.: *King John*, 1961.

HENRY III

NORGATE, K.: *The Minority of Henry III*, 1912.

POWICKE, F. M.: *King Henry III and the Lord Edward*, 2 vols. 1947.

EDWARD I

JENKS, E.: *Edward Plantagenet*, 1923.

MORRIS, J. E.: *The Welsh Wars of Edward I*, 1901.

PLUCKNETT, T. F. T.: *Legislation of Edward I*, 1949.

SALZMAN, L. F.: *Edward I*, 1968.

(SEELEY, R. B.): *Life and Reign of Edward I*, 1872.

TOUT, T. F.: *Edward I*, 1920.

EDWARD II

JOHNSTONE, H.: *Edward of Carnarvon 1284-1307*, 1946.
TOUT, T. F.: *The Place of the Reign of Edward II in English History*, 2nd ed., 1936.

EDWARD III

LONGMAN, W.: *Life and Times of Edward III*, 2 vols., 1869.
MACKINNON, J.: *History of Edward III*, 1900.

RICHARD II

HUTCHISON, H. F.: *The Hollow Crown*, 1961.
STEEL, A.: *Richard II*, 1941.
WALLON, H.: *Richard II*, 2 vols., Paris, 1864 (in French).

HENRY IV

DAVIES, J. D. G.: *King Henry IV*, 1935.
WYLIE, J. H.: *History of England under Henry IV*, 4 vols., 1884-98

HENRY V

DAVIES, J. D. G.: *Henry V*, 1935.
KINGSFORD, C. L.: *Henry V, the typical mediæval hero*, 1923.
MOWAT, R. B.: *Henry V*, 1919.
WYLIE, J. H. AND WAUGH, W. T.: *The Reign of Henry V*, 3 vols., 1914-29.

HENRY VI

BAGLEY, J.: *Margaret of Anjou, Queen of England*, 1948.
BLAKMAN, J.: *Memoir of Henry VI*, 1919.
CHRISTIE, M. E.: *Henry VI*, 1922.

EDWARD IV

SCOFIELD, C. L.: *The Life and Reign of Edward the Fourth,* vols., 1923.
STRATFORD, L.: *Edward IV,* 1910.

RICHARD III

GAIRDNER, J.: *Life and Reign of Richard III,* 1898.
KENDALL, P. M.: *Richard the Third,* 1955.
MARKHAM, C. R.: *Richard III,* 1906.

NOTES TO THE TEXT

These notes are intended to give references for facts of importance not easily to be found in the standard works already mentioned.

INTRODUCTION

p. 33 Empress Maud—see the late Earl of Onslow's biography: *The Empress Maud*, 1939.

CHAPTER I. HENRY II

The main authorities for personalia are: Gerald the Welshman: *Works*, ed. J. S. Brewer, J. F. Dimock and G. F. Warner (Rolls Series, 8 vols.), 1861-91; *Itinerary and Description of Wales*, translated in Everyman's Library, No. 272. Read especially H. E. Butler: *The Autobiography of Giraldus Cambrensis*, 1937. Walter Map: *De Nugis Curialium*, ed. M. R. James (Anecdota Oxoniensia, Mediæval and Modern Series, XIV, 1914); and translation (Cymmrodorion Record Series, IX), 1923.

p. 48 Eleanor of Aquitaine—F. McM. Chambers, " Some Legends concerning Eleanor of Aquitaine ", in *Speculum*, XVI, 1941, p. 459ff.

p. 50 Henry's early visits to England—A. L. Poole in *English Historical Review*, XLVII, 1932, p. 447ff.

p. 51 Eleanor's Courts of Love—A. Kelly, " Eleanor of Aquitaine and her Courts of Love ", in *Speculum*, XII, 1937, p. 3ff.

p. 53 Geoffrey of Monmouth—*History of the Kings of Britain*, ed. A. Griscom, 1929. Translation in Everyman's Library, No. 577.

p. 54 Edric Wild—Map: *De Nugis*, Dist. II, xii.

p. 54 Map's Poems—T. Wright: *Latin Poems attributed to Walter Mapes* (Camden Soc., XVI), 1841.

London—Translation of FitzStephen by Professor H. E. Butler in F. M. Stenton: *Norman London* (Historical Association Leaflet, Nos. 93, 94), 1934.

Chester—*Liber Luciani de Laude Cestrie*, ed. M. V. Taylor (Record Soc. of Lancashire and Cheshire, LXIV), 1912.

On John of Salisbury and his circle read Canon Roger Lloyd's delightful book *The Golden Middle Age*, 1939.

p. 55 "Modern" luxury—A. Kelly in *Speculum*, XII, quoting
Recueil des Historiens de la France, XII, p. 450.

Winchester illumination and painting—W. Oakeshott: *Th
Artists of the Winchester Bible*, 1945; T. Borenius and E. W
Tristram: *English Mediæval Painting*, 1927; E. W. Tristram: *English Mediæval Wall Painting—the Twelfth Century*, 1945.

CHAPTER II. RICHARD I

p. 59 The King's Latin—*Autobiography of Giraldus*, p. 282.

p. 63 Henry II's will—J. Nichols: *Wills of the Kings and Queens*,
pp. 7-10.

p. 68 Richard's letter—J. O. Halliwell: *Letters of the Kings of
England*, I, p. 7.

p. 74 Heraldry—Lions (not *three* lions) were painted on the shield
of Geoffrey Plantagenet at his marriage in 1127, and appear
on his enamel portrait of about 1151. See A. R. Wagner:
Heraldry in England (King Penguin Books, No. 22), 1946,
p. 6 and Plate I.

CHAPTER III. JOHN

p. 76 Whitewashing—G. K. Chesterton: *A Miscellany of Men*,
1912, "The Mediæval Villain", pp. 228-34.

Ireland—*Autobiography of Giraldus*, p. 118.

p. 81 Mr. H. G. Richardson suggests (*English Historical Review*,
LXI, 1946, p. 289ff.; LXV, p. 360ff.) that John's marriage to
Isabella was due to deliberate policy. If so, it is another
example of John's genius for doing the wrong thing. See
also *E.H.R.*, LXVII, p. 233ff.

CHAPTER IV. HENRY III

p. 91 Lincoln Cathedral—G. K. Chesterton: *A Miscellany of
Men*, "The Architect of Spears", pp. 208-13.

p. 95 The details of this chapter are from the *Calendar of Liberate
Rolls*, 3 vols., 1226-40, 1240-5, 1245-51. Extracts concerning building from the Rolls up to 1269 will be found in T. H.
Turner: *Domestic Architecture in England . . . to the end
of the Thirteenth Century*, 1851.

p. 102 Numbers at Oxford—G. G. Coulton: *Mediæval Panorama*,
1940, p. 409.

p. 104 It is worth quoting Sir F. M. Powicke's summing-up, which I had not seen when I wrote this chapter (*King Henry III and the Lord Edward*, 1947, II, p. 589): "Henry had rarely found the peace for which his nature must have craved. Even his great days had their annoyances. He had never been free from his exacting people. Yet he had held his own, with the uneasy persistence and the reluctant submission to hard facts of the querulous realist. The old man left his kingdom greater than it was when, a fair-faced child, he rode from Devizes to be crowned at Gloucester. England was more united, more prosperous, more richly endowed, more beautiful in 1272 than it was in 1216."

CHAPTER V. EDWARD I

In this chapter, besides the works mentioned in the Bibliography, I have used L. F. Salzman: *English Life in the Middle Ages*, 1926.

p. 112 European peace—Edward's greatest work for European peace, the mediation of Bordeaux between France, Aragon, Naples, and Sicily in 1287-8, is described by Tout: *Edward the First*, pp. 98-101.

p. 114 note Alfonso's boat—Public Record Office, E.101/467/9.

p. 118 Edward's violent temper is evidenced by the Wardrobe Book for 1296-7 (British Museum Add. ms. 7965, f. 15v.) quoted by Professor Hilda Johnstone in *Edward of Carnarvon*, p. 124: "To Adam the King's goldsmith for a great ruby and a great emerald bought to set in a certain coronet of the countess of Holland, the King's daughter, in place of two stones which were lost when the King threw the coronet in the fire." But there is ample proof that Edward's wrath soon cooled, and that he never bore a grudge.

p. 119 Child Murder—The cases of 1232 (Winchester), 1255 (Lincoln), 1276 (London), 1290 (Oxford) at least are mentioned in official records. H. L. Strack's defence to the accusation (*The Jew and Human Sacrifice*, 1909) is much weakened by the fact that it fails to mention the Lincoln case of 1255, which is reported in considerable detail on various Chancery rolls.

p. 122 Edward's resumption of power—(R. B. Seeley): *Life and Reign of Edward I*, 1872, pp. 254-7.

p. 123 Elegy—T. Wright: *The Political Songs of England, John to Edward II* (Camden Soc.), 1839, pp. 246-50. Sir Charles Fortescue-Brickdale has recently published an excellent translation of the *Commendatio* or elegy printed in Stubbs's *Chronicles of Edward I & II* (Rolls Series), 1883, II, xviii,

3-21—" A Gloucestershire Rector's Lament for Edward I ",
in *Transactions* of the Bristol and Gloucestershire Archæo-
logical Society, LXI, 1939, pp. 188-95.

CHAPTER VI. EDWARD II

p. 124 Books—H. Johnstone, " Isabella, the She-Wolf of France ",
in *History*, N.S., XXI, 1936-7, p. 214.
Poem—The text, from Longleat Collection, *Tractatus varii
Theologici*, f. 76.v, is printed with a translation by P. Studer
in *Modern Language Review*, XVI, 1921, 34-46.
p. 125 The King's pursuits—H. Johnstone, " The Eccentricities of
Edward II ", in *English Historical Review*, April 1933.
p. 126 The Scots orphan—H. Johnstone in *History*, 1936-7, p. 212.
The King's attitude—J. O. Halliwell: *Letters of the Kings
of England*, I, p. 23; *Antiquaries Journal*, VIII, 1928, p. 123.

CHAPTER VII. EDWARD III

The main sources for this chapter will be found in Longman.
p. 134 Queen Philippa—G. G. Coulton: *Mediæval Panorama*, 1940,
p. 644.
p. 138 Fourteenth-century War—W. Longman: *Life & Times of
Edward III*, I, pp. 84, 133; *Rotuli Parliamentorum*, II, p.
96b.
p. 140 German journey—R. Pauli: *Pictures of Old England*, 1861,
p. 151
p. 144 Letter to the Infante Pedro—M. A. E. Green: *Lives of the
Princesses of England*, III, pp. 257-8 (from *Foedera*, III, 172).
p. 146 John Arderne—D'A. Power: *English Medicine and Surgery
of the 14th Century*, 1912; *Treatises of Fistula* (Early English Text Society, 139), 1910; Westminster Abbey Muni-
ments, No. 19,356.
p. 147 Edward III and the fishermen—*Calendar of Fine Rolls,
1347-56*, p. 214.

CHAPTER VIII. RICHARD II

p. 153 Richard's books—E. Rickert, " King Richard II's Books " in
The Library, 4 S., XIII, 1932-3, p. 144.
Richard and Music—G. Hayes: *King's Music*, 1937, p. 34;
S. H. D. Holton, " Richard the Redeless " in *Transactions* of
the Royal Historical Society, N.S. x., 1896, p. 142.

p. 153 note Dancing—F. Devon: *Issues of the Exchequer*, 1837, p. 212; *John of Gaunt's Register, 1379-84* (Camden 3rd S.), 1937.

p. 157 Richard as a neurotic—It has been shown by Mr. L. C. Hector (*English Historical Review*, Jan. 1953, LXVIII, pp. 62-5) that one of the main instances, quoted by almost all the authorities, of Richard's hysterical behaviour, rests on a complete misconception.

p. 157 Irish Question—J. O. Halliwell: *Letters of the Kings of England*, I, p. 51.

p. 160 Villein Education—*Rotuli Parliamentorum*, III, p. 294a. The Poor—W. E. Tate: *The Parish Chest*, 1946, p. 189, quoting Statutes 12 Ric. II, c. 7 (1388) and 15 Ric. II, c. 5 (1391), Statute of Mortmain II.

p. 161 Queen Elizabeth—H. B. Wheatley: *Historical Portraits*, 1897, p. 141.

CHAPTER IX. HENRY IV

p. 167 Henry's travels—L. T. Smith: *Expeditions to Prussia and the Holy Land made by Henry Earl of Derby* (Camden Soc., N.S., LII), 1894.

p. 168 Timur—H. Ellis: *Original Letters*, Series 3, I, pp. 54-8. Queen Joan—see A. R. Myers, "The captivity of a royal witch: the household accounts of Queen Joan of Navarre, 1419-21" in *Bulletin of the John Rylands Library*, XXIV, No. 2 and XXVI, No. 1.

p. 169 Will—J. Nichols: *Wills . . .*, p. 203.

CHAPTER X. HENRY V

p. 172 Heretic's execution—H. Ellis: *Original Letters*, Series 2, I, p. 89.

p. 173 Cambridge's appeal—Ellis, Series 2, I, p. 48.

p. 176 Mason's letter—C. Monro: *Letters of Queen Margaret of Anjou etc.* (Camden Soc., LXXXVI), 1863, pp. 19-21.

p. 178 Old Hall MS.—edited by Plainsong and Mediæval Music Soc., 3 vols., 1933-8. See also F. L. Harrison: *Music in Mediæval Britain*, 1958, p. 220ff.

CHAPTER XI. HENRY VI

The main authority for personal details is Blacman's Memoir. M.
Letts' *The Diary of Jörg von Ehingen*, 1929, reproduces a curious
portrait of Henry VI in *c.* 1455.

p. 179 note Woodblock signature—cf. W. J. Hardy: *The Hand-*
  writing of the Kings and Queens of England, 1893.

p. 180 Duchess of Gloucester—Ellis: *Original Letters*, Series 2,
  I, pp. 105-6. cf. R. Stewart-Brown, " The imprisonment of
  Eleanor Cobham, Duchess of Gloucester " in *Transactions*
  of the Historical Society of Lancashire and Cheshire,
  LXXXV.

p. 181 Henry's " Will "—see R. Willis and J. W. Clark: *The*
  Architectural History of the University of Cambridge, 1886,
  I, pp. 351-80.

p. 184 Pecock—see V. H. H. Green: *Bishop Reginald Pecock*, 1945,
  pp. 163, 173n.

CHAPTER XII. EDWARD IV

p. 196 Elizabeth's coronation is recorded in a contemporary manuscript, edited with much biographical matter in 1935 (G.
  Smith: *The Coronation of Elizabeth Wydeville*, London,
  Ellis, 29 New Bond Street). There are valuable references
  in the London Corporation Bridge Masters' Account Book,
  1460-84; extracts are printed in C. Welch: *History of the*
  Tower Bridge etc., 1894, p. 121.

p. 197 Edward's new grants—see especially *Calendar of Patent*
  Rolls, 1461-7.

p. 199 Conscription—for the Yorkist manifesto—see Scofield, I,
  p. 69n. The difference is that the old English levies were
  defensive, based on part-time training; the French fifteenth-
  century (and modern) conscripts are drafted into a full-time
  standing army, without territorial or defensive limitation
  of service. See also Sir John Fortescue: *The Governance of*
  England, ed. C. Plummer, 1885, p. 249, quoting I Edw. III,
  st. 2, c. 5 and 18 Edw. III, c. 7, " whereby no one was to be
  called upon to serve outside the limits of his own county,
  except in case of sudden invasion ". English parish accounts
  are full of entries referring to evasion of, and substitution
  for, militia service in the eighteenth and nineteenth centuries, and mediæval cases are referred to by G. C. Homans:
  English Villagers of the Thirteenth Century, Cambridge,
  Mass., 1942, p. 330.

p. 200 Tiptoft—see R. J. Mitchell: *John Tiptoft, 1427-70*, 1938.
p. 203 Edward to James III—J. O. Halliwell: *Letters of the Kings of England*, I, p. 125.

CHAPTER XIII. RICHARD III

Besides the standard works (from opposing standpoints) of Gaird-ner and Markham, some new light has been thrown by Professor A. F. Pollard, " Sir Thomas More's 'Richard III'" in *History*, January 1933, showing the unhistorical nature of More's work, and by the discovery of Mancini's contemporary account of the events of 1483, edited by C. A. J. Armstrong as *The Usurpation of Richard the Third* (Dominicus Mancinus ad Angelum Catonem de Occupatione Regni Anglie per Ricardum Tercium Libellus), 1936.

p. 207 Old Countess of Desmond—R. Chambers: *The Book of Days*, I, p. 149.
p. 208 Irish array—Ellis: *Original Letters*, Series 2, I, p. 123.
     Richard Plantagenet—Chambers: *The Book of Days*, II, p. 728; W. Hutton: *The Battle of Bosworth* (1788).
p. 210 Henry's letter—Halliwell: *Letters*, I, p. 169.

INDEX

Abelard, Pierre, 55

Abingdon, Henry, composer (*fl.* 1445-84), 181

Achard, Lord of Châlus, 75

Acre, Palestine, 65, 67-8, 72

Adam, miner, 97

Ælendis, Countess of Anjou, 25

Æthelred, the Unready, King of Wessex, 23

Agincourt, battle, 176, 192

Aimar, Viscount of Limoges, 75

Albertus Magnus, scientist, 117

Albigenses, 46, 48, 129

Alexander III, King of Scots, 120

Alfonso IX, King of Castile, 40
X, King of Castile, 112

Alfonso, son of Edward I, 114n.

Alfred, King of Wessex, 22-4, 66-7, 76, 111, 172, 191

Alnwick, Northumberland, 47

Aloysia, sister of Philip Augustus, 62, 66

Amboise, France, 25

Angers, France, 27, 83

Anglesey, 114

Angoulême, France, 49

Anjou, France, 24-8, 63, 80, 82, 99
House of, 24-8

Anne of Bohemia, Queen of England, 7, 155-6, 158, 161, 171, 219-20
Neville, Queen of England, 206

Antwerp, 140

Appellants, The, 156, 160n., 171-3

Aquileia, Italy, 72

Arabs, 61, 69-71

Aragon, 40

Architecture, 56, 61, 84, 91, 103, 135, 146, 153-4, 177, 187, 203

Arderne, John, surgeon, 146

Aremburg of Maine, Countess of Anjou, 26

Arghun, Ilkhan of Persia, 117

Arley Regis, Worcs., 55

Arsouf, battle, 69

Arthur, King of Britain, 66, 117
of Brittany, 32, 77, 80-2, 206

Arthurian Romance, 115

Arts, 89, 118, 125, 154-5, 203, 208, *see also* Gothic Art, Architecture, Books, Drama, Illuminated mss., Music, Painting, Sculpture

Arundel, Richard, Earl of, 156-7
Thomas, Archbishop of Canterbury, 159-60

Ascalon, Palestine, 70

Aston, Hugh, composer (*c.* 1480-1511), 204

Astrology, 47, 59, 200

Athelstan, King of Wessex, 32

Augustine, St. (354-430), 203
St. (*d.c.* 613), 26

Austria, 72

Auvergne, Dauphin of, 214-15

Avignon, 138

Avranches, Henry of, poet (*fl.* 1251), 101

Bacon, Roger, scientist (d. 1293), 91, 117

Fontana Paperbacks

Fontana is a leading paperback publisher of fiction and non-fiction, with authors ranging from Alistair MacLean, Agatha Christie and Desmond Bagley to Solzhenitsyn and Pasternak, from Gerald Durrell and Joy Adamson to the famous Modern Masters series.

In addition to a wide-ranging collection of internationally popular writers of fiction, Fontana also has an outstanding reputation for history, natural history, military history, psychology, psychiatry, politics, economics, religion and the social sciences.

All Fontana books are available at your bookshop or newsagent; or can be ordered direct. Just fill in the form and list the titles you want.

FONTANA BOOKS, Cash Sales Department, G.P.O. Box 29, Douglas, Isle of Man, British Isles. Please send purchase price, plus 8p per book. Customers outside the U.K. send purchase price, plus 10p per book. Cheque, postal or money order. No currency.

NAME (Block letters) _____

ADDRESS _____

_____

_____